14.00

Battlefield of the Second Day at Gettysburg

THE SECOND DAY AT GETTYSBURG

Essays on Confederate and Union Leadership

edited by

GARY W. GALLAGHER

The Kent State University Press

KENT, OHIO, AND LONDON, ENGLAND

© 1993 by The Kent State University Press, Kent, Ohio 44242
ALL RIGHTS RESERVED
Library of Congress Catalog Card Number 93-16146
ISBN 0-87338-481-4
ISBN 0-87338-482-2 (pbk.)
Manufactured in the United States of America

03 02 01 00 99 98 97 96 95 94   6 5 4 3 2

Library of Congress Cataloging-in-Publication Data
The Second day at Gettysburg : essays on Confederate and Union
leadership / edited by Gary W. Gallagher.
p. cm.
Continues: The First day at Gettysburg / edited by Gary W.
Gallagher.
Includes bibliographical references and index.
ISBN 0-87338-481-4 (cloth : alk. paper). ISBN 0-87338-482-2
(pbk. : alk. paper) ∞
1. Gettysburg (Pa.), Battle of, 1863. 2. Command of troops—Case
studies. I. Gallagher, Gary W. II. First day at Gettysburg.
E475.53.S46   1993
973.7'349—dc20   93-16146

British Library Cataloging-in-Publication data are available.

Contents

Introduction

GARY W. GALLAGHER

The essays in this book continue the evaluation of selected commanders during the Gettysburg campaign begun in *The First Day at Gettysburg: Essays on Confederate and Union Leadership*. The focus shifts to the second day of battle, which encompassed the famous struggles for Little Round Top, the Wheatfield, and the Peach Orchard, as well as the less well-known fighting along the slopes of Culp's Hill. The first day had progressed from a meeting engagement into a bitter contest between significant elements of both the Army of Northern Virginia and the Army of the Potomac, ending with triumphant Confederates driving Union defenders onto high ground south and southeast of Gettysburg. With the bulk of both forces present on July 2, R. E. Lee resumed the tactical offensive begun the previous day. These assaults by an army at the peak of its power and confidence matched in spirit and persistence any mounted previously by Lee's men and nearly gained success against each flank of the Northern line. Facing a series of crises highlighted by the spectacular disintegration of Daniel E. Sickles's Third Corps, George G. Meade's army repeatedly flirted with disaster before holding on in the end.

Events on July 2 ignited controversies relating to Confederate and Union generalship that have persisted for 130 years. On the Confederate side, a host of Lost Cause writers savaged James Longstreet for failing to launch his attack earlier in the day. Seeking to remove any taint of defeat from Lee as well as to wound Longstreet, whose Republican politics and willingness to criticize his old chief made him an easy target, prominent former Confederates such as Jubal A. Early, Fitzhugh Lee, and

John B. Gordon claimed that Lee had ordered his senior lieutenant to open the battle at dawn. They insisted that if Longstreet had struck the Union left in the morning—or even earlier in the afternoon—Southern infantry would have taken Little Round Top and rendered untenable the entire Union line. Assailed in print for several decades, Longstreet responded with accounts of the battle marked by errors, dissembling, and rancor. Many historians of the twentieth century, most notably Douglas Southall Freeman in his immensely influential biography of Lee, essentially repeated the arguments articulated by Longstreet's tormentors. Other scholars rallied to "Old Pete's" defense, among them Glenn Tucker, whose books on Gettysburg reached a wide audience, and William Garrett Piston, who turned a judicious eye toward the postwar controversies in his study of Longstreet.

The debate over Longstreet's role on July 2 inevitably involves an assessment of Lee's generalship in the wake of the first day's victory. The Confederate commander's decision to press for complete victory via a renewed offensive received the approbation of most Lost Cause writers of the late nineteenth and early twentieth centuries; similarly, Freeman suggested that Lee, far from home and facing an uncertain logistical situation, had no viable alternative. In contrast, Edward Porter Alexander, commander of Longstreet's guns in the action on July 2, vigorously argued that the Army of Northern Virginia should have taken up a good line and forced Meade to attack. Many modern historians agree with Alexander's opinion that Lee might easily have switched to the defensive and awaited an opportunity to deliver a decisive counterpunch.

The most acrimonious disagreement about Federal generalship on July 2 has centered on Daniel E. Sickles's decision to occupy an advanced position embracing the high ground at the Peach Orchard. As with the controversy that raged over Longstreet's behavior, nineteenth-century arguments about Sickles included heavy doses of politics and special pleading.

Anyone seeking to reach dispassionate conclusions about this aspect of the battle must use accounts by participants with great care.

The contributors to this book address a number of topics relating to command on the second day at Gettysburg. The first essay examines key questions concerning Lee's decision to order a new round of assaults. Did he have better options? Did he give free rein to his naturally aggressive personality? And is it fair to look at Gettysburg in isolation, or should Lee's decision be judged in the context of the history of the Army of Northern Virginia? William Glenn Robertson then reviews the case against Dan Sickles, taking into account the importance of reputation and clashes of personality as well as military factors such as the nature of the terrain and perceptions about the tactical situation. In the third essay, Robert K. Krick draws on wartime testimony unstained by Lost Cause propaganda to reassess Longstreet's actions. Finding a consistent pattern in Longstreet's behavior throughout the war, Krick reaches conclusions that are certain to provoke further debate.

The last two essays depart from such hotly contested historiographical ground. A. Wilson Greene looks at Henry W. Slocum and the Union Twelfth Corps. The senior Union corps leader, Slocum has received scant attention in the mammoth literature on Gettysburg. Greene offers a convincing portrait of a general unwilling or unable to act decisively and a corps that fell far short of achieving its full potential at Gettysburg. In the final essay, D. Scott Hartwig shifts the spotlight to the divisional level, where he reconstructs the chaotic experience of directing large numbers of men in mid–nineteenth century combat. Cast as attackers in a Union drama dominated by the tactical defensive, John C. Caldwell and his men performed admirably before factors beyond their control overwhelmed them. Hartwig suggests why good tactical plans often went astray—and why modern students should exercise care in criticizing Civil War commanders for failures on the battlefield.

As with *The First Day at Gettysburg*, the essays in this book reflect research in both easily accessible sources and a range of unpublished materials. Once again aware of the belief in some quarters that nothing remains to be said about Gettysburg (or about virtually any Civil War military operation for that matter), the authors sought to present interpretations that will challenge readers to look again at old questions, at the same time offering new evidence that enhances our understanding of the campaign. Gettysburg was a defining moment for both the Army of Northern Virginia and the Army of the Potomac. Because neither organization was ever quite the same afterward, commanders and their decisions influencing the course of the battle—and by extension the later histories of the armies—retain validity as subjects of investigation. Beyond this purely military dimension, of course, the result on the battlefield had a significant impact on civilians North and South as well as on European observers. Readers will quickly perceive that the essays in this book sometimes contradict one another—even when relying on the same evidence. The authors see that as a strength that points to the potential for continued investigation.

These essays represent revised versions of papers first delivered in June 1991 at the fifth annual conference on the Civil War at the Mont Alto campus of Pennsylvania State University. Once again, the gathering of a talented group of historians at Mont Alto provided a wonderful opportunity to learn amid very pleasant surroundings. Indeed, the Mont Alto conferences have come to represent a most welcome escape from increasingly hectic schedules. Will Greene, Scott Hartwig, Bob Krick, and Glenn Robertson good naturedly responded to a series of editorial demands and thus made possible the publication of this book. The wit and knowledge they expressed in the lecture room and on the ground at Gettysburg provided good reason to hope we can all get together again some day. George Skoch once again served as our cartographer, displaying his usual skill at turning rough sketches into finished maps that complement the essays very well. As with the essayists, he met every deadline without complaint. The help of all these individuals lightened the editor's load considerably.

"If the Enemy Is There, We Must Attack Him"

R. E. Lee and the Second Day at Gettysburg

GARY W. GALLAGHER

N o aspect of R. E. Lee's military career has sparked more controversy than his decision to pursue the tactical offensive at Gettysburg. Lee's contemporaries and subsequent writers produced a literature on the subject notable for its size and discordancy. Unwary students can fall victim to the hyperbole, dissembling, and self-interest characteristic of many accounts by participants. The massive printed legacy of the "Gettysburg Controversy," with its blistering critiques of James Longstreet and "Old Pete's" clumsy rejoinders, demands special care. Even many modern writers unfurl partisan banners when they approach the topic. Despite the size of the existing literature, Lee's decision to resume offensive combat on July 2 remains a topic worthy of study. Before passing judgment on his actions, however, it is necessary to assess the merits of earlier works—an exercise that underscores the contradictory nature of the evidence and the lack of interpretive consensus among previous writers.

The Army of Northern Virginia went into Pennsylvania at its physical apogee, supremely confident that under Lee's direction it could triumph on any battlefield. LeRoy Summerfield Edwards of the 12th Virginia Infantry struck a common note in a letter written near Shepherdstown on June 23: "[T]he health of the troops was never better and above all the *morale* of the army was never more favorable for offensive or defensive operations . . . victory will inevitably attend our arms in any collision with the enemy." British observer A. J. L. Fremantle detected a similar outlook when he spoke to a pair of officers from Louisiana on that same day. Recuperating from wounds suffered in fighting at Winchester during the march northward, these men gave Fremantle "an animated account of the spirits and feeling of the army. At no period of the war, they say, have the men been so well equipped, so well clothed, so eager for a fight, or so confident of success. . . ."[1]

Two weeks and more than twenty-five thousand casualties later the picture had changed considerably. The soldiers still believed in Lee, but they had lost their almost mystical faith in certain victory. Randolph H. McKim, a young Marylander in Richard S. Ewell's Second Corps, betrayed such sentiment in his diary shortly after Gettysburg: "I went into the last battle feeling that victory *must* be ours—that such an army could not be foiled, and that God would certainly declare himself on our side. *Now* I feel that unless He sees fit to bless our arms, our valor will not avail." Stephen Dodson Ramseur, a brigadier in Robert E. Rodes's division, reacted similarly to the shock of Gettysburg. "Our great campaign," wrote Ramseur a month after the battle, "admirably planned & more admirably executed up to the fatal days at Gettysburg, has failed. Which I was not prepared to anticipate." Although insisting that Gettysburg did not spell the doom of the Confederacy, he believed it foreshadowed other crises the South must overcome to gain independence. Ramseur looked "the thing square in the face" and stood ready "to undergo dangers and hardships and trials to the end."[2]

Staggering losses and a shift in morale thus grew out of Lee's decision to press for a decisive result on the field at Gettysburg. Some Southerners immediately questioned his tactics. "Gettysburg has shaken my faith in Lee as a general," Robert Garlick Hill Kean of the War Department wrote in his diary on July 26, 1863. "To fight an enemy superior in numbers at such terrible disadvantage of position in the heart of his own territory, when the freedom of movement gave him the advantage of selecting his own time and place for accepting battle, seems to have been a great military blunder. . . . and the result was the worst disaster which has ever befallen our arms—." Brigadier General Wade Hampton used comparably strong language in a letter to Joseph E. Johnston less than a month after the battle. The Pennsylvania campaign was a "complete failure," stated Hampton, during which Lee resorted to unimaginative offensive tactics. "The position of the Yankees there was the strongest I ever saw & it was in vain to attack it." Hampton had expected the Confederates to "choose our own points at which to fight" during the expedition, but "we let Meade choose his position and then we attacked."[3]

More restrained in his disapproval was James Longstreet, who informed his uncle Augustus Baldwin Longstreet confidentially in late July 1863 that the "battle was not made as I would have made it. My idea was to throw ourselves between the enemy and Washington, select a strong position, and force the enemy to attack us." Through such a defensive stance, thought Longstreet, the Confederates might have "destroyed the Federal army, marched into Washington, and dictated our terms, or, at least, held Washington and marched over as much of Pennsylvania as we cared to, had we drawn the enemy into attack upon our carefully chosen position in his rear."[4]

The early postwar years witnessed a rapid escalation of the debate over Lee's generalship at Gettysburg. Longstreet served as a catalyst for an outpouring of writing, the opening salvo of which appeared the year after Appomattox in William Swinton's *Campaigns of the Army of the Potomac.* A Northern journalist, Swinton interviewed Longstreet and drew heavily on his opinions to portray Lee's tactics at Gettysburg as misguided and contrary to a precampaign pledge to "his corps-commanders that *he would not assume a tactical offensive, but force his antagonist to attack him.*" Lee's assaults on the second day were a "grave error" explained by overconfidence in the prowess of his soldiers, fear that withdrawal without battle would harm morale in the Army of Northern Virginia and among Southern civilians, and contempt for the Army of the Potomac. Having "gotten a taste of blood in the considerable success of the first day," suggested Swinton in language similar to that used elsewhere by Longstreet, "the Confederate commander seems to have lost that equipoise in which his faculties commonly moved, and he determined to give battle."[5]

Other early postwar accounts also highlighted questions about Lee's aggressive tactics. Edward A. Pollard, the staunchly pro-Southern editor of the *Richmond Examiner* during the war, alluded in 1866 to "a persistent popular opinion in the South that Gen. Lee, having failed to improve the advantage of the first day, did wrong thereafter to fight at Gettysburg." Granting the "extraordinary strength" of the Federal position, Pollard nonetheless asserted that the superlative morale of Lee's army might have justified the attempt to drive Meade's army from the field.[6] James D. McCabe, Jr.'s, generally appreciative *Life and Campaigns of General Robert E. Lee*, also published in 1866, argued that after July 1 the Confederate army "had before it the task of storming a rocky fortress stronger than that against which Burnside had dashed his army so madly at Fredericksburg, and every chance of success lay with the Federals." Citing Swinton's work as corroboration, McCabe endorsed Longstreet's proposal to shift around the Federal left and invite attack from a position between the Union army and Washington. "There are those who assert that General Lee himself was not free from the contempt entertained by his men for the army they had so frequently vanquished, and that he was influenced by it in his decision upon this occasion," added McCabe in reference to Lee's resumption of assaults on July 2. "This may or may not be true. It is certain that the decision was an error."[7]

The interpretive tide turned in Lee's favor shortly after the general's death. Led by Jubal A. Early, a number of former

General Robert Edward Lee

(Francis Trevelyan Miller, ed. *The Photographic History of the Civil War.*
10 vols. New York: Review of Reviews, 1911, 2:235 [hereafter cited as
Photographic History])

Confederates eventually mounted a concerted effort in the Southern Historical Society's *Papers* and elsewhere to discredit Longstreet (whose Republicanism made him an especially inviting target) and prove Lee innocent of all responsibility for the debacle at Gettysburg. Speaking at Washington and Lee University on the anniversary of Lee's birth in 1872, Early disputed the notion that the Confederates should have refrained from attacking after July 1. "Some have thought that General Lee did wrong in fighting at Gettysburg," remarked Early in obvious reference to Longstreet's views, "and it has been said that he ought to have moved around Meade's left, so as to get between him and Washington. . . . I then thought, and still think, that it was right to fight the battle of Gettysburg, and I am firmly convinced that if General Lee's plans had been carried out in the spirit in which they were conceived, a decisive victory would have been obtained, which perhaps would have secured our independence."

As the most prominent member of the Lost Cause school of interpretation, Early won a deserved reputation as Lee's most indefatigable defender and Longstreet's harshest critic. He blamed defeat on Longstreet's sulking sloth in mounting the assaults on July 2. Lee expected the attacks to begin at dawn, insisted Early (a charge Longstreet easily proved to be literally untrue—though Lee certainly wanted the attacks to commence as early as possible); Longstreet began the offensive about 4:00 P.M., by which time Meade's entire army was in place. "The position which Longstreet attacked at four, was not occupied by the enemy until late in the afternoon," concluded Early, "and Round Top Hill, which commanded the enemy's position, could have been taken in the morning without out a struggle."[8]

Although few veterans of the Army of Northern Virginia spoke publicly against Lee during the postwar years, many did not share Early's views. Benjamin G. Humphreys, who commanded the 21st Mississippi Infantry in William Barksdale's

brigade on the second day at Gettysburg, revealed sharp disagreement with the Lost Cause writers in comments he scrib-
bled in the margins of his copy of Walter Taylor's *Four Years
with General Lee.* Humphreys deplored the "necessity of hunt-
ing out for a 'scapegoat'" to guarantee that the "'infallibility'
of Lee must not be called into question." The commanding
general "took upon himself all the blame for Gettysburg,"
observed Humphreys mockingly, "was that not an evidence of
his infallibility?"[9]

Lee himself said little publicly beyond his official report.
The fighting on July 1 had escalated from a meeting engagement to a bitter contest involving two corps on each side,
during the course of which the serendipitous arrival of Ewell's
leading divisions had compelled the Federals to withdraw
through Gettysburg to high ground below the town. "It had
not been intended to deliver a general battle so far from our
base unless attacked," wrote Lee in apparent confirmation of
Longstreet's assertion that he had envisioned acting on the
tactical defensive in Pennsylvania, "but coming unexpectedly
upon the whole Federal Army, to withdraw through the mountains with our extensive trains would have been difficult and
dangerous." Nor could the Confederates wait for Meade to
counterattack, "as the country was unfavorable for collecting
supplies in the presence of the enemy, who could restrain our
foraging parties by holding the mountain passes with local
troops." "A battle had, therefore, become in a measure unavoidable," concluded Lee, "and the success already gained gave
hope of a favorable issue."[10]

Lee offered the last hopeful statement despite a firm understanding of the terrain. "The enemy occupied a strong position," he conceded, "with his right upon two commanding
elevations adjacent to each other, one southeast and the other,
known as Cemetery Hill, immediately south of the town. . . .
His line extended thence upon the high ground along the
Emmitsburg Road, with a steep ridge in rear, which was also

Union Breastworks on Little Round Top
(Robert Underwood Johnson and Clarence Clough Buel, eds. *Battles and Leaders of the Civil War.* 4 vols. New York: The Century Company, 1887, 3:300 [hereafter cited as *Battles and Leaders*])

occupied. This ridge was difficult of ascent, particularly the two hills above mentioned as forming its northern extremity, and a third at the other end, on which the enemy's left rested." Stone and rail fences affording protection to defenders, together with generally open approaches three-quarters of a mile wide, complicated any plan of assault. Yet offensive thoughts dominated Lee's thinking. When Ewell declined to strike at

Union Artillery Positions on Cemetery Hill,
Culp's Hill in the Distance
(*Battles and Leaders* 3:310)

Cemetery Hill late on the afternoon of July 1, the commanding
general opted to await the arrival of Longstreet's two leading
divisions: "It was determined to make the principal attack
upon the enemy's left. . . . Longstreet was directed to place the
divisions of McLaws and Hood on the right of Hill, partially
enveloping the enemy's left, which he was to drive in."
A. P. Hill would engage the Union center with a demonstration,
while Ewell's troops would do the same on the enemy's right
with an eye toward exploiting any opening.[11]

Almost matter-of-fact in its explication of the reasons for
resuming attacks on July 2, Lee's report contains no hint that
he considered the decision a bad one. Five years after the battle,
he responded to a query about Gettysburg in a similar vein:
"I must again refer you to the official accounts. Its loss was

occasioned by a combination of circumstances. It was commenced in the absence of correct intelligence. It was continued
in the effort to overcome the difficulties by which we were
surrounded, and it would have been gained could one determined and united blow have been delivered by our whole
line."[12]

Several secondhand accounts also suggest that Lee never
deviated from the tenor of his report. Colonel William Allan,
former chief of ordnance in the Second Corps, made notes of
a conversation with Lee on April 15, 1868, wherein Lee talked
passionately about Gettysburg. Lee had hoped to avoid a general battle in Pennsylvania, recorded Allan, but "Jeb" Stuart's
absence caused the opposing forces to stumble into one another on July 1. The commanding general "found himself engaged with the Federal army therefore, unexpectedly, and had
to fight. This being determined on, victory w[oul]d have been
won if he could have gotten one decided simultaneous attack
on the whole line." Lee also observed that his critics "talked
much of that they knew little about" and, in a likely reference
to William Swinton's book, stated that he doubted Longstreet
ever said Lee "was under a promise to the Leut. Generals not
to fight a general battle in Pa. . . . He never made any such
promise, and he never thought of doing any such thing."[13]

Nearly two years later, Lee again "spoke feelingly" about
Gettysburg with Allan. "Much was said about risky movements," noted Allan. Lee believed that "everything was risky
in our war. He knew oftentimes that he was playing a very
bold game, but it was the only *possible* one." This justification
of risk, though not specifically tied to any phase of the campaign, certainly could apply to Lee's pursuing assaults after
the first day. As in his earlier pronouncements on the subject,
Lee seemed content with his principal decisions. He still maintained that Stuart's failure had precipitated the fighting, and
the fact that he "never c[oul]d get a simultaneous attack on
the enemy's position" sealed the result.[14]

Accounts by Brigadier General John D. Imboden and Major John Seddon further buttress an image of Lee as comfortable with his tactical conduct at Gettysburg. Early on the morning of July 4, wrote Imboden in the 1880s, he met with Lee at army headquarters outside Gettysburg. The conversation turned to the failed assaults on July 3: "I never saw troops behave more magnificently than Pickett's division of Virginians did to-day in that grand charge upon the enemy," averred Lee. "And if they had been supported as they were to have been . . . we would have held the position and the day would have been ours." It is reasonable to infer from this passage that Lee also viewed the resumption of the offensive on July 2 as correct. Major Seddon, a brother of the Confederate secretary of war, met with Lee shortly after Gettysburg and subsequently related his conversation to Major General Henry Heth. Heth quoted Seddon as stating that Lee acknowledged a heavy loss at Gettysburg but pronounced it "no greater than it would have been from the series of battles I would have been compelled to fight had I remained in Virginia." After making this observation, Lee rose from his seat and with an "emphatic gesture said, 'and sir, we did whip them at Gettysburg, and it will be seen for the next six months that *that army* will be as quiet as a sucking dove.'"[15]

A smaller body of evidence portrays Lee as subject to doubts about his tactical moves at Gettysburg. Perhaps best known is Fremantle's description of Lee's response to Brigadier General Cadmus M. Wilcox as the latter brought his brigade out of the fight on July 3: "Never mind, General, *all this has been MY fault*—it is *I* that have lost this fight, and you must help me out of it in the best way you can."[16] Whether or not Lee meant the entire battle when he spoke of "this fight," his comment can be extended to the decision to keep attacking after July 1. In early August 1863, Lee informed President Davis that he was aware of public criticisms of his generalship at Gettysburg. "I do not know how far this feeling extends in the army," wrote Lee. "My brother officers have been too kind to report it, and so far the troops have been too generous to exhibit it. It is fair, however, to suppose that it does exist, and success is so necessary to us that nothing should be risked to secure it." Offering to step down as commander of the army, Lee implicitly recognized that he had erred in Pennsylvania: "I cannot even accomplish what I myself desire. How can I fulfill the expectations of others?"[17]

Two additional vignettes, though both hearsay, merit mention. Henry Heth remembered after the war that he and Lee discussed Gettysburg at Orange Court House during the winter of 1863–64. "After it is all over, as stupid a fellow as I am can see the mistakes that were made," said the commanding general somewhat defensively. "I notice, however, my mistakes are never told me until it is too late, and you, and all my officers, know that I am always ready and anxious to have their suggestions." Captain Thomas J. Goree of Longstreet's staff recalled in an 1875 letter to his old chief a similar episode at Orange Court House in the winter of 1864. Summoned to Lee's tent, Goree found that the general had been looking through Northern newspapers. Lee "remarked that he had just been reading the Northern official reports of the Battle of Gettysburg, that he had become satisfied from reading those reports that if he had permitted you to carry out your plans on the 3d day, instead of making the attack on Cemetery Hill, we would have been successful."[18] Because Longstreet first argued for a movement around the Federal flank on July 2, it is possible that in retrospect Lee also considered the assaults of the second day to have been unwise.

Many later writings about Gettysburg by Confederate participants followed furrows first plowed by Jubal Early and his cohorts in their savaging of James Longstreet. They insisted that Longstreet disobeyed Lee's orders to attack early on July 2, dragged his feet throughout that crucial day, and was slow again on July 3. Had "Old Pete" moved with dispatch, the Confederates would have won the battle and perhaps the war. No questioning of Lee's commitment to bloody offensive action after July 1 clouded the simplistic reasoning of these authors, typical of whom was former Second Corps staff officer James Power Smith. In a paper read before the Military History Society of Massachusetts in 1905, Smith recounted the conference among Lee and his Second Corps subordinates on the evening of July 1. Events of that day dictated further attacks, stated Smith. "There was no retreat without an engagement," he affirmed. "Instead of the defensive, as he had planned, General Lee was compelled to take the offensive, and himself endeavor to force the enemy away. It was not by the choice of Lee nor by the foresight of Meade that the Federal army found itself placed on lines of magnificent defence." Persuaded that Ewell's corps lacked the power to capture high ground on the Union right, Lee concluded that Longstreet would spearhead an effort against the enemy's left on July 2. "Then with bowed head he added, 'Longstreet is a very good fighter when he gets in position, but he is *so slow.*'" This last comment, a staple of the Lost Cause canon with no direct supporting evidence from Lee's own hand, anticipated the further argument that Lee's sound planning ran aground on the rock of Longstreet's lethargic movements.[19]

Longstreet defended himself against his tormentors ineptly, launching indiscreet counterattacks that often strayed widely from the truth and provoked further onslaughts against his character and military ability. One notorious example of his poor judgment will suffice: "That [Lee] was excited and off his balance was evident on the afternoon of the 1st," claimed Longstreet in his memoirs, "and he labored under that oppression until enough blood was shed to appease him." Such statements provoked a massive response from Longstreet's critics, creating a body of evidence that would damn him in the eyes of many subsequent historians.[20]

The writings of Brigadier General Edward Porter Alexander stood in notable contrast to the emotional approach of many

Colonel Edward Porter Alexander
(*Photographic History* 5:61)

former Confederates. Easily the most astute military analyst among Lee's lieutenants, he sometimes is perceived as an apologist for Longstreet because he served for much of the war as chief of artillery in the First Corps. In fact, Alexander probed in brilliantly dispassionate fashion Lee's generalship at Gettysburg. He thought a casual reading of Lee's report "suggests that the aggressive on [the] second day seemed forced upon him, yet the statement is very much qualified by the expression 'in a measure,' & also by the reference to the hopes inspired by our partial success." Alexander bluntly declared that "no real difficulty" prevented Lee's shifting to the defensive on July 2 and maneuvering in such a manner as to force Meade to attack. Lee's reference to his trains failed to impress Alexander, who as the army's former chief of ordnance possessed an excellent grasp of the difficulties of moving large numbers of wagons.

With an engineer's love of precision, Alexander reckoned "it a reasonable estimate to say that 60 per cent of our chances for a great victory were lost by our continuing the aggressive. And we may easily imagine the boon it was to Gen. Meade . . . to be relieved from the burden of making any difficult decision, such as what he would have had to do if Lee had been satisfied with his victory of the first day; & then taken a strong position & stood on the defensive." Expressing astonishment that "the strength of the enemy's position seems to have cut no figure in the consideration [of] the question of the aggressive," Alexander labeled Meade's good fortune "more than impudence itself could have dared to pray for—a position unique among all the battlefields of the war, certainly adding fifty per cent to his already superior force, and an adversary stimulated by success to an utter disregard of all physical disadvantages. . . ."

These opinions aside, Alexander believed that victory eluded the Confederates on July 2 only because Longstreet's assaults began so late. Professing no doubt that the offensive could have started sooner, he expressed equal certainty that "Gen. Lee much desired it to be made very much earlier." Longstreet's preference to await the arrival of Evander M. Law's brigade, to which Lee acceded, and the delay occasioned by Southern infanty near Black Horse Tavern coming into view of Federal signalmen on Little Round Top slowed the flanking march. Present on the field the entire time and "apparently consenting to the situation from hour by hour," Lee bore a major portion of responsibility for the late opening of the attacks by Alexander's reading of the evidence.[21]

Modern writers have continued to explore Lee's choice to resume offensive operations on July 2. Easily the most influential of Lee's biographers is Douglas Southall Freeman. After discussing Lee's conferences with Ewell and Longstreet on the evening of July 1, Freeman asked, "But was it wise to attack at all? What alternatives were there?" Freeman listed four available courses of action: Lee could take up a defensive position on the field and invite attack from Meade; he could retreat to the western side of South Mountain; he could move around the Union left as Longstreet urged, placing the army between the Federals and Washington; or he could mount another series of attacks in the hope of achieving a complete victory. The first two alternatives Freeman dismissed quickly with a paraphrase of Lee's official report. The third he termed impractical, citing the opinions of "nearly all military critics"—the roster of whom included Jubal Early, William Allan, Armistead L. Long, and other stalwart members of the Lost Cause school of interpretation. With unintended irony, Freeman admitted in a footnote that George G. Meade "was the only critic who agreed with Longstreet. He said that Longstreet's proposal was . . . the step he feared Lee would take. . . ."[22]

Freeman thus brought himself to the fourth option. Once again paraphrasing Lee, he concluded: "Strategically, then, Lee saw no alternative to attacking the enemy before Meade concentrated, much as he disliked to force a general engagement so early in the campaign and at such a distance from Virginia."

Tactically, Freeman approved of Lee's plan to use the divisions of McLaws and Hood to deliver the heaviest blow on the Union left, with Ewell's corps doing what it could against the enemy's far right. Little did Lee know, contended Freeman, that as he anticipated another day's combat his plans already were being undone. In a statement worthy of Jubal Early, Lee's great biographer closed his chapter on July 1: "The battle was being decided at that very hour in the mind of Longstreet, who at his camp, a few miles away, was eating his heart away in sullen resentment that Lee had rejected his long-cherished plan of a strategic offensive and a tactical defensive." That sullenness manifested itself in a performance on July 2 so sluggish "it has often been asked why Lee did not arrest him for insubordination or order him before a court-martial." Freeman answered that an absence of qualified officers forced Lee to make do with Longstreet, warts and all, even as he lamented the absence of "Stonewall" Jackson.[23]

Other historians offer a mixture of praise and censure for Lee's decision to attack on July 2. Clifford Dowdey, whom one reviewer aptly called "the last *Confederate* historian," endorsed Lee's offensive inclination, observing that Lee apparently never thought of shifting to the defensive. Dowdey emphasized the need for a quick Confederate triumph: "[Lee's] thinking was shaped by the background of the South's waning strength, by the present illustration of the attrition in high command, and by the need for a decisive victory away from home. . . . His men were driving the enemy, and, though Ewell had kept them from clinching the victory today, Lee thought only of how to complete it the next day." Poor execution robbed the army of success on July 2, but the decision to seek that success had been correct.[24] Frank E. Vandiver echoed Dowdey, with the twist that a spell of ill health in Pennsylvania rendered Lee edgy and more inclined to seek a quick resolution. His physical ailments and Longstreet's stubbornness left Lee "generally irritated and he's determined that he is going to attack." "He has every reason for wanting to do that," judged Vandiver, "he has his army in Pennsylvania, it's at its finest strength and gear and this is the time to cast the die. Across the field is a Union general, George G. Meade, who has been in command of the Army of the Potomac only two weeks [sic], doesn't know much about his army and might be unready to fight a major engagement."[25]

Even the British historian J. F. C. Fuller, widely known as a severe critic of Lee, essentially accepted the rationale in the general's official report of the campaign. The "defective supply arrangements and the absence of his cavalry (to disengage himself) compelled him to fight," wrote Fuller, "and to fight an offensive action in place of a defensive one; for, as he had to live on the country, it was impossible for him to stand still for any length of time." Fuller believed that an inability to move and forage simultaneously ruled out Longstreet's option. This approval of the decision to attack on July 2 contrasted sharply with Fuller's estimate of Lee's tactical blueprint, which he considered "a thoroughly bad plan" with little prospect of success.[26]

H. J. Eckenrode and Bryan Conrad generally treated Lee favorably in their harsh biography of Longstreet (their real hero was Stonewall Jackson), but at Gettysburg these authors deviated from their usual pattern. They found that the commanding general "blundered into battle" and once committed "showed no genius in the manner in which he conducted it, making no feints and relying on frontal attacks on a formidable position."[27]

Few historians probed the questions of Gettysburg more judiciously than Edwin B. Coddington, Harry W. Pfanz, and Alan T. Nolan—yet their careful examinations produced differing conclusions. Coddington weighed Lee's options for July 2, took into account the explanations in his official report, and resolved that although Lee's expressed concern about his trains and living off the countryside had some validity, the general perhaps overstated the dangers of withdrawal. The key to Lee's action was psychological—he and his army would not retreat unless pushed. "They had just achieved a smashing success against a part of the Union army," wrote Coddington, "and now was the time for them to finish the job. The stakes were high, and they might never again have as good an opportunity." Coddington viewed the decision as perfectly in keeping with the pattern of offensive combat forged by Lee and his army in previous campaigns.[28]

Pfanz agreed that Lee's decision to keep attacking was reasonable. Longstreet's proposed flanking movement posed logistical problems, Stuart was unavailable to screen the march, and the whereabouts of much of the Union army remained unknown; moreover, a "shift to the left and away from the valley that sheltered the Confederate line of communications was virtually out of the question." A defensive stand would transfer the initiative to Meade, who might circumscribe Southern foraging while calling up Union reinforcements, and thus "did not seem a practical course of action." "In General Lee's words," Pfanz stated in summary, "a battle had, therefore, become in a measure unavoidable.'" Nolan disagreed strongly, attributing rationales for Lee's aggressive behavior after July 1 to an unpersuasive school of apologists for the Southern chief. "When all is said and done, the commentators' rationalizations of Lee's most daring offensive thrusts seem contrived," insisted Nolan. "Although these commentators are aware that Lee's efforts were unsuccessful, costly, and destructive to the South's chances of victory in the war, they are committed to the Lee tradition and seem to strain to absolve him."[29]

Lee's decision to pursue the offensive on July 2 manifestly has produced such cacophonous opinions as to confuse the most earnest student. But despite the contradictory shadow cast by this imposing mass of material—and accepting the fact that definitive answers are impossible at a distance of more than a century and a quarter—it remains worthwhile to train a close lens on the crucial questions: Was it reasonable for Lee to renew assaults on July 2? On the basis of his knowledge at the time, did aggressive tactics offer the best chance for the type of sweeping success on Northern soil that might propel the Confederacy toward independence?

The situation at the end of the first day of fighting is well known. Lee had arrived on the field early in the afternoon and, in the words of Walter H. Taylor of his staff, "ascertained that the enemy's infantry and artillery were present in considerable force. Heth's division was already hotly engaged, and it was soon evident that a serious engagement could not be avoided."[30] Only two of Heth's brigades actually had experienced serious fighting at that point, however, and Lee found himself witness to a meeting engagement rather than a general battle. It soon became apparent that the positioning of units from Richard S. Ewell's Second Corps, which were arriving on the northern end of the field, afforded the Confederates a tactical edge that Lee promptly exploited to good advantage. By 4:30 P.M., Southern attackers had driven the Federals to defensive lines along the high ground south of Gettysburg. Lee watched the action from atop Seminary Ridge, sensed the makings of a striking victory, and shortly after 5:00 P.M. instructed Ewell to seize the heights below town if practicable. For a variety of reasons, Ewell decided not to do so. Why Lee refused to commit some of A. P. Hill's troops—especially the fresh division of Richard H. Anderson—to a final joint assault with Ewell's brigades remains a mystery; the upshot was that daylight expired with Union troops firmly entrenched on Cemetery Hill.[31]

About 5:00 P.M., James Longstreet found Lee on Seminary Ridge. Dismounting and taking out his field glasses, Longstreet scanned the high ground that eventually would constitute the famous Union fish hook. Impressed by the strength of the enemy's position, Longstreet soon engaged Lee in an increasingly tense conversation. The only eyewitness testimony about this exchange comes from Longstreet, who left three versions that agree in substance but differ in detail. Longstreet suggested to Lee that the Confederates move around the Federal left and take up a defensive position between the Army of the Potomac and Washington; once situated, they could force Meade to attack them and then seek an opening for a counter-stroke. This proposed movement, claimed Longstreet in all of his later writings, conformed to an agreement between himself and Lee to pursue a strategic offensive but remain on the tactical defensive in Pennsylvania. He therefore was surprised at Lee's response: "If the enemy is there to-morrow, we must attack him." Loath to embrace aggressive tactics, Longstreet persisted in his arguments. But Lee did not "seem to abandon the idea of attack on the next day. He seemed under a subdued excitement, which occasionally took possession of him when 'the hunt was up'.... The sharp battle fought by Hill and Ewell on that day had given him a taste of victory."[32]

James Power Smith of Ewell's staff presently joined Lee and Longstreet with news that Jubal Early and Robert Rodes believed they could take the high ground south of Gettysburg if supported on their right. Thinking Hill's troops too exhausted for such duty, Lee asked Longstreet if the leading elements of the First Corps were near enough to assist. According to Smith, Longstreet "replied that his front division, McLaws, was about six miles away, and then was indefinite and noncommital."[33] Disappointed with Longstreet's response, Lee instructed Smith to tell Ewell "he regretted that his people were not up to support him on the right, but he wished him to take the Cemetery Hill if it were possible; and that he would ride over and see him very soon."[34]

Lest Smith's reading be deemed suspect because of his well-known antipathy toward "Old Pete," it is important to note that a trio of witnesses friendly to Longstreet also sketched a man deeply upset about the prospect of attacking on July 2. G. Moxley Sorrel of Longstreet's staff remembered that the lieutenant general "did not want to fight on the ground or on the plan adopted by the General-in-Chief. As Longstreet was not to be made willing and Lee refused to change or could not change, the former failed to conceal some anger." Raphael J. Moses, commissary officer of the First Corps, wrote in his unpublished autobiography that later in the evening Longstreet expounded at length to Fremantle about the enemy's position, insisting that "the Union army would have greater advantages at Gettysburg than we had at Fredericksburg." Fremantle himself noted that over supper on July 1, "General Longstreet spoke of the enemy's position as being 'very formidable.' He also said that they would doubtless intrench themselves strongly during the night."[35] Of Longstreet's deep misgivings there can be no doubt; nor is it likely that his words and gestures failed to convey his feelings to Lee.

Sometime after 5:30 P.M., Longstreet departed and Lee rode toward Ewell's end of the line. Lee must have worried about the attitude of his senior lieutenant, whose friendship he valued and upon whom he had relied heavily since calling him "the staff of my right hand" in the wake of the Seven Days.[36] Although he knew from a reconnaissance by Armistead L. Long of his staff that Federals held Cemetery Hill in strength, Lee also wondered why firing had slackened along the Second Corps front. He had instructed Ewell to take that high ground if possible, and his postwar conversations with William Allan clearly indicated deep dissatisfaction at Ewell's failure to press his assaults. Walter Taylor's memoirs confirm that Lee was unhappy: "The prevailing idea with General Lee was, to press forward without delay; to follow up promptly and vigorously the advantage already gained. Having failed to reap the full fruit of the victory before night, his mind was evidently occupied with the idea of renewing the assaults upon the enemy's right with the dawn of day on the second."[37]

Lee thus reached Second Corps headquarters north of Gettysburg in a testy mood. He and the principal commanders of

Major General Jubal Anderson Early
(*Photographic History* 10:245)

Stonewall Jackson's old corps gathered after dusk in the arbor of a small house near the Carlisle road. The ensuing conversation deepened Lee's frustration with his lieutenants. "It was evident from the first," recalled Jubal Early in the fullest eyewitness account of the meeting, "that it was his purpose to attack the enemy as early as possible the next day." Early maintained that "there was not the slightest . . . difference of opinion" about Lee's idea of continuing the offensive; however, all three Second Corps leaders argued against their troops spearheading the assaults. They had been impressed with the strength of Cemetery Hill, which Ewell's official report characterized as "a commanding position." Early took the lead in pointing to the Union left as the most vulnerable target.[38] Because Lee believed two of A. P. Hill's divisions had been fought out on July 1, the response of Ewell and his subordinates meant that the First Corps, headed by a suddenly peevish Longstreet, would perform the hardest work the following day.

Early averred in a controversial part of his account that Lee exhibited distress at the thought of relying on Longstreet: "When General Lee had heard our views . . . he said, in these very words, which are indelibly impressed on my memory: 'Well, if I attack from my right, Longstreet will have to make the attack;' and after a moment's pause, during which he held his head down in deep thought, he raised it and added: 'Longstreet is a very good fighter when he gets in position and gets everything ready, but he is *so slow*.'" This assertion, with its claim of precise accuracy nearly fifteen years after the alleged quotation was uttered, reeks of Lost Cause special pleading and lacks support from evidence closer to the event.[39] It is quite simply beyond belief that Lee would criticize his senior lieutenant in front of junior officers. Still, it is reasonable to assume that Lee did not relish the prospect of entrusting his assaults on July 2 to a man obviously opposed to resuming the offensive—and his facial expression may well have indicated as much to Early and the others.

Lee spent a long night working out details for the next day's fighting. Lack of enthusiasm among his subordinates for continuing the tactical offensive must have grated on him. The Army of Northern Virginia had built its formidable reputation on a series of impressive victories that with few exceptions included a large aggressive component. Had not the odds at the Seven Days or Second Manassas been less favorable for Southern success? And what of Chancellorsville? On all of those fields the army's offensive spirit had made the difference. Now Lee faced the prospect of planning a battle with substantive doubts regarding key Confederate commanders.

Although he strongly favored retaining the initiative, those doubts kept other options open. Longstreet's desire to flank the Federals remained on his mind. George Campbell Brown of Ewell's staff recalled in 1870 that Lee instructed him on the night of July 1 to tell Ewell "not to become so much involved as to be unable readily to extricate his troops." "I have not decided to fight here," stated Lee, "and may probably draw off by my right flank. . . . so as to get between the enemy & Washington & Baltimore, & force them to attack us in position."[40] During his meeting with the officers of the Second Corps, Lee had proposed moving their troops to the right but dropped the idea when Early argued, among other things, that it would hurt morale to give up ground won through hard combat. Lee returned to this idea later, however, sending Ewell orders "to draw [his] corps to the right." A second conference with Ewell, during which the corps chief expressed a willingness to attack Culp's Hill, persuaded Lee to leave the Second Corps in position on the left.[41] As stated before, the commanding general's final plan for July 2 called for Longstreet to make the principal attack against the Union left while Hill and Ewell supported him with secondary assaults against the enemy's center and right. Lee admonished Ewell to exploit any opportunity to convert his offensive into a full-blown attack.[42]

Few episodes in Lee's career reveal more starkly his natural aggressiveness. He had examined closely the imposing Federal position later described so graphically in his official report. Even the most optimistic scenario would project heavy casualties in an attempt to seize that ground. Jedediah Hotchkiss's journal records that on the morning of July 2, Lee discussed the upcoming assault at Second Corps headquarters and was not "very sanguine of its success. He feared . . . a great sacrifice of life." Lee knew from prisoners that two Union corps had been defeated on July 1, but he lacked information about the location of the bulk of the enemy's forces. In the absence of sound intelligence from his cavalry, he surmised only that the balance of Meade's army "was approaching Gettysburg."[43] His senior subordinate had disagreed sharply with the suggestion that offensive operations be resumed on July 2. Officers in the Second Corps were willing enough for Longstreet's soldiers to mount assaults but preferred a supporting role for their own men. In sum, powerful arguments could be raised against continuing the offensive.

Why did Lee choose to overlook all of them? His own explanations are unconvincing. Raphael Moses mentioned that Lee objected to Longstreet's flanking maneuver "on account of our long wagon and artillery trains"; as noted above, Lee also asserted in his official report that "to withdraw through the mountains with our extensive trains would have been difficult and dangerous." Lee further postulated a logistical crisis should he take a defensive position and await Meade's attack—his men had stripped the immediate region clean of supplies, and the enemy might use local troops to frustrate Southern efforts to forage on a large scale.[44]

Porter Alexander countered both of these points in one telling passage. "Now when it is remembered that we stayed for three days longer on that very ground, two of them days of desperate battle, ending in the discouragement of a bloody repulse," wrote the artillerist in the 1890s, "& then successfully withdrew all our trains & most of the wounded through the mountains; and finding the Potomac too high to ford, protected them all & foraged successfully for over a week in a very restricted territory along the river . . . it does not seem improbable that we could have faced Meade safely on the 2nd at Gettysburg without assaulting him in his wonderfully strong position." David Gregg McIntosh, like Alexander an artillerist who held Lee in the highest esteem, similarly dismissed the obstacles to Lee's pulling back on July 2: "The fact that he was able to do so after the battle, justifies the belief that Longstreet was right in his opinion that an attack in front was not advisable, and that General Lee committed an error in determining upon that course."[45]

Lee's notion that local units posed a serious threat to his army strains credulity. Jubal Early's memoirs captured the attitude of Confederates in the Army of Northern Virginia toward such troops. Describing a clash with soldiers of the 26th Pennsylvania Militia several days before the battle of Gettysburg, "Old Jube" identified them as "part of Governor Curtin's contingent for the defence of the State, . . . [who] seemed to belong to that class of men who regard 'discretion as the better part of valor.'" It was a good thing the regiment fled quickly, added Early sarcastically, "or some of its members might have been hurt, and all would have been captured." Those who did fall into Southern hands received paroles the next day and were "sent about their business, rejoicing at this termination of their campaign." George Templeton Strong of the United States Sanitary Commission took an equally derisive view of the Pennsylvania militia. On learning that they were mustering in strength, Strong wrote an acidic entry in his diary on June 30: "Much good they would do, to be sure, in combat with Lee's desperadoes, cunning sharp-shooters, and stark, hard-riding moss troopers."[46] Furthermore, correspondence on July 2–3 among Secretary of War Stanton and various Union commanders involved with local troops leaves no doubt about the ineffectiveness of the latter.[47] Had Lee decided to forage on either side of the South Mountain range, it is almost certain that his soldiers could have handled local Federal troops with impunity.

Even offensive moves by a combination of local forces and units from the Army of the Potomac—a remote possibility due to problems of transportation and morale among the former— should not have given Lee undue pause. His decision to attack on July 2 betrayed confidence that his soldiers could take a strong position from the enemy. It makes no sense to assert that those men would fail to hold a position against attacks from the same foe. Porter Alexander turned to a quotation from Stonewall Jackson in emphasizing this point: "We did sometimes fail to drive them out of position, but they *always* failed to drive us."[48]

What of Lee's dismissal of Longstreet's proposed flanking movement? Possible weaknesses in the plan must be given consideration (though Lee did not mention any in his report). If Longstreet envisioned a strategic rather than a tactical shift around Meade's left, the Army of Northern Virginia might have opened its own left flank to the Federals. Moreover, lines of supply and communication west of South Mountain might have been somewhat vulnerable.

But no such dangers would have obtained had Lee remained on the victorious field of July 1. As Porter Alexander put it, "We had a fine defensive position on Seminary Ridge ready at our hand to occupy. It was not such a really *wonderful* position as the enemy happened to fall into, but it was no bad one, & it could never have been successfully assaulted." To the west lay even stronger ground in the passes of South Mountain. A fragment of Lee's army had been driven from such gaps on September 14, 1862; however, the Army of Northern Virginia in July 1863 possessed the numbers and morale to hold the eastern face of the mountain indefinitely, all the while foraging in the lush Cumberland Valley. Had Lee fallen back to South

Mountain "with all the prestige of victory," thought Alexander, "popular sentiment would have forced Meade to take the aggressive."[49] The likely result of Northern assaults would have been a bloody repulse followed by some type of Confederate counterattack. Readily at hand was the example of Second Manassas, where Jackson had fixed the Federals with assaults on August 28, 1862, gone on the defensive the next day, and set the stage for Longstreet's smashing counterattack on the thirtieth.

The difficulty of Meade's situation after July 1 should be kept always in mind. Abraham Lincoln and the Republicans could not tolerate for long the presence of the most famous Rebel army on Northern soil. As early as June 14, a day before the first elements of the Army of Northern Virginia crossed the Potomac at Williamsport, Secretary of the Navy Gideon Welles sketched a very uneasy Union leadership. Noting "scary rumors abroad of army operations and a threatened movement of Lee upon Pennsylvania," Welles described Secretary of War Edwin M. Stanton as "uneasy" and Lincoln as fearful that thousands of Federal troops in the Shenandoah Valley would be lost—"Harper's Ferry over again." The next day Welles mentioned a "panic telegraph" from Pennsylvania's governor, Andrew G. Curtin, and rumors of Rebels in Chambersburg, Pennsylvania: "I can get nothing satisfactory from the War Department. . . . There is trouble, confusion, uncertainty, where there should be calm intelligence."[50]

The onus was on the Federals to force Lee away from Pennsylvania. Meade's initial orders underscored his responsibility as head of "the covering army of Washington as well as the army of operation against the invading forces of the rebels." Should Lee menace either Washington or Baltimore, stated General in Chief Henry W. Halleck in a telegram to Meade on June 28, "it is expected that you will either anticipate him or arrive with him so as to give him battle."[51] The crucial part of this order is that Meade was *to give* battle rather than simply await the enemy's moves. Lee's comment that a battle had become "in a measure unavoidable" after July 1 applied far more realistically to Meade than to himself.

Clearly a number of factors militated against Lee's attacking on July 2. Just as clearly, a defensive posture might have opened the way for a decisive counterattack. The prudent decision would have been to shift to the defensive following the tactical victory on July 1. From such a posture, Lee would retain great freedom of action following a likely Union attempt to defeat the Army of Northern Virginia through offensive tactics. The Confederates could have stayed north of the Potomac for a protracted period of time, thus adding logistical and political accomplishment to any military success. Finally, had Lee opted for the tactical defensive after the first day's battle, thousands of men shot down in assaults on July 2–3 would have been in the ranks for further service.

But acceptance of these statements does not prove that Lee made a foolish decision. A victory on Northern soil might aggravate internal dissension in the North and thus weaken Union resolve. Within the context of dwindling Confederate manpower (a state of affairs Lee's aggressive generalship had helped to produce), there was reason to believe the Army of Northern Virginia would never again face the Army of the Potomac on such relatively equal terms. Lee had seen his men perform prodigious feats on a number of battlefields—most recently against intimidating odds at Chancellorsville. The overriding influence in his choosing to resume the offensive on July 2 might have been a belief that the splendid Southern infantry could overcome the recalcitrance of his lieutenants, the difficulties of terrain, and everything else to achieve great results. Lee's subsequent comments that failures of coordination brought defeat suggest that he never doubted his soldiers might have won the fight. Fourteen years after the campaign, Henry Heth said simply, "The fact is, General Lee believed the Army of Northern Virginia, as it then existed, could accomplish anything."[52]

Ample testimony about soaring confidence in the Army of Northern Virginia lends credence to Lee's opinion, none more dramatically than Fremantle's description of morale on the night of July 1. Over supper that evening, recorded Fremantle, Longstreet discussed the reasons attacks might fail; however, in the ranks "the universal feeling in the army was one of profound contempt for an enemy whom they have beaten so constantly, and under so many disadvantages." Lee's great faith in his own men implied a degree of scorn for the Federals, an attitude noted by Fremantle's fellow foreign observer, Captain Justus Scheibert of the Prussian army: "Excessive disdain for the enemy . . . caused the simplest plan of a direct attack upon the position at Gettysburg to prevail and deprived the army of victory."[53]

If Lee did experience any regret about his decision to remain on the offensive after the first day's victory, perhaps it stemmed from a sense that he had asked the men to do so much despite obvious signs of trouble among his top lieutenants. Two of Lee's statements at the time illustrate this point. He wrote Mrs. Lee on July 26, 1863, that the army had "accomplished all that could reasonably be expected." "It ought not to have been expected to perform impossibilities, or to have fulfilled the anticipations of the thoughtless and unreasonable," admitted the general in a sentence that could well be taken as self-criticism. Five days later Lee wrote a preliminary report for Adjutant General Samuel Cooper in which he praised the "heroic valor and fortitude" of his troops. "More may have been required of them than they were able to perform," he acknowledged, "but my admiration of their noble qualities and confidence in their ability . . . has suffered no abatement. . . ."[54]

R. E. Lee confronted a crucial choice on the evening of July 1, 1863. His selection of the tactical offensive for July 2 reflected his predilection for aggressive action. Porter Alexander thought even Napoleon failed to surpass "some of the deeds of audacity to which Gen. Lee committed himself" and saw Gettysburg as an example of Lee's unnecessarily taking "the most desperate chances & the bloodiest road."[55] Without question Lee *did* gamble a very great deal on the throw of his offensive dice after July 1. He ruled out defensive maneuvers that might have opened breathtaking possibilities, and in the process he bled the future offensive edge from his magnificent army. It is not unfair to state from the safe confines of historical perspective that Lee erred in his decision. Many of his own contemporaries realized as much at the time. But it *is* unfair to look at the grisly result and argue that his actions were entirely unreasonable. Momentum and morale count heavily in warfare, and it was probably those two factors that motivated Lee to a significant degree. Had Southern infantry solidified the first day's victory through successful assaults on July 2, as they almost did, many of Lee's critics would have been silenced.

The Peach Orchard Revisited
Daniel E. Sickles and the Third Corps on July 2, 1863

WILLIAM GLENN ROBERTSON

W arfare ranks among the most complex of human endeavors. Participants must take into account a wide variety of variables, including terrain, weather, technology, and human frailties, all of which combine to produce a particular outcome. Not the least of warfare's complexities stems from the interaction of personalities among senior commanders. In any army in any century leaders have had their friends and their enemies, equals and subordinates they could trust and those they could not. Strong personalities breed strong reactions, both positive and negative. Such interpersonal relationships always affect the outcome of great events, far more in fact than participants usually admit. So it always has been, and so it always will be, as long as humans make war on each other in an organized manner. Obvious to contemporaries, this important web of interpersonal relationships often disappears from view after a conflict unless individuals choose to illuminate the relationships in their writings. Even when described in memoirs and other postwar accounts, these relationships often become distorted, generating claims and counterclaims that increasingly obscure the original issues and circumstances.

In seeking to reconstruct and analyze past events, historians must be aware of the relationships among senior officers and the frequent distortions of those relationships in postwar writings. Some historians unfortunately become parties in the debate rather than honest brokers, doing little more than

33

perpetuating the arguments of principals with whom they have come to identify. Objective truth is thus obscured rather than illuminated. Was Major General Ambrose E. Burnside as incompetent as conventional wisdom would have it? Probably not, as a recent biography argues. Was Major General Benjamin F. Butler as lacking in morality and military skills as his detractors, contemporary and otherwise, have so loudly proclaimed? Again, probably not. Historians should strive to meet the admittedly difficult test of viewing senior commanders with strong personalities and controversial records as impartially as possible. These officers should not be caricatured as either heroes or villains but should be seen as complex personalities interacting with others of a like nature in extremely stressful situations. Only in this manner can their decisions be analyzed dispassionately and understood.

Among senior commanders on both sides in the American Civil War, Major General Daniel Edgar Sickles enjoyed one of the most colorful careers. Sickles gained notoriety years before he donned a Federal general's uniform. His spirited personality and mixed reputation generated friends and enemies alike. He brought this baggage with him to Gettysburg, where his bold decision on the battle's second day added to the controversy already swirling about him. For various reasons that decision continued to generate debate long after the battle. Partisans gathered on both sides of the issue and quickly skewed the arguments of the principals. Even today Dan Sickles and his Gettysburg decision have the power to excite passions, as the most judicious student of the subject, Richard Sauers, has admitted. It is time to look again at Sickles's actions on July 2, 1863, with as much objectivity as possible. What was the context within which Sickles operated? What actions did he take? What were the results of those actions? What result might a different decision have generated?[1]

Born on October 20, 1819, in New York City, Daniel Edgar Sickles was the son of prominent patent lawyer George Garrett

Major General Daniel Edgar Sickles
(Courtesy of the Library of Congress)

Sickles and his wife Susan Marsh. Blessed with a nimble intelligence and boundless self-confidence, young Sickles vexed his parents by running away from home several times. An effort to instill discipline by sending him to boarding school in Glens Falls, New York, at the age of fifteen failed. Leaving school after an altercation with a teacher, Sickles worked as a printer's helper for more than a year before returning to New York City. There he soon began to associate with an unsavory crowd and to indulge in what would become a lifelong proclivity to dally with women of ill repute. His parents sought to separate him from his friends by moving the family to New Jersey, but Sickles again left home. Realizing that he could not bring his wayward son back to the family fold by force, George Sickles offered forgiveness and the promise of a free education. For two years Dan lived in the household of Lorenzo Da Ponte, a family friend who endeavored to prepare him for college. In the same household were the Antonio Bagiolis and their infant daughter Teresa, who eventually would become Sickles's wife. Sickles entered New York University during his second year with the Da Pontes.

When Da Ponte died suddenly, Sickles lost interest in college and pursued an entirely new path. He left school and studied law in the office of Benjamin F. Butler, President Martin Van Buren's attorney general, while beginning a long association with Democratic party politics at Tammany Hall. Admitted to the bar in 1843 at the age of twenty-four, Sickles soon gained a reputation as a rake, a spendthrift, and a partisan politician of high visibility. Election to the New York state assembly in 1847 offered a new arena to Sickles, who scandalized polite society by escorting a known prostitute into the legislative chambers. Sickles ignored censure by his peers, and both his political and legal careers prospered. On September 27, 1852, Sickles and Teresa Bagioli were married against the wishes of both families. She was sixteen and he almost thirty-three. Anyone who believed that marriage would transform Sickles's life-style experienced swift disappointment. In the words of one biographer, Sickles was a man of such "violent, undisciplined impulses" that he could hardly be expected to alter his behavior overnight, and indeed he did not.[2]

In 1853 Sickles took the position of confidential secretary to James Buchanan, newly appointed minister to Great Britain. Viewing Buchanan as a rising political figure, Sickles determined to advance along with his new superior even if it cost him money and entailed an absence from his pregnant wife. He cut quite a swath in England until July 1854, when he publicly refused to toast the health of Queen Victoria at an Independence Day banquet. This diplomatic faux pas, a backstage role in the abortive and infamous Ostend Manifesto, and an increasing need for more income led to Sickles's return to the United States late in 1854. Resuming his law practice, his political career, and his philandering where he had left them in 1853, he was elected to the New York state senate in 1855. Buchanan returned from abroad to run for president in 1856, while Sickles ran for Congress. Both were elected, but for different reasons neither would find the prize worth having. Buchanan soon began to struggle with the Union's greatest crisis; Sickles fell into a domestic squabble.[3]

Sickles's life-style in the nation's capital followed a predictable pattern. He lived far beyond his apparent means, continued his rakish indiscretions, and generally made himself notorious in Washington society. Re-elected in 1858, he immersed himself even more fully in political intrigue while Teresa languished at home. Some time in the spring of 1858 she began an affair with Philip Barton Key, the handsome U.S. attorney for the District of Columbia and son of Francis Scott Key. Eventually much of Washington came to know of their trysts, though Sickles did not learn of the affair until February 26, 1859. He confronted Teresa on that date, and she signed what amounted to a full confession. On seeing the unsuspecting Key signaling to Teresa the next day, Sickles rushed out of his house and shot him to death. Arrested and tried for murder, Sickles was acquitted in April. His successful defense rested on a plea of temporary insanity (by some accounts the first use of this defense), strong circumstantial evidence to the contrary nonwithstanding. Sickles created even greater comment when he accepted Teresa back into his household in July 1859. Surprisingly, few blamed Sickles for Key's demise, but fewer still could accept his decision to forgive Teresa.[4]

Most of Washington society ostracized Sickles, who completed his term in Congress under a cloud. Too realistic to make another race for office, Sickles returned to New York City in early 1861 to resume the practice of law. Thus he was relatively unencumbered when the secession crisis turned from words to acts of violence in April 1861. At the suggestion of a political friend, Sickles decided to raise a regiment. Authority from the governor of New York to raise one regiment soon mushroomed into authority to raise a brigade of five regiments. Sickles and his friends quickly recruited the brigade, calling it the Excelsior Brigade, and after considerable political and financial difficulty saw it accepted into Federal service in late July 1861. Assigned to a division commanded by Brigadier General Joseph Hooker, Sickles quickly fell into disfavor with his superior (they would later become friends). Further problems arose when the Senate refused to confirm his appointment as brigadier general. Fast political footwork and astute lobbying finally brought Sickles the coveted star on May 13, 1862, but his beloved Excelsior Brigade already had sailed to the Virginia Peninsula.[5]

Sickles's late arrival in the theater of war caused him to miss the battle of Williamsburg, the only significant action for the Excelsior Brigade during the Peninsula campaign. Present but only lightly engaged at Seven Pines, Oak Grove, Glendale, and Malvern Hill, the brigade nevertheless shared the accolades bestowed on Hooker's division by friendly newspapermen. Hooker himself praised Sickles's performance in combat. The brigade acquitted itself well at Second Bull Run in August 1862 while Sickles was absent in New York on recruiting duty. In the reorganization following that battle, Hooker rose to command the First Corps and Sickles took charge of Hooker's old division in the Third Corps. Although the division spent the Antietam campaign in reserve at Alexandria, Sickles's star continued to ascend with Hooker's. On November 29, 1862, Sickles was promoted to the rank of major general. His division again remained in reserve and saw little action at the Battle of Fredericksburg in December. More significant for Dan Sickles, the disaster at Fredericksburg prompted the Lincoln administration to select a new commander for the Army of the Potomac. Major General Joseph Hooker, Sickles's old superior and now his patron, replaced Burnside in late January 1863.[6]

Known for his aggressive fighting qualities as well as for an arrogant and dissolute life-style, Hooker skillfully reorganized the army. Sickles received command of the Third Corps on February 5, 1863, becoming the only non–West Pointer among the seven corps chiefs and the only one lacking experience at that level of responsibility. Hooker had seen Sickles in action on the Peninsula and remained confident that the New Yorker would acquit himself well. Others in the Army of the Potomac expressed doubts about Sickles's promotion. Indeed, many regular army officers objected to Hooker's appointment. Riddled with, and often hampered by, internal politics, the officer corps of the Army of the Potomac prepared for the next campaign in a sour mood.

More judicious than most of his peers, Major General George G. Meade of the Fifth Corps spoke of the situation to his wife in late January: "As to Hooker, you know my opinion of him, frequently expressed. I believe my opinion is more favorable than any other of the old regular officers, most of whom are decided in their hostility to him." "I believe Hooker is a good soldier," continued Meade, "the danger he runs is of subjecting himself to bad influences, such as Dan Butterfield and Dan Sickles, who, being intellectually more clever than Hooker, and leading him to believe they are very influential, will obtain an injurious ascendancy over him and insensibly affect his conduct." Meade further underscored his opinion of Butterfield and Sickles in February, when he wrote that "such gentlemen as Dan Sickles and Dan Butterfield are not the persons I should select as my intimates, however worthy and superior they may be." The cause of Meade's distaste for Sickles is unknown, but the latter's life-style and lack of professional military education must have played a large role.[7]

The Army of the Potomac embarked on the Chancellorsville campaign in late April 1863 burdened with a divided officer corps. For once Sickles's command found itself heavily engaged. Occupying the right center of Hooker's perimeter around the Chancellorsville crossroads on May 2, Sickles's troops discovered what ultimately proved to be the march of Stonewall Jackson's corps around the Union flank. Sickles advanced aggressively to deal with the Confederates, only to be recalled by Hooker. That evening the massive Confederate column rolled up the Federal right. Strongly positioned on dominant terrain at Hazel Grove, Sickles's Third Corps held its ground but became increasingly exposed by the morning of May 3. Although Sickles wanted to remain at Hazel Grove, Hooker ordered the Third Corps to withdraw to Fairview. In military terms Hazel Grove was an excellent place from which to dominate Fairview with artillery, a fact soon discovered by Confederates. Blasted by Southern guns at Hazel Grove, the Third Corps and the Army of the Potomac withdrew even farther, eventually leaving the field altogether. The Army of the Potomac had suffered another crushing defeat, but this time Dan Sickles's men had fought as long and as hard as any of the army's units. Losses in the Third Corps amounted to 4,119 killed, wounded, or missing, the largest total for any corps on the Chancellorsville field itself, as even Meade grudgingly admitted.[8]

The debacle of Chancellorsville exacerbated existing fractures in the command structure of the Army of the Potomac. Hooker had called a conference of his corps commanders late in the battle to seek their advice. Although a majority recommended an advance instead of a retreat, Hooker had withdrawn the army to its camps. Meade was among those favoring an advance. When he learned after the battle that Hooker was misrepresenting his position, Meade confronted his superior and asked for corroboration from his fellow corps leaders. He received satisfaction from all but Sickles, who, ever the Hooker partisan, reported that by the end of the conference Meade had waffled on the question. Meade's reaction to Sickles's response is unknown but can easily be surmised. As the Army of the Potomac moved northward in the early stages of what would become the Gettysburg campaign, most of its senior leaders had taken sides on the larger question of Hooker's leadership. Chief of Staff Daniel Butterfield and Sickles stood as Hooker's principal defenders. Notable among Hooker's detractors were Major General John F. Reynolds of the First Corps and George Meade. When a minor dispute over the Federal garrison at Harpers Ferry supplied a pretext, the Lincoln administration removed Hooker on June 28, 1863, and replaced him with Meade.[9]

Meade's rise to supreme command brought not only a fresh face to army headquarters but also an entirely new faction to control of the Army of the Potomac. Although he kept Dan Butterfield as chief of staff for a time, Meade soon dispensed favors to his friends at the expense of those considered to be Hooker's sycophants. Prominent among Meade's friends were John Reynolds and Second Corps chief Winfield S. Hancock. Sickles headed the list of Meade's enemies. Perhaps Sickles's lack of professional military education or his close association with the discredited Hooker explained Meade's attitude. Given

Meade's strict personal rectitude, the root cause of his distaste more likely could be traced to Sickles's unsavory private reputation. Whatever the underlying reasons, Sickles found himself subordinate to a man whose behavior toward him would be coldly correct at best and actively hostile at worst. Sickles would have to be careful—behavior foreign to the New Yorker—with Meade in charge of the army. Meade himself took charge in the midst of a dangerously fluid situation. All eyes would be on him, especially those of the Hooker faction represented by Sickles. Burdened by this personal baggage, the two men soon found themselves engaged in the greatest military campaign of their lives and about to commence a personal conflict that would end only with their deaths.[10]

As might be expected, Meade and Sickles began their relationship inauspiciously. Bad weather, poor maps, lack of knowledge about the enemy, and a general malaise among the Federal troops hampered Meade's efforts to move the army northward. June 29 proved especially frustrating because most of the corps fell short of their assigned objectives. Only Reynolds's First Corps met its target. Not only was Hancock's Second Corps delayed three hours but its failure to march on time caused the Fifth Corps to lag even farther behind. In response, Meade wrote understandingly to Hancock with no hint of a rebuke. When the commander of the Twelfth Corps reported that he was being delayed by the trains of the Third Corps, however, Meade instructed his assistant adjutant general to inform Sickles that "the train of your corps is at a stand-still at Middleburg, and delaying, of course, all movements in the rear. [General Meade] wishes you to give your immediate attention to keeping your train in motion."[11]

Apparently the more Meade thought about Sickles's lack of success on June 29, the more he believed this relatively gentle rebuke was not sufficient. On June 30, Sickles received the following more pointed note from army headquarters:

Major General George Gordon Meade
(*Photographic History* 10:169)

The commanding general noticed with regret the very slow movement of your corps yesterday. It is presumed you marched at an early hour, and up to 6 P.M. the rear of your column had not passed Middleburg, distant from your camp of the night before some 12 miles only. This, considering the good condition of the road and the favorable state of the weather, was far from meeting the expectation of the commanding general, and delayed to a very late hour the arrival of troops and trains in your rear. The Second Corps in the same space of time made a march nearly double your own. Situated as this army now is, the commanding general looks for rapid movements of the troops.

Sickles's reaction to this note is unrecorded, but he scarcely could have mistaken the tone and its import. His friend Joe Hooker no longer commanded the Army of the Potomac. In addition, the reference to Hancock, who stood high in Meade's estimation, must have been especially galling in light of the problems caused by Hancock's failure to meet his marching goal on June 29.[12]

Sickles received a series of confusing and contradictory orders from either Meade or his designated representatives over the next two days. On June 30, Meade empowered his friend Reynolds to coordinate the movements of three corps, including that of Sickles. Sickles received several conflicting orders that day from both Reynolds and Meade. Rather than fall further into Meade's bad graces, Sickles reported the contradictions to army headquarters and waited for Meade to indicate his preferred course of action. A similar situation prevailed on July 1—Meade's Pipe Creek Circular mandated that the Third Corps remain at Emmitsburg, whereas a message from Reynolds summoned the corps northward to Gettysburg, leaving Sickles again undecided as to his proper course of action. Sickles acted promptly when additional messages from Gettysburg on July 1 announced that Reynolds was dead, that Major General Oliver O. Howard was in charge, and that Howard wanted the Third Corps to march north. Leaving one brigade from each of his two divisions at Emmitsburg, he moved toward Gettysburg with the remainder of his corps and notified Meade of his actions. En route to Gettysburg, Sickles received another message from Meade confirming the original order to remain at Emmitsburg. Sickles disregarded this message, continuing his march on the grounds that events had changed the context within which Meade had issued the instructions.[13]

Sickles arrived at Gettysburg via the Emmitsburg Road with two brigades of Major General David B. Birney's First Division at about 6:00 P.M. on July 1. Moving on a parallel track west of the Emmitsburg Road, Brigadier General Andrew A. Humphreys's Second Division stumbled into Confederates near Black Horse Tavern and did not join the corps bivouac on Cemetery Ridge until approximately 2:00 A.M. on July 2. Meade reached the Federal positions on the hills just south of Gettysburg a little after midnight. His actions on that trying day were not those of a man completely sure of himself or his situation. The enemy had been discovered and momentarily checked, the army was concentrating on Gettysburg, and the situation was quite stable by the end of the day on July 1. But Meade had not been solely responsible for this outcome. However necessary, his delegation of responsibility to Reynolds had introduced a level of confusion into the command structure that could have had serious consequences. From any point of view other than that of a Meade partisan, the new army commander's performance over the preceding forty-eight hours had been less than inspirational. Certainly from the perspective of Dan Sickles, Meade's actions thus far had encouraged little confidence in his leadership.[14]

Some time before sunrise, Meade rode along his line to get some idea of its contours. His route first took him southward from Cemetery Hill along Cemetery Ridge toward Little Round Top. Turning northward before he reached the Round Tops, Meade surveyed the area of Culp's Hill on his right. His ride complete, he used a hastily drawn map to indicate positions for the infantry corps then on the field or soon to arrive.

The Twelfth, Eleventh, and First Corps would hold the Federal right on the hills nearest Gettysburg. Hancock's Second Corps came next, occupying the northern end of Cemetery Ridge, and Sickles's corps extended Hancock's line southward. In taking the specified position, Sickles was to relieve Brigadier General John W. Geary's Second Division of the Twelfth Corps, which would then march to Culp's Hill to rejoin its parent unit. The Fifth Corps would remain behind the front line as the army's reserve pending arrival of Major General John Sedgwick's large Sixth Corps. Having thus designed a satisfactory line, Meade ordered his chief of staff to draft a contingency plan should the army have to retreat. Meade could see Confederates only opposite his right and center and understandably concentrated his attention on those sectors. Nevertheless, between 6:00 and 7:00 A.M., he sent his son and aide, Captain George Meade, to check the position of the Third Corps on the army's left.[15]

Riding southward from army headquarters, young Meade found Sickles's command post just west of the Taneytown Road. The captain failed to see Sickles, who was inside his tent, but heard from a staff officer that the Third Corps remained out of position because Sickles was unsure of the ground the army commander wished him to occupy. Captain Meade hastened back to his father with this disturbing information. General Meade then forcefully reiterated his earlier directions to Sickles: move the Third Corps to the left of Hancock's Second Corps and occupy the position formerly held by Geary's division of the Twelfth Corps. Upon returning to the Third Corps, Captain Meade delivered his father's message to Sickles himself. Sickles retorted that his men were already in motion, but that Geary's supposed position had been a simple bivouac area with no clearly defined front line. Captain George E. Randolph, Sickles's chief of artillery, then asked Captain Meade to convey a request to army headquarters for Brigadier General Henry J. Hunt, the army's chief of artillery, to survey the new location for gun positions. As Sickles left to join his four brigades, Captain Meade rode back to his father's headquarters. Approximately two hours later, about 9:00 A.M., Sickles's last two brigades arrived from Emmitsburg to bring the corps to full strength.[16]

General Meade became increasingly preoccupied with the army's right as the morning progressed. Confederate units continued to mass openly on that end of the line. Rather than await an assault, Meade briefly contemplated launching a spoiling attack but abandoned the idea because of the broken nature of the terrain around Culp's Hill. His focus nonetheless remained on his right flank until Sickles arrived at army headquarters at about 11:00 A.M. Sickles reported his continuing uncertainty about the position assigned his corps. Meade repeated that the Third Corps should extend its line southward on Cemetery Ridge from the left of the Second Corps through Geary's old position toward the Round Tops. Apparently satisfied, Sickles asked Meade if he might post his two divisions according to his own discretion. Meade responded affirmatively, with the caveat that his lieutenant observe the general defensive scheme already outlined. In parting, Sickles reiterated the earlier request that General Hunt visit the new position to assess its suitability for artillery. Meade agreed, and Hunt left army headquarters with Sickles.[17]

Instead of taking Hunt directly south along Cemetery Ridge, Sickles guided him in a southwesterly direction along the Emmitsburg Road. They rode to a peach orchard that stood on rising ground approximately fifteen hundred yards west of Geary's old position, where Sickles stated that he much preferred to deploy his corps so as to encompass the high ground around the orchard. Standing some forty feet higher than the position Meade identified, the orchard, argued Sickles, clearly dominated the line then held by the Third Corps. Hunt generally agreed that the Peach Orchard ridge offered potential, especially if the Federals mounted an offensive from their left. He also pointed out deficiencies in the proposed position: the line was too long, the resulting salient could be attacked simultaneously from two directions, and both flanks of the Third Corps would be in the air. Pressed by Sickles for authorization to move the Third Corps forward to the new line, Hunt refused to assume authority rightfully belonging to Meade. He did, however, agree to inform Meade of the situation. Before departing, Hunt also suggested to Sickles that a reconnaissance of the woods west of the Emmitsburg Road might be both prudent and fruitful. The artillery chief then headed toward Cemetery Hill via Devil's Den.[18]

Acting on Hunt's suggestion, Sickles ordered General Birney to dispatch a scouting party into the woods beyond the Emmitsburg Road. Birney detailed four companies of Colonel Hiram Berdan's First U.S. Sharpshooters, supported by a small infantry regiment, to undertake the mission. Upon entering Pitzer's Woods, the sharpshooters encountered Confederate pickets and drove them northward until a Confederate battle line appeared. Forced into a hasty retreat, the sharpshooters returned across the Emmitsburg Road with startling news of Confederates swarming into the woods to the west. Berdan's report convinced Sickles that strong Confederate forces were moving to his left. Should he fail to act quickly, enemy guns might deploy on the coveted Peach Orchard ridge and place the Third Corps in another Hazel Grove–Fairview situation. Believing that the merits of the Peach Orchard salient outweighed its disadvantages, and concluding that there was no time to lose, Sickles decided to occupy the high ground without waiting for Meade's permission. Even before Berdan reported the results of his reconnaissance, Sickles had begun to advance units of the corps piecemeal. Now, about 2:00 P.M., he ordered the remainder of the corps forward. Humphreys's division occupied the right of the salient along the Emmitsburg Road with one brigade in line, one in support, and one in reserve. On Humphreys's left, Birney placed all three of his

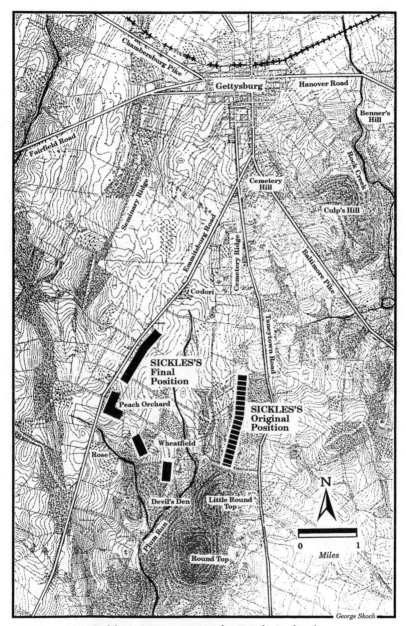

Sickles's Movement to the Peach Orchard

brigades in line—a futile attempt to stretch his division from the Peach Orchard to Little Round Top.[19]

Meade dispatched a message at 3:00 P.M. summoning all of his corps commanders to a conference at army headquarters. Before Sickles arrived, Meade learned from Brigadier General G. K. Warren, his chief engineer, that the Third Corps was not in its assigned position. Sickles appeared at the conference just as Meade prepared to ride to the Third Corps sector. Instructed to return to his command immediately, Sickles preceded Meade back to the vicinity of the Peach Orchard. Meade and part of his staff arrived shortly to see that only rapid remedial action would prevent the isolation of the Third Corps from the remainder of the army. When Sickles offered to return his divisions to their old position, Meade initially ordered him to do so but changed his mind when Confederate artillery opened fire on the Third Corps. Telling Sickles to remain where he was, Meade directed the Fifth Corps and a division of the Second Corps to come to the aid of the Third Corps. He also arranged for more artillery to support Sickles, then rode to the rear to expedite the movement of reinforcements. Before any of the reinforcing units could arrive, a heavy attack by two divisions of Lieutenant General James Longstreet's Confederate corps smashed into the Federal troops in the Peach Orchard salient and drove them back in confusion. During the attack Sickles was gravely wounded in the leg and taken from the field. Ultimately the damaged limb required amputation, ending Sickles's field career.[20]

As he recovered gradually, Sickles harbored the idea that he could return to his beloved command. That hope ended on October 18, 1863, when Sickles visited Meade and asked to resume leadership of the Third Corps. Pointedly referring to Sickles's physical incapacity, Meade declined to reinstate the New Yorker. With his path blocked by a man he had long disliked, Sickles returned to Washington to ponder his next move. Major General Henry W. Halleck completed his report of events at Gettysburg in November 1863. No friend of Sickles, Halleck demonstrated open sympathy for Meade: "General Sickles, misinterpreting his orders, instead of placing the Third Corps on the prolongation of the Second, had moved it nearly three-quarters of a mile in advance—an error which nearly proved fatal in the battle." Soon made public, these words struck a blow at Sickles's vulnerable pride. He resolved to even the score against his enemies, casting about for a forum in which to air his own version of events on July 2.[21]

Sickles chose to make his primary case in a series of hearings held by the Joint Committee on the Conduct of the War. Chaired by Senator Benjamin Wade, the seven-member committee had the reputation of bias against most West Pointers. Neither Halleck nor Meade was a favorite of the committee, so Sickles's testimony against Meade in early 1864 fell on friendly ears. The general's statements before the committee masterfully presented his interpretation of events at Gettysburg through a complex blend of truth, half-truth, and occasional falsehood. Subsequent testimony from Generals Abner Doubleday and Daniel Butterfield generally reinforced Sickles's case against Meade. Meanwhile, an author cloaked by the pseudonym "Historicus" vigorously argued Sickles's side of the story in several widely read articles in the *New York Herald*. Meade responded by twice giving testimony before the committee utterly at variance with that of Sickles; however, he followed advice to remain silent in the face of the barrage from "Historicus." About the same time, on March 24, 1864, the Third Corps was abolished and its units transferred into other corps. This consolidation, carried out for reasons totally separate from the Meade-Sickles controversy, ensured that Sickles would never again stand at the head of his old unit. With the Third Corps gone, Sickles increased his determined effort to keep fresh the memory of its greatest day.[22]

Several factors thus combined to keep the controversy over Sickles's conduct at Gettysburg before the public and eventually the historical community. They included the bitter animosity between partisans of Meade and Hooker in the Army of the Potomac, the political agenda of the Joint Committee on the Conduct of the War, the abolition of the Third Corps, and, by no means least, Dan Sickles's desire for self-justification and self-promotion. Meade died in 1872; Sickles lived until 1914 and vigorously defended his actions at Gettysburg until the end. Although the thrust of his defense changed at various times, Sickles's arguments usually boiled down to four contentions. First, major elements of the Army of Northern Virginia were clearly shifting to his left. This statement was true but not for the reasons Sickles alleged, because the forces his reconnaissance encountered were not part of Longstreet's later movement. Second, Meade's orders to Sickles were either nonexistent or vague. In fact, Meade had given Sickles verbal orders that, although general, were specific enough for the Third Corps eventually to reach Geary's sector. Third, Meade desired Sickles to occupy an exceedingly poor position. Here Sickles scored his strongest point, because the ground was lower than terrain to both the west and south and was too extensive for the Third Corps to hold in strength. Finally, Sickles portrayed Meade as a weak commander planning a retreat from the field at Gettysburg. In this, too, Sickles was wrong. Nevertheless, throughout the remainder of his life, Dan Sickles served to all who would listen this mixture of fact, partial truth, and error.[23]

Time and historical fashion have not served Sickles well since his death. For all his flaws, Meade has become the victor of Gettysburg, the man who defeated Robert E. Lee. Meade enjoys an image as the Army of the Potomac's most successful battle commander, if only because he led it for the remainder of the war. In contrast, Sickles is remembered more for his flamboyant personality and his peccadillos than for any pos-

itive characteristics as a soldier. His performance at Chancellorsville rarely emerges from the shadow of the far greater
debacle suffered by his patron Hooker. Indeed, the movement
of the Third Corps to the Peach Orchard salient on July 2,
1863, and its subsequent retreat from that position define Sickles's military career in the public mind. Sickles may have
vanquished Meade in the former's lifetime, but Meade's partisans have won in the end. Their victory has been so complete
that a modern defense of Sickles's actions may be likened to
the proverbial tilting at windmills. But a case can be made for
Dan Sickles without resorting to his characteristic bombast.
The assessment that follows constitutes just such a case.

Both George Meade and Dan Sickles carried mental baggage
to Gettysburg that hampered their smooth cooperation in the
crisis. Enmity between them reached far back and was
exacerbated by Meade's elevation to succeed Hooker. Meade's
plans and actions proved tentative during his first few days in
command of the army. Although it may have been necessary
under the circumstances, his reliance on favorites such as
Reynolds and Hancock led to the issuance of conflicting orders
from multiple sources. The image Meade projected, especially
to those predisposed to dislike him, was thus scarcely au-
thoritative. He had yet to solidify his hold on either the Army
of the Potomac or its quarrelsome command structure. It
would not be surprising, therefore, for Sickles to question
Meade's judgment and rely on his own if circumstances seemed
to warrant such a course of action. Moreover, only two months
earlier Sickles had been ordered to relinquish a strong position
at Hazel Grove and forced to occupy an inferior one at Fairview
with unfortunate results. With his own judgment seemingly
vindicated so recently, he could be expected to assert it again
in similar circumstances—especially in opposition to orders
from a new commander he hardly respected.[24]

When Sickles received Meade's instructions to occupy
Geary's old position on the southern extension of Cemetery

Ridge early on July 2, he apparently understood what Meade intended but found the prospect unpleasant. Geary's men had held low ground in relation to the surrounding terrain, especially that to the west where the Peach Orchard ridge rose at least forty feet higher. Fields of fire to the west of Geary's position also were seriously limited. Clearly preoccupied with his right, Meade had made only a cursory investigation of the terrain to his left. Little Round Top dominated the ground southward beyond Cemetery Ridge, but Sickles believed he lacked enough troops to reach that eminence and occupy it in force. Berdan's reconnaissance to the west of the Peach Orchard ridge yielded information that added to Sickles's concern. With the enemy apparently moving around his left flank, dominant terrain reminiscent of Hazel Grove in his front, and his own confidence in Meade's judgment minimal, Sickles eventually concluded that he must take the situation into his own hands. Once he selected a course of action, he implemented it without much reference to the remainder of the Army of the Potomac.[25]

From the perspective of the Third Corps, Sickles's advance to the Peach Orchard ridge made sense. It could have been the right move from the Army of the Potomac's perspective, too, if coordinated with Meade and adjacent units in time to adjust the overall Federal defensive alignment. Executed unilaterally, however, Sickles's movement was decidedly improper. Unfortunately, the personalities of Sickles and Meade, and the peculiar chemistry between them, ensured that Sickles would act unilaterally. Sickles clearly should have made a greater attempt to coordinate his advance with army headquarters. Equally clearly, Meade should have paid more attention to his left. Neither commander took these actions, which in hindsight appear so reasonable, and thus the two divisions of the Third Corps broke their connection with the Second Corps on their right and occupied the Peach Orchard ridge. There Longstreet's late afternoon assaults found them; there the

Third Corps suffered severely; there Dan Sickles lost both his leg and his field command forever.[26]

What if Sickles had obeyed Meade's orders and simply prolonged the Federal line southward along Cemetery Ridge? Any answer to this hypothetical question must be purely speculative, but some results seem probable. First, Sickles's corps likely would not have occupied Little Round Top in strength. Just north of Sickles, Hancock's Second Corps, with 11,347 men, held a front of approximately 1,300 yards. With only 10,675 soldiers, Sickles almost certainly would not have covered a front of 1,500 yards—the distance necessary to hold the crest of Little Round Top in force. Second, the flaws on the left of Meade's line probably would not have been addressed in a timely fashion. Thus Warren might not have visited Little Round Top and brought forward the reinforcements that saved the position. Third, much of the ground on the Federal left for which Longstreet's men fought fiercely would have fallen to the Confederates with only the slightest resistance. Given these hypothetical changes to actual events, it is quite possible that the Army of the Potomac might have lost the Round Tops and the southern end of Cemetery Ridge. Such a disaster might in turn have triggered the loss of Meade's entire fish-hook position.[27]

The foregoing possibilities suggest that Sickles's movement to the Peach Orchard ridge can be interpreted as fortuitous. His seemingly outrageous action forced Meade to address the situation on his left at a crucial time. The advance also threw Confederate attackers off stride. Further, the defense of a critical point always should begin forward of its final protective line, and Sickles's new position was forward of Little Round Top. The cost of Sickles's action was great, but quite possibly, even probably, the movement accomplished more than if the Third Corps had defended the line originally envisioned by Meade. It must be stated, however, that Sickles erred in the way he executed his decision. An advance coordinated with the remainder of the Army of the Potomac would have brought the advantages of the Peach Orchard position without the detrimental effects of an unsupported move by a single corps. Unfortunately, the absence of trust and respect between Meade and Sickles precluded such a rational solution to the problem.

The entire episode has been clouded since 1863 by issues of politics and personality that hinder unbiased analysis. It is time to put aside such extraneous issues. When Sickles's scandalous prewar behavior, postwar bombast, and special pleading are discounted and the case is considered solely on its merits, the results of the Third Corps advance to the Peach Orchard salient speak for themselves. Dan Sickles was not perfect on July 2, 1863, but neither was he the military buffoon so often portrayed.

"If Longstreet . . . Says So, It Is Most Likely Not True"

James Longstreet and the Second Day at Gettysburg

ROBERT K. KRICK

When General James Longstreet died in 1904, he had long since passed his optimum life span for Confederate image building. Had the bullet that maimed the general in the Wilderness on May 6, 1864, killed him instead, there can be little doubt that a bronze equestrian Longstreet would stand on Richmond's Monument Avenue today. Through four postwar decades, however, the contentious Longstreet launched a steady flood of attacks against his former Confederate colleagues, often straying from the demonstrable truth and regularly contradicting his own accounts from one article to the next. When a Petersburg newspaper called Longstreet's poison-pen ventures the "vaporings of senility and pique,"[1] it echoed the views of millions of Southerners. The general's modern supporters insist that in analyzing his war record, we must ignore his late-life posturing, and in fact that is both appropriate and readily achievable in weighing his style during the 1860s. On the other hand, although the senility doubtless was something new, the pique was not a sudden anomaly, sprung whole from the postwar ground. The change in Southern attitudes toward James Longstreet after the war came in large part because he survived to reveal glimpses of his soul that left observers repulsed, rather than simply in response to his postwar political maneuvering. The record shows that Longstreet operated at times during the war with an unwholesome and unlovely attitude. He had a tendency to be small minded and mean spirited, and he behaved in that fashion to the detriment of his army on a number of occasions, including during the second day at Gettysburg.

By December 1861, James Longstreet had experienced a meteoric rise in rank. A few months earlier he had been a major and paymaster in the U.S. Army; now he was a major general of infantry. No one in the army had fared better and most had done far less well. No observers had thought of heaping calumny on Longstreet's head for any reason—justified or not. He was in no way controversial. He was, nevertheless, a confirmed sulker—apparently entirely of his own volition, without having been forced to it by a hostile public opinion, because none such existed. A young Texan on his staff, who was friendly with Longstreet and remained so into old age early in the twentieth century, described Longstreet's tendency to pout in a letter written to his mother that month: "On some days [Longstreet is] very sociable and agreeable, then again for a few days he will confine himself mostly to his room, or tent, without having much to say to anyone, and is as grim as you please." The general behaved that way when he was unwell, as might be expected, but he also acted in that fashion when "something has not gone to suit him. When anything has gone wrong, he does not say much, but merely looks grim." The staff had learned to expect this behavior and did not "talk much to him" before finding out if he was in "a talkative mood."[2] It would be hard for a Longstreet detractor, convinced of his tendency to sulk, to fabricate a more telling description of the general's demeanor when "something [had] not gone to suit him."

A member of J. E. B. Stuart's staff described Longstreet's personal style at about the same time. W. W. Blackford and Stuart boarded for a time at the same house in Fairfax Court House with Longstreet. Blackford wrote: "Longstreet . . . impressed me then as a man of limited capacity who acquired reputation for wisdom by never saying anything—the old story

Lieutenant General James Longstreet
(*Photographic History* 10:244)

of the owl. I do not remember ever hearing him say half a dozen words, beyond 'yes' and 'no,' in a consecutive sentence, though often in company with his old companions of the old army." A civilian woman who had dinner with Longstreet the following year described his gruff performance as being "shy and embarrassed in manner."[3]

Longstreet's stolid persona often produced in observers the certainty that he must surely be a bulwark in a storm. The general did perform in just that manner for the Army of Northern Virginia on a number of crucial occasions. His style, however, may also have been mixed with more than a tincture of the dullard. Was Longstreet a quiet genius or just quietly slow? A bulwark or a dullard? He probably combined elements of both. At West Point, where one of his roommates was the notorious John Pope, Longstreet displayed no hint of mental agility. He finished fifty-fourth among fifty-six graduates in the class of 1842. His worst mark was fifty-fifth in Ethics, behind even the spectacularly unethical Earl Van Dorn.[4]

The phenomenon of dullard as bulwark is a familiar one in military history. In a wonderfully droll eighteenth-century book of satirical advice to army officers, a British veteran commented on the syndrome: "Ignorance of your profession is . . . best concealed by solemnity and silence, which pass for profound knowledge upon the generality of mankind." Longstreet's own dear friend both before and after the war, Ulysses S. Grant, is among the prominent Americans most often discussed in that vein. An English diplomat commented that Grant, during his attempts to cope with the duties of president, could not "deliver himself of even the simplest sentence." During the midst of the Belknap scandal, Grant appeared to James A. Garfield so indifferent to the mess and its resultant turmoil that Garfield wrote in his diary: "His imperturbability is amazing. I am in doubt whether to call it greatness or stupidity."[5] Opinions vary, and always will, about the characteristics of long-dead historical figures. If there was

.something of the dullard in James Longstreet's mix, it probably served him well on some occasions, just as the misanthropic tunnel vision of Longstreet's bête noire, "Stonewall" Jackson, proved to be an asset in that officer's aggressive military behavior. The sullen side of Longstreet's dull personality, however, contributed to his military failures.

A popular and appropriate query posed by Longstreet supporters runs something like this: If the general was given to sulking, and was otherwise deficient in dedication and deportment, why were he and Lee on such good terms? To quote Gary W. Gallagher, from his essay in this book, Longstreet was a man "whose friendship he [Lee] valued." Lee's calm, poised style included an ingenuous element that accepted individuals at face value. He also recognized that the raw material at hand was the best to be had in his country. Lee concluded a May 1864 review of the performance of a brigadier general by posing the query, "Besides, whom would you put in his place?"[6] In any event, there is ample evidence that Lee was genuinely fond of Longstreet, and of course he valued his subordinate's high services to the army. It is interesting to speculate how Lee would have reacted had he known the extent of Longstreet's disloyalty, or whether he in fact was aware of the situation. Because Lee declared that he did not believe Longstreet would say such things—precisely the things Longstreet said repeatedly for thirty years after Lee's death— when he heard rumors of them, he probably remained unaware of Longstreet's distaste for him.

The true nature of the corps commander's feelings for Lee stands out beyond any shadow of doubt in a letter written by Longstreet to Joseph E. Johnston on October 5, 1862. Just four months earlier, Lee had taken over Johnston's army as it crouched beneath the gates of Richmond, having just been beaten at Seven Pines—a battle in which, not coincidentally, Longstreet had conspired with Johnston to transfer blame dishonestly to an innocent colleague. Now Lee had completely remade the face of the war, having driven the enemy army from the verge of his own capital and pursued it across the Potomac. Longstreet clearly wanted his pliant collaborator back, and professed to know that the army preferred to be rid of Lee (an idea either patently dishonest or else breathtakingly out of touch with the ranks): "I feel that you have their hearts more decidedly than any other leader can ever have. The men would now go wild at the sight of their old favorite." Speaking for himself, Longstreet quailed at the prospect of being stuck longer with Lee: "I cant become reconciled at the idea of your going west." Could Johnston find some means to return to the army even in a subordinate role, Longstreet had "no doubt but the command of the entire Army" would fall to him "before Spring." Having been thus blunt, the disgruntled general implied that he would love to say more: "Cant always write what we would like to say." While laboring under Lee's misrule, Longstreet and his staff had used captured champagne to drink to Johnston "whenever we opened a bottle" but thought of Johnston "more seriously at other times."[7] Had Lee seen this missive, or learned of its contents indirectly (as he may have done), it probably would have made not one whit of difference in his dealings with Longstreet.

There can of course be no grounds for denying Longstreet the right to dislike Lee or to prefer Joseph E. Johnston. His distaste for Lee does put him in the rather select, if not exclusive, company of Roswell S. Ripley, apparently the only other general officer who actively disliked the army commander after he began active operations in June 1862. Longstreet's anti-Lee posture wins for him the approval of his modern soul mates, historians eager to debunk Lee's wartime status in the South. More important for present purposes is the degree to which the subordinate disdained the superior, as an element in considering Longstreet's response to those instances when he did not get his way.

A traditional folk saying summarizes how alarmingly easy it is to fool yourself, how readily you may fool a superior, but how impossible it is to fool subordinates over the long term. Stonewall Jackson's world view left him unpopular with virtually every immediate subordinate; basking in his reflected glory was far more comfortable among officers and men a layer or more away from his difficult presence. None of Jackson's bruised officers ever expressed much doubt, however, about their general's whole-hearted commitment to the tasks at hand—which was, in fact, the cause of much of the abrasion in the first place.

A great many of James Longstreet's subordinates liked and admired him, including such clever and thoughtful fellows as E. P. Alexander and G. Moxley Sorrel. Those two men also provide some pointed critique of his attitude at Gettysburg. Longstreet's own favorites included generals such as Robert Toombs, who deserves consideration as at least a finalist for designation as worst general officer in the Army of Northern Virginia. According to one of his staff, Longstreet "had a high opinion of Toombs, and I heard him say that if Toombs had been educated at West Point . . . he would have been as distinguished as a soldier as he was as a civilian." Longstreet also "was exceedingly fond" of George E. Pickett, perhaps because the younger man was one of the few antebellum graduates of West Point with a worse scholastic record than his own. Sorrel recalled how "taking Longstreet's orders in emergencies, I could always see how he looked after Pickett, and made us give him things very fully; indeed, sometimes stay with him to make sure he did not get astray." A third favorite was General Louis T. Wigfall (to whom Longstreet was, in his own words, "strongly attached"), a military failure as pronounced as any in the army, excepting, always, Toombs.[8]

Others of Longstreet's subordinates displayed considerable discomfort with the corps commander's attitude. Cadmus Marcellus Wilcox served long and faithfully as a brigade commander for the first half of the war, and then as a major general at the head of a division during the rest of the conflict. In November 1862 he was anxiously seeking a means to leave Longstreet's corps, presumably because of discontent with its commander. The details are not clear because Lee typically destroyed his half of the correspondence with Wilcox and then gently persuaded the disgruntled general to look beyond local issues to the good of the army and the country. Wilcox's attitude toward Longstreet is anything but indistinct in two letters he wrote soon after the war, which apparently never have been published. Writing to a fellow First Corps general, the usually reticent Wilcox declared emphatically, "I never had any respect for Longstreet's ability for I always knew he had but a small amount." Furthermore, Wilcox had "always regarded him as selfish & cold harted [sic], caring for but little save his own self." General Wilcox insisted that at Frayser's Farm and Williamsburg, the brigade commanders suffered under Longstreet's absence from the front "& we brigadiers talked of it." To Wilcox's chagrin, Longstreet "is spoken of as the hard & stubborn fighter, his troops did fight well, but not from any inspiration drawn from him & he of course gets the credit of it."[9]

As Longstreet fell into steadily greater disfavor after the war, he adopted the expedient of blaming his difficulties on individuals hostile to him because of political considerations and his other unpopular postwar traits. His modern supporters believe that whole-souled admiration for the general only faded after the war for irrelevant reasons, and under the prompting of consciously dishonest Lost Cause myth makers. Longstreet might be viewed as a man far ahead of his times, with his very 1990s-like stance of insisting that having outraged much of the community by one set of actions, he was immune to criticism for anything else: obviously everyone hated him and therefore must be ignored as prejudiced; citing a recidivist's chronic misdeeds is unfair, we are told. The innocence-

through-unpopularity motif might in fact obtain in some instances. Longstreet really did a thorough job of making himself
unlovable, and prompted some outraged hyperbole in the process. Cadmus Wilcox, however, was anything but a controversialist. He was about the quietest man of his rank in
the matter of postwar speaking and writing and quarreling.
Wilcox's private letters to a friend of Longstreet's—not to some
fiendish Lost Cause journal—scarcely can be impeached as
polemics. Right or wrong, General Wilcox simply and privately
thought little of Longstreet's ability and appreciated even less
his "selfish & cold harted" attitude.

Major General Lafayette McLaws of Georgia was among the
most pointed detractors Longstreet ever earned. His position
is the more remarkable because for a long time the corps
commander viewed McLaws as a special protégé. McLaws provides key testimony about his chief at Gettysburg and Knoxville below, but this generic commentary on Longstreet's
"contemptible mode of procedure" summarizes his notions:
"You can follow Longstreet's career, from the First battle of
Manassas to the close of the war, and you will see that the
first act, in any engagement, was to call for reinforcements;
not that any reinforcements were needed, but that was his
policy." McLaws knew from close experience that Longstreet's
reports "will lay the blame of failure . . . upon some one else,
and in case of real fiasco he will undertake to do something
where success is impossible and find faults and lay the blame
of the failure in his last venture upon some one else he has
a spite against. All this is to draw attention away from his
own mismanagement of the real issue."[10]

The best example of the blame-shifting technique cited
by McLaws was Seven Pines. In a fantastic display of poor
planning, miscommunication, and arrant ineptitude, James
Longstreet left the presence of Joseph E. Johnston with instructions to march northeastward up the Nine Mile Road to
implement the army commander's sloppy and casual battle

Major General Lafayette McLaws
(*Photographic History* 10:115)

plan but somehow contrived in befuddlement to head more than ninety degrees away from his intended goal. No major battle in Virginia includes any more bizarre confusion. In the process Longstreet blocked for long hours the route of troops under General Benjamin Huger who were earmarked for triggering the attack. Some have suggested that Longstreet consciously scrambled the plan in order to reach an area where distinction might be found, but that seems highly unlikely. McLaws noted that Longstreet "disobeyed his orders (supposed to be from stupidity)." Far more significant than the peculiar events was Longstreet's apparently instinctive reaction to blame it all on a convenient bystander. With Johnston's connivance, he succeeded in blaming Huger—who had been most directly wronged—as the author of the confusion! As Douglas Southall Freeman has noted, "Longstreet, whose conduct at Seven Pines was most subject to question, emerged not only without blame but also with prestige increased."[11] Huger proved to be a fortuitous choice as scapegoat, as he soon demonstrated a genuine tendency toward sluggishness.

Later that summer Longstreet had occasion to refine his technique. When his friend and subordinate Robert Toombs disobeyed orders and left a ford on the Rapidan unguarded, a Federal cavalry column slipped through unnoticed. The Yankees very nearly captured J. E. B. Stuart at Verdiersville. Stuart thought that the cavalrymen were Fitzhugh Lee's troopers, whom he expected to arrive soon. Although this relatively minor incident caused some inconvenience to the army, it hardly warranted the historiographical counteroffensive launched by Longstreet. He spread the word that Lee, who was among the victims of the malfeasance by Longstreet's friend Toombs, was really the culprit, and escalated the result so egregiously that he later subscribed to the amusing premise that Lee "lost the Southern cause" on that largely forgotten morning. Longstreet later explained that all of the Virginia cavalrymen required guidance. Stuart in particular needed "an older head"—no doubt Longstreet had himself in mind—"to instruct and regulate him."[12]

Debate raged postwar about whether Longstreet disobeyed Lee in delaying his offensive at Second Manassas, where the armies met ten days after Fitz Lee lost the war at Verdiersville. Supporters of the First Corps commander continue to insist that his delay in executing Lee's wishes at Second Manassas was the right thing to do. But they can hardly cling to the notion that Longstreet was not dragging his feet, since he calmly admitted to doing so. "I failed to obey the orders of the 29th," he boasted, "and on the 30th, in direct opposition to my orders, made the battle from my position and won it." In describing tactical developments on the field, Longstreet gerrymandered them through an arc of nearly 180 degrees in a display of either extraordinary sloppiness or blatant dishonesty.[13]

Judging from his letter to Joe Johnston quoted above, Longstreet obviously believed from the early days of his association with Lee that he knew better how to run the army. That belief apparently had grown by the summer of 1863 to include warwide strategic concepts, according to Longstreet's postwar declarations. The corps commander claimed to have been brimming with unbeatable options for forays into Tennessee, Ohio, and other such exotic latitudes, but Lee was immune to reason. A contemporary letter from Longstreet to McLaws hints that the lieutenant general's hindsight was much crisper than his foresight. McLaws hoped to get back to the vicinity of Georgia and his family—the direction in which Longstreet's strategic vision was supposed to be gamboling. Longstreet thought he might be able to work it out, but if McLaws went south and west, he must remember that "we want every body here that we can get and . . . you must agree to send us every man that you can dispense with during the summer particularly."[14] That would seem to indicate that Longstreet's strategic vision about the poor chances in Lee's theater were somewhat more auto-biographical than contemporary.

Longstreet's version of his dismayed abandonment of the various better ideas includes two remarkable words. After badgering Lee about Cincinnati, Vicksburg, and other such chimeras, Longstreet "found his [Lee's] mind made up not to allow any of his troops to go west. I then *accepted* his prop-osition to make a campaign into Pennsylvania, *provided* it should be offensive in strategy but defensive in tactics" (em-phases added). That a corps commander would use words of that sort in describing the decisions of his army's head reveals a phenomenal degree of cocky disrespect. Lee of course had not struck such a "bargain," and in the event behaved without respect to the nonexistent pact. Longstreet later professed to know somehow that Lee had missed his only real chance to breach successfully this pseudocartel when he overlooked a great opportunity at Brandy Station, "when he could have caught Hooker in detail, and, probably, have crushed his army."[15]

General Longstreet's corps fought one of the war's most desperate engagements on July 2, 1863, on the Confederate right at Gettysburg. Despite the corps's brave and stubborn perform-ance, its commander came in for bitter criticism for his at-titude and behavior on that crucial day. There was generously ample basis for such criticism, but as controversy swirled around the subject some of the general's detractors—most notably the Reverend William Nelson Pendleton—produced inaccurate and misleading testimony. The nature and processes of the controversy itself have become controversial, but this essay inquiring particularly into the nature of Longstreet's at-titude must focus on primary evidence.

Longstreet did not want Lee to take the initiative on July 2. He made that unmistakably clear to his superior, but Lee determined that the army must find the best possible spot at which to seek a continuation of the striking success it had won the previous day. After an often-discussed series of conferences with Lee, some of them turbulent, Longstreet faced the simple fact that he must move to the right and attack. He accepted that responsibility in the poorest possible grace. Had Tom Goree been writing to his mother on this day he most certainly could have duplicated his December 1861 letter: when "something has not gone to suit him. . . . [he] merely looks grim." James Longstreet spent most of July 2 "without having much to say to anyone, and . . . as grim as you please," in accordance with Goree's earlier description.

One early and striking manifestation of Longstreet's sullen execution of his orders has not received much attention in the voluminous literature on Gettysburg. His two divisions faced a long and uncertain march to their intended destination. The march surely would take considerable time under the best of circumstances. Inevitably such moves involved delays. Given the urgency of the situation, celerity (to use one of the favorite words of the sorely missed T. J. Jackson) clearly was in requisition. Longstreet ignored that patently obvious imperative from the outset. Evander M. Law's brigade of Alabama troops, one of eight brigades scheduled for the march, was not yet up. Longstreet insisted on waiting for its arrival. As he reported officially to Lee, "I delayed until General Law's brigade joined its division." Even then he was not ready, having "*after* his arrival" (emphasis added) to "make our preparations." While the clock inexorably ticked off moments potentially golden for the South, Longstreet lounged with division commander John B. Hood "near the trunk of a tree" and explained to Hood that General Lee "is a little nervous this morning; he wishes me to attack." Hood's description of this relaxed encounter, written after the war to Longstreet himself, concluded ominously: "Thus passed the forenoon of that eventful day. . . ."[16]

Had Longstreet insisted on awaiting Law's arrival at the line of departure before launching his attack, he might have been able to make a weak case; though under the circumstances that afternoon, a delay in attacking to augment the force by one-eighth would not have made good sense, especially given the en echelon arrangement that was used. He was not waiting to attack, however, but merely to *begin* a complicated march. Law of course would have arrived at the jump-off point for the march long before his turn came to fall in at the end of the column. Longstreet simply was dragging his feet.

Once the march finally began, on a dismally tardy schedule, the sulking corps commander put on a display of pettiness of heroic proportions by pretending to think that he could not direct his own troops. Captain Samuel Richards Johnston, engineer officer on Lee's staff, had reconnoitered early that morning in the area toward which Longstreet was grudgingly headed. Beginning at about 4 A.M., Johnston rode over the ground between Willoughby Run and Marsh Creek leading east toward the Emmitsburg Pike. He examined the terrain between the pike and the Round Tops, rode over the slopes and to the crests of those soon-to-be-famous knobs, crossed the Slyder farm, and returned. When the scouting captain reached headquarters, General Lee "was surprised at my getting so far, but showed clearly that I had given him valuable information." Lee suggested that Captain Johnston join Longstreet's column on its march; any other use of the man best informed about the ground would have been criminally negligent. The army commander of course gave his staff captain no special authority. In fact, he gave him "no other instructions" at all beyond joining Longstreet. Johnston thought it was about 9 A.M. when he joined Longstreet, and added what everyone else well knew: "He did not move off very promptly—nor was our march at all rapid. It did not strike me that Genl Longstreet was in a hurry to get into position. It might have been that he thought hurry was unnecessary."[17]

Longstreet decided to play an ugly game with the misguided Lee—and with thousands of unfortunate soldiers and the destiny of a mighty battle—by taking the ludicrous position that

Sam Johnston really commanded the march. He was Lee's man on the spot, and this wholly silly march and attack were Lee's idiotic idea, so let him have his way and then we'll just see who really knows best! No episode in the army's long history, which included more than a few displays of temper and spite and small-mindedness, can measure up to this exhibition by Lieutenant General Longstreet. More than two hundred officers in the marching column outranked Sam Johnston, if in fact his staff rank could be counted at all in the face of line commanders. To make matters even worse, this tragicomic affair unfolded without Johnston knowing that he was the stalking horse for the pouting corps commander.

When the head of the marching column passed Black Horse Tavern it quickly came to a point where the narrow road crawled over a high knoll. At its top, the Confederates would come in clear view of Federals on Little Round Top. Sam Johnston innocently told Longstreet that this would "discover your movements to the enemy," but Longstreet had no comment. He watched as the column went over the crest into view of the Federals and halted. The knoll with the naked crest actually extended only a short distance in either direction. Porter Alexander moved his large artillery battalion around the far edge of the knoll without a second thought. When he noticed the infantry not only failing to follow his example but also halted in clear view of Little Round Top—thus canceling both secrecy and speed—he was astonished. The infantry never did follow Alexander's simple and convenient route. Instead they retraced their steps and went on a great looping detour that covered, Alexander noted disgustedly, "four miles to get less than one."[18] The spectacle of a corps under arms, groping its way without a commander at a crucial moment, makes one of the most pathetic vignettes in the army's annals.

Longstreet's little game, with his own rules developed as he went, eventually allowed him to assume command of Hood's division but not that of McLaws. Under this system,

Longstreet could declare that he "did not order General
McLaws forward, because, as the head of the column, he had
direct orders from General Lee to follow the conduct of Colonel [sic] Johnston. Therefore, I sent orders to Hood, who was
in the rear and not encumbered by these instructions." All of
this petty and dishonest posturing dramatically exacerbated
the tendency of Longstreet's command to move with what
some observers thought was unwonted sluggishness even under ordinary circumstances. A member of General Ewell's staff
remarked of operations during July that "Longstreet was . . .
himself notorious for moving slowly, & McLaws' Divn of his
Corps was . . . the slowest of Longstreet's troops & a clog on
the whole Army." An engineer officer who had nothing to do
with Longstreet and expressed no opinion of any sort about
him referred to him as "Old Snail" in a routine diary entry
during July, as though that were his common nickname.[19]
Troops with that marching tendency were particularly vulnerable to the sort of sulky delaying action that Longstreet
employed on July 2.

Why did Lee not accompany his grumpy subordinate, insist
on greater organization and speed of movement, and make his
presence felt at the point of decision? Because he came to
Gettysburg with two brand-new corps commanders and neither of them was James Longstreet. He had already had cause
to be deeply concerned about Ewell, and Hill's inaugural attempt at corps command at Gettysburg had very little impact
on the battle. It must have been easy for Lee to decide to stay
near the sectors of his two tyros while leaving his one veteran
to operate with greater independence, as was Lee's preferred
system. Longstreet's admirer Porter Alexander concluded cat-
egorically: "There seems no doubt that had Longstreet's
attack. . . . been made materially sooner, we would have gained
a decided victory"; but Alexander says Lee somehow should
have done a better job of forcing Longstreet to conform to his
will. We can of course recognize that Lee's presence with

Longstreet was desperately needed, using hindsight, but that incomparable tool by definition was not in the army commander's arsenal. Lee was left to ask, according to one of his staff, "in a tone of uneasiness, 'what *can* detain Longstreet? He ought to be in position now.'" When Lee learned of the advance of Federal General Daniel E. Sickles to the Emmitsburg Pike he "again expressed his impatience."[20]

When at last the marching comedy of errors reached the vicinity of the Emmitsburg Pike opposite the Peach Orchard and the Round Tops, Longstreet for the first time could see the ground over which he was to attack. It obviously offered strong advantages to the defenders, if they were present in strength, but by the same token it offered equally alluring opportunity to the Confederates if they could occupy the high ground by some means. Longstreet had been stubbornly opposed to fighting on the offensive under any circumstances. His churlish behavior all day had resulted from that general conviction, not from any idea of the terrain, which he only now could see. As Porter Alexander aptly commented: "The long & the short of the matter seems to me as follows. Longstreet did not wish to take the offensive. His objection to it was not based at all upon the peculiar strength of the enemy's position for that was not yet recognized, but solely on general principles."[21]

As Longstreet's two strong and tested divisions neared action, the corps commander adjusted his horizon to the point that he was willing to resume his abdicated command of McLaws. Captain Sam Johnston would have been relieved to relinquish the command, we can suppose, had he ever known that he had it in the first place. It might have appeared that the lieutenant general was prepared to go back to work in the interests of his faithful and trusting riflemen who were about to head into mortal combat, but in fact his taste for charade and for self-fulfilling prophecy had only been whetted. The most pressing question facing the corps, which should have occupied the energies of its commander, was how to align the troops and commit them to battle. Longstreet abdicated that responsibility and insisted that Lee's plan, now long stale and necessarily only a general guide in any event, be rigidly honored. It had become apparent that Lee knew far less well than Longstreet how to win a battle, and here was an irresistible opportunity to prove it to him.

The division and brigade commanders, together with some aggressive regimental officers, had looked at the zone of attack eagerly and with pragmatic eyes. Some of them quickly discerned that the Federal left dangled amorphously in a large and vaguely defined region north of Round Top. John B. Hood, whose division stood on the far right, at once requested permission to turn that flank. Longstreet refused to entertain any such deviations from Lee's plan, which he now suddenly endowed with a categorical aura. To alter it would be to impair the lesson Lee needed to learn. Hood later reminded Longstreet how he had urged "that you allow me to turn Round Top and attack the enemy in flank and rear." Longstreet replied curtly, "Gen'l Lee's orders are to attack up the Emmettsburg [sic] road." A second heartfelt plea met a similar response. "A third time I dispatched one of my staff to explain fully," Hood recalled, "and to suggest that you had better come."[22] Longstreet refused to go look for himself or to consider any alternatives. To do so would have been to exercise corps command, and he was not yet ready to climb off his high horse.

Moxley Sorrel confirmed Hood's account of his desperate attempts to operate intelligently. Hood "begged me to look at" his division's plight, Sorrel remembered, "report its extreme difficulty, and implore Longstreet to make the attack another way." The staffer complied, but elicited the same answer from Longstreet. McLaws was not involved in the vain attempt to move around the right, but his superior found opportunity nastily to force him too into misguided positions as a means of venting his spleen. Longstreet in fact never denied having refused to consider alternatives. He actually reiterated his position as a means of clarifying Lee's bad plan; that was the point of the whole business. "General Hood appealed again and again for the move to the right," Longstreet confirmed."[23]

What Hood wanted to do, Longstreet insisted, "had been carefully considered by our chief and rejected in favor of his present orders."[24] Longstreet had the genetic equipment to be naturally, as well as intentionally, obtuse. In this instance he certainly was employing a calculated density rather than his ample native supply. He and Lee had disagreed over whether it was desirable—to say nothing of practicable—to relocate the army in some miraculous fashion to a point between Gettysburg and Washington. That would have been more or less to the Federal strategic left (if not right in the midst of their approaching columns). In rejecting that visionary notion, Lee of course was offering no comment of any sort about moving against the Federals' tactical left on the battlefield. The whole movement of July 2 was aimed toward just that target. Lee always left the means of committing a corps to action up to its commander, certainly when out of his presence and almost invariably even when he was nearby. He had refused to attempt to relocate his army southeastward into a different county; that had nothing at all to do with relocating its tactical arrangements in the same direction—or in any other—by the width of a pasture or two or a few hundred yards of woods.

Among the most telling indictments of Longstreet's behavior are the words of two of his intimates, one who remained so for life and one who broke with him on the spot. Both Moxley Sorrel and Lafayette McLaws commented pointedly on their superior's attitude on this dark and bloody day. Sorrel stayed on close terms with his chief to the end of his life but could not conceal some surprise about how Longstreet acted on July 2. The lieutenant general "failed to conceal some anger. There was apparent apathy in his movements. They lacked the fire and point of his usual bearing on the battlefield." Sorrel admitted to imagining Lee's horror about "what was going on to the disadvantage of the army," then reined himself in with a visible jolt: "This is all I shall permit myself to express on this well-worn . . . subject."[25]

Lafayette McLaws stood high among James Longstreet's favorites on July 1. Just a few weeks before, he had been Longstreet's candidate for a lieutenant generalcy and command of one of the new corps. To the end of his life Longstreet grumbled about the dark Virginian plot that gave those billets to Ewell and A. P. Hill instead of to McLaws. By the end of July 2, however, the veteran division commander had been so revolted by his chief's behavior that he was unable to abide his further patronage. The two generals remained at loggerheads and wound up in open conflict later in the war. Their hostility extended unabated through McLaws's life, despite some periods of superficial postwar rapprochement. After the feud erupted, McLaws's testimony must be viewed in that context, though it remains more important than would be admitted by the school of thought that suggests that no one could effectively criticize Longstreet because so many hated him.

The misbegotten tendency to flick away attacks on Longstreet's behavior as the work of a dishonest postwar cabal just will not stand up in considering McLaws's most pointed description of July 2. It came in the intimate forum of a letter to his wife, and was written not in the grip of some 1880s political frenzy but on July 7, 1863. "General Longstreet is to blame for not reconnoitering the ground and for persisting in ordering the assault when his errors were discovered," he told Mrs. McLaws. "During the engagement he was very excited, giving contrary orders to every one, and was exceedingly overbearing." In consequence, McLaws said, "I consider him a humbug, a man of small capacity, very obstinate, not at all chivalrous, exceedingly conceited, and totally selfish."[26] A stronger bill of particulars would be difficult to contrive. If McLaws's description is in any wise accurate, and it seems to be substantially correct, James Longstreet's deportment stands in stark and ugly contrast next to the selfless devotion shown by the thousands of men who were bleeding and dying that afternoon under his direction—or, more accurately, his lack of direction.

A striking and fascinating comparison can be made between the actions of James Longstreet on July 2 and those of Stonewall Jackson on May 2 at Chancellorsville. On May 2, 1863, Lee chose to send his ranking subordinate on an extended march toward his enemy's most exposed flank on the second day of battle. Lee remained with the fixing element of his army to supervise its less experienced leaders, assigned to the maneuver element the key tactical responsibility, and instructed the commander of the maneuver element to attack the enemy flank at a specific point at which it apparently rested. In the event, Jackson managed his march with his accustomed energy and skill; Lee remained with the static element of the army and succeeded in bemusing the Federals opposite him; Jackson accepted the tactical responsibility eagerly; and, most significantly, when Jackson reached the enemy flank and found the situation somewhat different than what had been expected, he altered the tactical plans without a moment's hesitation and realized in consequence a staggering victory.

The situation facing Lee at Gettysburg two months later to the day was not identical, but it was analogous to an interesting degree. He again chose on the second day of battle to send his ranking subordinate toward what he believed to be the most vulnerable enemy flank. He remained with the static element of his army to supervise its inexperienced leaders, expected the point of decision to be where his maneuver element struck, and surely expected the lieutenant general on the scene to seek the best possible terms when he attacked at the end of a careful and rather risky march. Longstreet, of course, prosecuted the march execrably (or Captain Johnston unwittingly did, if you will). The most arresting parallel between the two days is the way in which Jackson, as was his custom, sought—and found—the best way to accomplish the purpose for which so much effort and risk had been incurred. In doing so Jackson received timely advice from a number of subordinates, most notably Fitzhugh Lee. Longstreet not only sulkily failed to seek out the best means of accomplishing his assigned task but also refused to countenance intelligence toward that end voluntarily supplied by subordinates. When he ostentatiously announced to all listeners, then and later, that Lee's bad plan must be followed, Longstreet was delineating as starkly as any critic ever could the chasm that separated his attitude from that of Stonewall Jackson. The contrast is an unpleasant one not only in theoretical fashion but particularly because it was drawn in the blood and suffering of thousands of his own men, and at a time that caused immense damage to his country.

Longstreet's demeanor on July 3 affecting the major assault on that day is another subject and beyond the scope of this essay. Later on the third, as the army contemplated disengagement, the general displayed further confusion and pique affecting McLaws. In an episode that has not received much attention, Longstreet again thrashed angrily about, giving more of what McLaws had called "contrary orders to everyone." McLaws promptly obeyed the first set of new orders, although he remonstrated against their pertinence with Moxley Sorrel; this obviously was not the week to seek sweet reason from Longstreet. After a time Sorrel came back and asked whether McLaws could resume his original position. McLaws of course reminded the staff officer of their earlier discussion. Sorrel responded, "Yes, I gave you the order to retire and it was given to me by Genl. Longstreet himself, but he now denied having given it!" Generals Law and Benning were also victims of this unusual proceeding and compared disgruntled notes with McLaws. A few weeks later, McLaws recalled, he wrote to Longstreet seeking an explanation and received the response that the corps commander "had no recollection concerning the orders."[27]

No better credo could be imagined for a subordinate in disagreement with his superior than one Longstreet himself wrote, or claimed to have written, on July 24, 1863. In a letter that Longstreet published as written to his uncle, he declared: "I consider it a part of my duty to express my views to the commanding general. If he approves and adopts them, it is well; if he does not, it is my duty to adopt his views, and to execute his orders as faithfully as if they were my own."[28] It is difficult to imagine a more prudent guideline for application to circumstances such as Longstreet faced at Gettysburg. Only the most intransigent of the general's supporters can cling to the notion, however, that he executed Lee's orders in Pennsylvania "as faithfully as if they were my own." Was his July 24 letter the special pleadings of a guilty conscience?

In terms of strategy and tactics, Lee's army suffered most at Gettysburg because of the unwonted absence of J. E. B. Stuart and his skilled mounted men. It suffered next, both chronologically and with regard to impact, from the sloth and equivocation of Richard S. Ewell on July 1. Longstreet's uncertain opportunities lost in the midst of an unseemly sulk on July 2 can only be reckoned as third behind those more crisply defined shortcomings. The salient difference is that evidently Stuart and Ewell were not displaying petty personality traits as they strove in vain.

A peculiar footnote to the Gettysburg controversies cropped up late in the nineteenth century when General Cullen A. Battle publicly reported that a formal court of inquiry actually convened to examine the campaign. General William Mahone presided, according to Battle, who claimed to have been appointed recorder for the court. In its verdict the court "censured both Stuart and Longstreet, but General Lee suppressed the report, and took the blame upon himself."[29] General Battle's account must be classified as falling among the bizarre satellite claims that cluster tenaciously around the larger Gettysburg controversies.

Longstreet's career after Gettysburg included further refinement of his blame-shifting techniques. It also included what must have been for him the startling lesson that fondness for the tactical defensive cannot be readily translated into battlefield results. Twice during the war, Longstreet had the chance to operate on a large scale independent of Lee's oppressive damper on his creative skills. Not long before Gettysburg the ambitious corps commander had led a strong force in a campaign around Suffolk. Such initiatives as Longstreet found occasion to use included no tactical defensive; cooperative Federals proved to be in short supply. Federal General John G. Foster, who faced Longstreet, was hardly a commander of legendary proportions, but he was able to restrain any impulses he might have had to cooperate with Longstreet. The Suffolk command produced no striking results for Longstreet and might be classified as an embarrassment rather than a humiliation. Longstreet earned humiliation in ample doses in Tennessee later in the year.

During the last week of November 1863, Longstreet tasted the bitter dregs of total defeat around Knoxville. His attack on Fort Sanders—not only a tactical offensive but a brutal frontal assault—cannot be adjudged anything other than a pathetic exhibition of ineptitude. No large veteran contingent of Army of Northern Virginia troops experienced anything so grotesque during the war, even during its closing hours. The few dozen Federals in the fort routed the thousands of attackers with great slaughter. The Northern assaults on Marye's Heights on December 13, 1862 (probably the only battle that really suited Longstreet, first and last), look like classic practice of military science compared to Fort Sanders. It is impossible to imagine R. E. Lee or T. J. Jackson—or Robert E. Rodes, William Dorsey Pender, S. Dodson Ramseur, John B. Gordon, or William Mahone, for that matter—caught up in so dreadful a situation.

After Knoxville even Longstreet must have admitted to himself that his cherished dreams of independent success were only cloud castles. He had been rebuffed by one John G. Foster at Suffolk, and then humiliated by Ambrose E. Burnside, of all people, for it was the inept Burnside who tormented Longstreet at Knoxville. The solution, once again, was to distribute blame amongst whatever targets came to mind. It seemed obvious to blame them for lack of enthusiastic support of their commander; after all, Longstreet knew with conviction that subordinates who lacked enthusiasm could foul up operations pretty thoroughly. The general put in arrest Generals McLaws, Evander M. Law, and Jerome B. Robertson. These sweeping arrests outstripped the record of the notoriously litigious Stonewall Jackson, who, though harsh and fond of courts, had no need of scapegoats.

Writing at the time, McLaws declared, "The charges were forced on him by public opinion & he attempts to make me a blind to draw public inquiry from his complete failure in the whole Tennessee campaign. . . . When it is considered that Gen. L . . . has nothing to recommend him as a commander, but the possession of a certain Bullheadedness, it is mortifying when one feels that he is allowed to tyranise, as he is doing." After the war McLaws summarized Longstreet's conduct of the campaign harshly but essentially accurately: "He was so out-witted and his movements so timid and managed as to conform exactly to those of the enemy, and as the enemy must have wished him to order, so as to give them every success and bring disaster and shame upon us."[30]

Longstreet sought to avoid charging McLaws formally, which he must have known would lead to embarrassment. He attempted merely to arrest his subordinate without either charges or a trial. McLaws insisted on being charged and tried, and Longstreet was indeed embarrassed by the results. Confederate court-martial transcripts survive only in collections of personal papers, but fortunately most of the documents from this court have been preserved. Longstreet charged McLaws with six specific misdeeds. Five of them misrepresented objective facts—facts that many thousands of veterans of the attack knew to be entirely contrary to Longstreet's claims. One specification damned McLaws, for instance, because he "failed to attack at NW corner [of Fort Sanders] where there was no ditch." More than fifty men who took part in Longstreet's absurd attack testified unanimously that McLaws did precisely what Longstreet claimed that he did not do. The sixth charge was subjective enough to be beyond substantive proof either way. The court ruled against McLaws on that single issue and in his favor on the other five, but the War Department overturned even that vague stricture, and censured Longstreet for his fiddling with the proceedings of the court.[31]

Tactical offensives in the Civil War, and perhaps in most military epochs, required a good deal more from their commanders than did defensive arrangements—more coordination, diligence, moral force, breadth, grasp, and strength of purpose and mind. This is not to postulate that they were the preferable alternative, because they surely were not. A cooperative foe such as Burnside at Fredericksburg only turned up intermittently. Meanwhile the initiative regularly required taking the offensive; witness even the defensive oracle Longstreet staggering helplessly into an offensive mode at Knoxville. Neither Longstreet nor his special hero Joe Johnston ever managed an offensive well in independent campaigning. When the two kindred spirits collaborated at Seven Pines, "no action in the war was planned with such slovenly thinking or prepared so carelessly," in the apt words of Clifford Dowdey (who may have overlooked Knoxville in choosing his superlative). "Johnston's aversion to details . . . was typical of him," and of Longstreet's feeble offensive gesture too.[32] Lassitude and whatever else went into the formula left Longstreet incapable of managing an offensive campaign when he—even he—recognized no alternative. That may well have affected his attitude throughout the war.

On the eve of the 1864 Wilderness campaign, Longstreet rejoined Lee's army with far more relief and gratitude than he could have imagined when he left to do great things on his own. The McLaws results, which must have embarrassed Longstreet, were published in Richmond the day Grant crossed the Rapidan. At the same time, General Law, one of McLaws's fellow sufferers, was preparing to file formal charges against Longstreet on several counts, including "conduct unworthy of an officer and gentleman in making a false report of the fight" at Wauhatchie. Law had caught Longstreet in another *"infamous lie,"* and he told McLaws, "If you will cover the Knoxville Campaign in your charges, I believe we can oust him." "Longstreet," Law insisted, "is most certainly on the wane both in, and out of the army."[33] In fact the general was on his way out of the army by means of convalescent leave.

Longstreet arrived in the Wilderness on the second day of battle, May 6, 1864, from a bivouac far to the southwest. Some sources suggest that Lee was dismayed over the tardiness of that arrival, including G. W. C. Lee quoting his father, C. S. Venable to Longstreet himself, and H. B. McClellan of Stuart's staff. The morning of the sixth proved to be Longstreet's last with the army for many months, as he fell dangerously wounded, the victim of a mistaken volley fired by Confederates in the tangled thickets of the Wilderness.

When Longstreet returned to duty during the autumn of 1864, Lee must have eagerly welcomed the return of his seasoned lieutenant and best corps commander. Whether Longstreet ever recovered his full ability to control his corps remains uncertain. Early in 1865 (on Lee's fifty-eighth birthday, in fact), the commanding general sent an inspection summary to Longstreet that expended nearly one thousand words in criticism of the condition of the First Corps. Although it no doubt was primarily a staff-to-staff communiqué, the document bore Lee's signature and was addressed to the corps commander. It cited "unsatisfactory" reports, officers who "have failed to do their duty," and units "lax in discipline" and "unsoldierly & unmilitary." The letter exhorted Longstreet in stern phrases: "Prompt measures must be taken"; "I desire that you will give particular attention . . . and exact unceasing effort"; "I desire you to correct the evils . . . by every means in your power"; "I beg that you will insist upon these points"; and, "this should be at once corrected."[34]

As Lee's senior subordinate, Longstreet enjoyed the applause of most officers and enlisted men, but at least a few of them felt that his late-war performance let them down. A novice artillerist declared on March 19, 1865, that he considered Longstreet "the poorest general we have." Another man in the same eighty-man battery wrote later, "For a few months near the close of the war . . . to our great regret we had to serve under Longstreet."[35] Neither artillerist ever earned an epaulet as military critic, but their unease suggests that Longstreet's 1865 aura as seen from the ranks was not quite what it once had been.

James Longstreet spent nearly four decades after the war assailing his former comrades in arms, beginning just slowly enough to avoid open assaults on Lee until after the death of the former army commander in 1870. When Lee heard the first mutterings about Longstreet's fabulous assertions and criticisms, he simply refused to believe that his former subordinate had said such "absurd" things.[36] Longstreet reached vitriolic high gear soon after Lee's death and maintained his momentum ever after. When the aging general's first wife died (she had been a Virginian, remarkably enough), he married a young woman—born the year of Gettysburg—who was herself a born controversialist and who acted on the general as kerosene would on a raging blaze.

At his death in 1904, Longstreet was one of the most thoroughly loathed men in the South. Many who found Longstreet's behavior distasteful would have echoed the mature judgment of Dr. Hunter Holmes McGuire, who read the general's mean-spirited memoir "more in sorrow for the man than indignation at his bad taste and temper." A substantial body of observers also shared McGuire's empirical conclusion: "If Longstreet . . . says so, it is most likely not true."[37]

Had General Longstreet died at the head of his corps on May 6, 1864, he surely would stand tall in the pantheon of Confederate heroes. We would see him in bronze on more than one battlefield, and probably in Richmond as well. The mortal wounds inflicted on Longstreet's reputation therefore seem to some observers to be the result of what he did after the war. The hurtful impact, however, came not from postwar deeds but from the vistas Longstreet unveiled in the long life left to him. His longevity gave him numerous opportunities to bare his soul—the same one with which he had been saddled during the war—and the view was not a savory one.

Lieutenant General Richard Taylor surveyed the Gettysburg controversy a few years after the war with interest and some detachment. As a son of a president of the United States, a brother-in-law of the president of the Confederate States, and a general officer who served in the Virginia theater, Taylor was blessed with exemplary connections in high circles. He had gone west well before Gettysburg, so had no vested interest in the specific details under debate. He did know the principle figures well enough, however, to offer a lively and apposite comment:

> A recent article in the public press, signed by General Longstreet, ascribes the failure at Gettysburg to Lee's mistakes, which he [Longstreet] in vain pointed out and remonstrated against. That any subject involving the possession and exercise of intellect should be clear to Longstreet and concealed from Lee, is a startling proposition to those having knowledge of the two men.[38]

"A Step All-Important and Essential to Victory"

Henry W. Slocum and the Twelfth Corps on July 1–2, 1863

A. WILSON GREENE

E very Civil War battle produced a gallery of heroes and rogues—commanders whose conspicuous valor, bold gambles, or fatal errors pursue them through history to their everlasting glory or shame. At the Battle of Gettysburg, the Army of the Potomac certainly conformed to this pattern. On one side proudly stand the likes of Brigadier General John Buford, Major General Winfield Scott Hancock, and Colonel Joshua L. Chamberlain, whereas on the other lurk the blemished visages of Major General Oliver Otis Howard, Major General Daniel E. Sickles, and Brigadier General Alexander Schimmelfennig.[1]

Usually absent from either list are the ranking officers of the Twelfth Corps. Major General Henry W. Slocum and his eight subordinate commanders have attracted less attention from Gettysburg scholars than the leaders of any other Union corps. Despite this neglect, some observers have credited Slocum's corps with crafting the Union victory, none more eloquently than Oliver Otis Howard: "The most impressive incident of the great battle of Gettysburg," wrote the Eleventh Corps commander in 1894, "was Slocum's own battle.... Slocum's resolute insistence the afternoon of July 2nd and his organized work and battle the ensuing morning, in my judgment prevented Meade's losing the battle of Gettysburg. It was a grand judgment and action; a step all-important and essential to victory."[2]

Major General Henry Warner Slocum
(*Photographic History* 10:177)

Was Howard correct in ascribing a critical role to the Twelfth Corps at Gettysburg? If so, what part did Slocum and the rest of the relatively anonymous hierarchy of his corps play on July 1–2? Did they render service that altered the outcome of North America's most famous battle?

The Twelfth Corps embarked on the Gettysburg campaign after suffering nearly three thousand casualties in the Battle of Chancellorsville.[3] Henry Warner Slocum, thirty-five years old and from Onondaga County, New York, led the corps at Chancellorsville as he had since October of the previous year. Slocum graduated seventh in the class of 1852 at West Point, having roomed part of the time with Philip H. Sheridan. After a brief career in the Old Army, Slocum resigned to practice law but maintained connections with the New York state militia. Shortly after the fall of Fort Sumter, he offered his sword to the Union, reentering the service as colonel of the 27th New York Infantry.[4]

Admirers praised Slocum's manner, which "inspire[d] faith and confidence," and noted that his sparkling brown eyes contributed to a "magnetic power over his troops."[5] A less-impassioned assessment might mention that the beardless Slocum lacked dash, loved discipline and order, and gained the respect, if not the devotion, of his men. Nothing in Slocum's record prior to the Gettysburg campaign either cast doubt on his military skills or marked him for higher responsibility.

Slocum's command consisted of only two divisions. The First Division belonged to Brigadier General Alpheus S. Williams, whose published letters make him familiar to modern students. "Old Pap" hailed from Connecticut and earned a degree from Yale, but after extensive travel abroad he settled in Michigan and established a Detroit law practice. Williams served in the Mexican War and presided over the state military board in the spring of 1861. A temporary replacement for the mortally wounded Major General J. K. F. Mansfield as Twelfth Corps commander at Antietam, he returned to his division

Brigadier General Alpheus Starkey Williams
(*Photographic History* 10:85)

after the battle. Fifty-two years old in early summer 1863, Williams sported a luxuriant beard embellished by extravagant mustachios rivalling the hirsute splendor of fellow brigadier John C. Robinson.[6]

The three brigades of Williams's division experienced considerable reorganization following Chancellorsville. The 28th New York and 128th Pennsylvania mustered out of the First Brigade in May, and the brigade commander, Brigadier General Joseph F. Knipe, temporarily left the field nursing a bothersome wound sustained the previous August at Cedar Mountain. The army consolidated the Second Brigade with the First's remaining two regiments and named Colonel Archibald L. McDougall of the 123d New York as commander of this new First Brigade. Gettysburg would be the only battle at which McDougall exercised so high an authority.[7] The Third Brigade remained intact under the able direction of Brigadier General Thomas H. Ruger of New York. Like Slocum, the thirty-year-old Ruger was a high-ranking graduate of West Point who resigned his commission to practice law. Ruger settled in Janesville, Wisconsin, and reentered the army as lieutenant colonel of the 3d Wisconsin, one of six western regiments in the corps at Gettysburg.[8]

The other division of the Twelfth Corps, known as the White Stars, served under Brigadier General John White Geary. This Pennsylvanian, in keeping with the coincidental character of the corps, also possessed a legal background. His law career, however, would be eclipsed by politics. After volunteer duty with Winfield Scott in Mexico, Geary moved to California where he became the first mayor of San Francisco. In 1856, at age thirty-seven, he received an unenviable appointment as territorial governor of turbulent Kansas; the strains of this office led him to an early retirement at his Pennsylvania farm. Geary raised a regiment in 1861 and advanced steadily through the ranks to divisional command.[9]

Brigadier General John White Geary
(Courtesy of the National Archives)

The Second Division experienced little organizational change between Chancellorsville and Gettysburg. Colonel Charles Candy led the First Brigade, a unit comprised entirely of Ohioans and Pennsylvanians. Twenty-nine years old and a native of Lexington, Kentucky, Candy had served a decade as an enlisted man in the regular army when the war commenced. Commissioned an officer in the volunteers, he would eventually receive a brevet promotion to brigadier general, making him one of the few soldiers to rise from private to general during the course of the war.[10]

Colorful Thomas L. Kane held the official command of the Second Brigade. Yet another lawyer, Kane had earned a reputation before the war as an ardent abolitionist and principal in the Underground Railroad. Following an eventful period with the Mormons in Utah, Kane returned to his native Pennsylvania, founded a village he named after himself, and recruited the famous Pennsylvania Bucktails. A bout with pneumonia after Chancellorsville forced Kane to leave the field temporarily and entrust his brigade to Colonel George A. Cobham of the 111th Pennsylvania. The thirty-seven-year-old Cobham, perhaps because he was an Englishman, did not practice law but earned his living as a bridge builder and contractor.[11]

The Third Brigade consisted of five New York regiments led by Brigadier General George Sears Greene of Rhode Island. One observer described this unit as "the best brigade of the biggest state led by the best general of the smallest state." Sixty-two years old, Greene had graduated second in the West Point class of 1823 and lost his wife and three children during one seven-month period at Fort Sullivan, South Carolina. He resigned his commission in 1836 to pursue civil engineering in New York. Greene's troops called their commander "Pop" and deeply respected him as a stern authority figure.[12]

The Twelfth Corps, smallest in the army at only nine thousand soldiers and officers present for duty,[13] marched north on June 29 from Frederick, Maryland. Entering Pennsylvania the next day, the troops arrived hot and dusty at Littlestown about 2:00 P.M. Although Pennsylvanians generously dispensed refreshments and encouraging words to the tired troops, General Williams most vividly remembered the provincialism of the locals: "The inhabitants are Dutch descendants and quite Dutch in language. . . . The people are rich, but ignorant of everybody and [every] thing beyond their small spheres. They have immense barns, looking like great arsenals or public institutions, full of small windows and painted showily. Altogether, they are a people of barns, not brains."[14]

As some soldiers mustered for pay, word came that Rebel cavalry had attacked Union horsemen to the north. The Twelfth Corps quickly prepared to go to their cavalry's assistance, but by the time the men hurried through Littlestown the alarm had been cancelled. The corps made a comfortable camp about one mile northeast of town on the road to Hanover. From army headquarters, Major General George G. Meade then instructed Slocum to become familiar with the roads between Littlestown, Gettysburg, and Major General John F. Reynolds's position farther west, and informed Slocum of Confederate movements toward Gettysburg.[15]

July 1 dawned, according to one soldier, "wet and lowery." Following "a hasty breakfast of coffee, crackers and pork," elements of Williams's division left their bivouacs about 5:00 A.M. The corps retraced its route to Littlestown then gained the Baltimore Pike leading northwest toward Gettysburg about ten miles distant. By 9:00 A.M. the last units of Geary's division had commenced what everyone described as a leisurely march.[16]

The pace proved so casual, in fact, that members of the 66th Ohio of Candy's brigade found an opportunity for a little spontaneous recreation. William Henry Harrison Tallman remembered stopping at a farm house along the road where he and his comrades "squandered our shin plasters for soft bread, butter, apple butter, and a cheese the like of which I never smelled before. This cheese was made up in round balls about the size of a regulation baseball and [when] broken open perfumed the air for rods around us. Then commenced a lively pelting of each other with the cheese balls and the odor in and around our company was dense enough to cut with a knife."[17]

Slocum's immediate goal, as specified in orders communicated by Meade the previous day, was the hamlet of Two Taverns, a six-mile march and more than halfway to Gettysburg. The only event that disturbed the tranquility of this movement, cheese-ball battles notwithstanding, came from the north in the form of "the dull booming of cannon" heard by some of the troops. Slocum later described the sounds as cavalry carbines occasionally accompanied by artillery rather than the racket caused by a general engagement.[18] Williams's vanguard reached Two Taverns in midmorning and Geary's leading units arrived about 11:00 A.M., filing to the west of the road and encamping on a small hill.[19]

The day had grown uncomfortably muggy, and some of the pickets posted around the camp collapsed from heatstroke. The men sought solace from the weather in their rations and by gossiping, "the air . . . full of the rumors which circulate so freely when a battle becomes imminent." The air also resounded with the unmistakable echo of combat. "Heavy and continuous firing in the direction of Gettysburg" gradually grew more rapid. "The cannonading became more and more furious as the minutes passed," according to a Wisconsin soldier, "until in the distance it sounded like one continual roll of thunder."[20] Some listeners climbed to the tops of nearby barns where the bursting of shells could be plainly detected; others witnessed "smoke from the cannon and the little puffs in the air" from high points at the bivouac itself.[21]

The men completed their meal and some had begun the regular monthly inspection when a civilian dashed up to Slocum's headquarters with word of "a great battle" in progress at Gettysburg. The general dispatched Major Eugene W. Guindon of his staff to ride north and investigate this report. Guindon soon observed what other witnesses had seen from their lofty vantage points at Two Taverns, returning to Slocum with confirmation of the citizen's veracity.[22]

Meanwhile, Edmund R. Brown of the 27th Indiana saw no fewer than three couriers arrive at Two Taverns, "their horses in a lather and jaded, prov[ing] that they had come a distance and ridden fast." Brown identified them as emissaries from Major General Oliver O. Howard, in command of Union forces at Gettysburg. In fact, Howard had sent a message to Slocum at 1:00 P.M.: "Ewell's corps is advancing from York. The left wing of the Army of the Potomac is engaged with A. P. Hill's corps."[23]

In response to this corroborated intelligence, the Twelfth Corps resumed its northward march on the Baltimore Pike but arrived too late to participate in the desperate defense mounted by Howard north and west of Gettysburg. Howard's strategy on the afternoon of July 1 depended in large part on the timely arrival of the Twelfth Corps, which he knew to be located only five miles to the southeast. Did Howard have reason to expect help from Slocum, and if so, why did it not materialize?

The most apposite document in this inquiry is Meade's famous Pipe Creek Circular, which was sent to Slocum on July 1.[24] The circular clearly stated Meade's intention to assume a defensive position along northern Maryland's Pipe Creek in the event of certain contingencies. First, the enemy would have to attack. Thanks to the civilian's report and Howard's messengers, Slocum knew early in the afternoon that a battle had been joined near Gettysburg. He did not know until later that the Confederates had initiated the action. Second, and more important, Meade wrote that the time for the withdrawal could "only be developed by circumstances" and that those circumstances would be "at once communicated to these headquarters and to all adjoining corps commanders." In other words, in the event of a Confederate assault, Reynolds would make the determination whether or not to retreat. Moreover, Meade specifically allowed for a Union advance by concluding his circular with the admonition that "developments may cause the commanding general to assume the offensive from his present positions."[25]

To be sure, Slocum's position at Two Taverns was consistent with Meade's instructions. Although it is clear that many Twelfth Corps soldiers heard the sounds of battle even before they reached the village, it is possible that the rolling terrain caused Slocum to misidentify the distant noise as cavalry skirmishing. When specific word of the engagement arrived from Howard and the civilian, however, Slocum apparently hesitated to either order his troops forward or, more negligently, take a short ride to find Howard and ascertain the facts for himself.[26]

In referring to Howard's messengers, one of Slocum's biographers observed that this "call did not give sufficient reason for Slocum to answer it immediately as desired inasmuch as Howard, as well as Slocum, had received a copy of the circular directing retreat on Pipe Creek." Under orders not to precipitate a general engagement elsewhere, Slocum occupied the place designated by his commanding officer, and "like the faithful, obedient commander that he was, he remained at his post of duty." This explanation simply misreads the intent of the Pipe Creek Circular. Moreover, Slocum's defenders then turn their argument on its head by praising the general's flexibility when he finally did direct his corps forward once convinced that its presence was necessary at Gettysburg.[27] A more critical historian, Samuel Bates, concluded that "General Meade anticipated, that if the forces in advance were attacked, any corps within supporting distance would go to their assistance; that it would act upon the Napoleonic principle, 'March to the sound of the enemy's guns.'" This Slocum did not instantly do and thus Bates held Slocum accountable for a measure of Howard's discomfiture.[28]

Slocum defended himself against this accusation by mentioning that none of his subordinates criticized his actions on July 1. "If all, or even any of these officers . . . had known at the time that the 12th Corps was kept idle, while two other corps were engaged with the enemy at a point only five miles distant, would not some of them, Yea! would every one of them have denounced the commander of the idle corps?" In fact, no one in Slocum's corps questioned his generalship on July 1—his loyal subordinates, it should be added, lacked crucial information that would warrant second guessing their chief's actions that day. In contrast, Howard's brother Charles penned a letter a week after the battle decrying Slocum's willingness "to demonstrate the fitness of his name Slow Come." Generals Howard, Meade, and Abner Doubleday would fault Slocum in later years, but without acrimony.[29]

Howard's couriers probably reached Two Taverns shortly after 1:30 P.M. Although Geary claimed his division resumed the march at 2:00, reliable accounts from officers on Williams's and Geary's staffs, among others, state that the corps left Two Taverns between 3:00 and 4:00.[30] Once Slocum issued the order to advance, the movement commenced rapidly. "Between three and four P.M.," remembered William Tallman, "the order was given to fall in. From the sound of the bugle at the head of the division we knew it meant hurry up."[31]

The northbound troops encountered wounded soldiers and Confederate prisoners as well as residents of varying loyalties. One "hard-featured woman" rushed toward the passing column with evident delight. In the midst of enthusiastic hand shaking and expressions of welcome, a United States flag passed by, causing, as a Massachusetts soldier remembered, "a new idea to dawn upon [the woman]. In a tone of great disgust she said, 'I thought you were Rebs' and without another word turned her back on us. . . . It is fair to presume, that . . . she immediately proceeded to bake bread and sell to the soldiers at one dollar per loaf."[32]

Personally exhorting his men to march as rapidly as possible, Slocum learned en route of Reynolds's death.[33] He turned command of the corps over to "Pap" Williams and rode on ahead of his troops. The soldiers pressed forward in the afternoon heat, some collapsing along the roadside and many divesting themselves of playing cards and other nonessential items.[34]

About 5:00 P.M., a time when Howard had restored a viable defense line on Cemetery Hill, the head of Williams's division approached a crossroads one mile south of Rock Creek and two miles from the cemetery. Ordered by Slocum's couriers to move to the right of Gettysburg and informed by his own staff officers of a "high bare hill" to the east, Williams determined to occupy the eminence. Moving on a "narrow winding path" toward this elevation, called Benner's Hill, Williams soon reached the Hanover Road. He saw Benner's Hill looming

before him but learned that Confederates had beaten him to
it. The Michigander countermarched a short distance then
deployed his men to assault the hill. Ruger's brigade had begun
its advance, meeting no opposition, when orders came from
Slocum to return to the Baltimore Pike. Williams obeyed and
quietly withdrew his division.[35]

Meanwhile, Geary pushed ahead, intending to report to General Howard for duty on Cemetery Hill. The Pennsylvanian
failed to locate Howard but found Winfield Scott Hancock,
now in temporary command of the army until Slocum appeared, who told him to occupy a range of hills south of town
on the Union left. Geary detached Kane's brigade as a reserve
at the base of Cemetery Hill and marched with Candy's and
Greene's troops toward Little Round Top.[36] The 5th Ohio and
147th Pennsylvania of the First Brigade took position on or
near the rocky crest that would prove so critical the following
day. Geary's skirmishers ranged as far west as the Emmitsburg
Road, and the division commander extended his right northward to connect with the left of the First Corps.[37]

Combat on the first day had ended by then. Williams deployed his men along the Baltimore Pike northeast of where
they had turned off on their aborted adventure toward Benner's
Hill. Geary's men remained on the Union left from Little
Round Top north along Cemetery Ridge. Except for the blood-
less charge at the base of Benner's Hill, the Twelfth Corps saw
no action on July 1.[38]

This might not have been the case had Slocum reacted more
quickly to the fighting at Gettysburg. Based on actual distances
and the rate of march achieved by the corps, it is reasonable to
believe that portions of Slocum's command could have reached
Cemetery Hill about the time Howard's battle lines evaporated
north and west of town. It is unlikely that Slocum's men could
have prevented the Union retreat, although historian Edwin B.
Coddington believes that Williams might have deployed at
Gettysburg in time to protect the First and Eleventh corps in

their final, costly withdrawal.[39] Because Lieutenant General Richard S. Ewell declined to test Union defenses on Cemetery Hill in the late afternoon of July 1, the potential value of the Twelfth Corps becomes moot. Had Slocum's forces arrived earlier, however, Ewell's oft-criticized decision would be significantly less controversial.

General Slocum's personal behavior compounds the indictment against his generalship. Howard's calls for help contained implicit and explicit requests for Slocum to ride forward and consult with him. Slocum ignored these entreaties, although he did canter ahead of his men when he met Captain Addison G. Mason of Meade's staff. Mason informed Slocum of Reynolds's death (if someone else already had not) and passed on Meade's desire that he "push forward with all dispatch."[40] Slocum still refused to press on. He next met Major Charles Howard, the general's aide-de-camp, on the Baltimore Pike about a mile from Cemetery Hill. The younger Howard implored Slocum to repair to his brother's command post and take responsibility for the fight. Slocum declined, lamely citing his belief that Meade wished not to bring on a general engagement.[41]

Lieutenant Colonel Charles H. Morgan, Hancock's chief of staff, then rode south from Cemetery Hill to oversee the arrival of the Twelfth Corps. Morgan met Slocum en route, and the general heard again, this time on Hancock's authority, that his presence was desired at the front. Slocum "objected to taking command on the ground that General Hancock had been specially selected over his head to do so, and had become familiar with the position and the location of the troops," remembered Morgan. Slocum explained further that he "did not care under the circumstances to assume the command which might make him responsible for a condition of affairs over which he had no control."[42]

Some historians explain Slocum's behavior as a reflection of his understanding of Meade's defensive and geographic preferences or point to Meade's failure to order his subordinate to assume command on the field by virtue of seniority.[43] Such arguments are unconvincing. If Slocum felt justified, albeit tardily, to commit his regiments to combat, he surely should have met his obligation to exert personal leadership. He never had displayed this type of hesitation, if not outright cowardice, during the Civil War and never would again, but his performance on July I certainly tarnishes his record.

Morgan finally persuaded Slocum to discharge his duty by informing the general that Meade's order naming Hancock as temporary field commander included instructions for Hancock to surrender his authority the moment Slocum appeared. The Twelfth Corps commander arrived on Cemetery Hill after 6:00 P.M. and finally relieved Hancock. Howard officially recognized Slocum's primacy when the two met some minutes later.[44] Meade arrived from Taneytown after midnight and assumed control from Slocum. At this juncture, Slocum returned to command of his corps, a responsibility technically discharged since late in the afternoon by Williams.[45] About midnight, General Kane rolled up in an ambulance after a harrowing trip from Baltimore. He reported to his brigade early the next morning but in a few minutes ordered Colonel Cobham to resume command. Kane remained "gallantly but unofficially" with his troops for the rest of the battle, "too feeble to resume the arduous duties of his post."[46]

As the first rays of light brightened the eastern sky on July 2, Geary received orders to move to the right from Little Round Top and southern Cemetery Ridge, leaving the defense of the Union left to the Third Corps.[47] His goal was Culp's Hill, a prominent eminence rising 180 feet above the surrounding terrain eight hundred yards southeast of Cemetery Hill. A thick blanket of second-growth hardwoods covered this rocky knob (which certainly was not the "mountain" described euphemistically by some Confederates), and huge boulders littered its slopes and crest.[48]

Geary's men arose at daybreak and noticed the "hazy and mysterious appearance" of Third Corps troops who had arrived during the night and were now "sleeping on the ground or groping about preparing food to eat." After pausing to consume a little breakfast of their own, Greene's Empire Staters countermarched through the fields they had tramped the day before, crossed the Baltimore Pike, and arrived on Culp's Hill about 6:00 A.M.[49] Greene's fourteen hundred men formed at right angles to Brigadier General James S. Wadsworth's division of the First Corps, extending Wadsworth's line from the crest down the south slope of Culp's Hill. A heavy growth of timber, relatively free from brush, covered their position, and the granite ledges and boulders provided good cover for riflemen. Greene's line extended about fifteen hundred feet, with the 78th on the left, followed in order by the 60th, 102d, 149th, and 137th. His right rested above a pronounced ravine that bisected the hill four hundred yards from its summit.[50]

Kane's brigade, nine hundred strong under the de facto command of Colonel Cobham, moved somewhat later from its reserve position near Powers Hill and formed on Greene's right. Cobham deployed his regiments to conform to the descending military crest of the ridge south of the ravine, causing his left to project at a forty-five-degree angle from Greene's right. The 109th and 111th Pennsylvania regiments, in that order, extended Geary's line from the ravine to a modest knob six hundred feet south. The 29th Pennsylvania formed as a brigade reserve in the rear.[51] Candy's was the last of the Second Division's brigades to shift to the right. The Ohioans and Pennsylvanians left their positions at the north of Little Round Top about 8:00 A.M. and formed behind Greene. The 28th Pennsylvania advanced along with detachments from the Third Brigade to serve as skirmishers on the west bank of Rock Creek.[52]

While Geary's White Stars moved to the right, Williams and Slocum met briefly at Williams's bivouac. The corps commander instructed his subordinate to advance again toward the

Hanover Road to make contact with the Fifth Corps, then arriving from the east. Williams promptly obeyed, and Ruger's brigade deployed in line of battle facing north. A Fifth Corps division soon appeared to join Williams's men in a relatively harmless exchange of fire with Confederate infantry. At 8:00 A.M., Slocum ordered Williams to withdraw the First Division and place it on Geary's right. Williams rode ahead of his troops to reconnoiter the ground he would occupy and met Geary at Culp's Hill. The two officers then examined the terrain and Geary's recently established line.[53]

Ruger and McDougall, meanwhile, marched their brigades back to the Baltimore Pike, crossed Rock Creek, and before 11:00 A.M. moved into the woods between the south slope of Culp's Hill and the creek. McDougall and his brigade led the way across a three hundred-foot-wide marshy swale watered by Spangler's Spring and clambered up the gentle southern slope of Culp's Hill. The New Yorker deployed his six regiments in two lines. The 123d New York, 20th Connecticut, and 46th Pennsylvania occupied the front from left to right, the 123d linking up with Cobham's Pennsylvanians. The 3d Maryland, 145th New York, and 5th Connecticut took cover behind a stone wall some forty paces behind their comrades. The right of the 46th Pennsylvania and 5th Connecticut did not quite reach the swale.[54]

Ruger's brigade moved to the Baltimore Pike in the wake of McDougall's men. An old woman stood along the road offering words of support to the soldiers in what a Wisconsin man remembered as a strong Pennsylvania Dutch accent: "Dot ish right, poys, go and drive dose fellows off. Dey has shtole enough around here." Her comments "amused and encouraged the men in that hour of high excitement," wrote the veteran. Colonel Nirom M. Crane, a New York banker, led the 107th New York across the headwaters of Spangler's Spring and onto the low base of Culp's Hill. The future Antietam cartographer Ezra A. Carman followed with the 13th New Jersey, forming on the right of the 5th Connecticut behind the stone wall.[55] The 2d Massachusetts also may have crossed the swale initially but eventually deployed in a moderately thick elevated forest, known as McAllister's Woods, between the swale and Rock Creek. The 3d Wisconsin filed in on the right of the Bay Staters, and the 27th Indiana completed the line. Ruger's brigade formed a rough arc on the morning of July 2—the 107th New York, 13th New Jersey, and 2d Massachusetts protected the swale from opposite sides, with the Badgers and Hoosiers facing east and south toward Rock Creek, guarding the right flank of the corps.[56]

By the time Ruger completed these dispositions, Brigadier General Henry Hayes Lockwood's brigade, freshly arrived from Baltimore and assigned for duty with the Twelfth Corps, had arrived on the field and extended Ruger's line toward the Baltimore Pike. A native of Delaware who graduated from West Point in 1836, Lockwood had left the army after one year to accept a teaching position at the Naval Academy. Only a stint of active duty aboard a vessel off the California coast during the Mexican War interrupted Lockwood's antebellum academic pursuits in Annapolis. In 1861 he became colonel of the 1st Delaware and subsequently commanded the Eastern Shore District of the Middle Department, a military backwater if ever one existed.[57]

In mid-June, Lockwood's brigade consisted of three regiments charged with defending Baltimore from Lee's rampaging legions. The 1st Maryland Eastern Shore Regiment, a three-year unit raised expressly to protect Federal interests in that part of the state, would not arrive at Gettysburg until July 3. The 1st Maryland (Regiment) Potomac Home Brigade numbered 739 men on the eve of battle and was one of four such outfits originally formed to guard the Potomac Valley, the B&O Railroad, and other Union resources in the Free State. Colonel William Pinckney Maulsby, a forty-seven-year-old lawyer from Frederick, led this oversized but inexperienced unit. The 150th

New York, known as the Dutchess County Regiment, completed Lockwood's brigade. It recruited in late 1862 under the slogan "come in out of the draft," and its six hundred troops looked to thirty-year-old farmer John Henry Ketcham for leadership. Like their comrades in the brigade, soldiers of the 150th had seen no serious combat.[58]

The 1st Maryland and 150th New York left Belger Barracks in Baltimore on June 25 (the 1st Maryland Eastern Shore would not leave until the 27th) and marched toward Frederick. They reached Monocacy Bridge in two days and encamped, watching awestruck as the Army of the Potomac, a "vast enginery of war," filed into and through the area. Like many green troops, Lockwood's men had overpacked their knapsacks. Veterans in Meade's army "guyed and blackguarded" the novices unmercifully for being so encumbered, and the newcomers quickly shed their excess baggage before heading north toward Pennsylvania.[59]

Lockwood's brigade arrived at Littlestown on July 1 in the wake of the Twelfth Corps. Its thirteen hundred rookies formed in line on the road to Gettysburg at 3:00 A.M. the next morning, were on the move by dawn, and reached the battlefield after a forced march. General Williams recently had completed his consultation with Geary about deploying the corps when Lockwood reported. The divisional commander, who never had met Lockwood and knew little about his abilities, found his new subordinate "a very pleasant gentleman" and ordered the brigade to take position along Rock Creek extending the right of Ruger's brigade. This allowed Williams to anchor his right flank on the Baltimore Pike.[60]

By late in the morning, the six brigades of the Twelfth Corps covered nearly a mile of front from the crest of Culp's Hill to (but not across) the swale at Spangler's Spring, through McAllister's Woods, and along the west bank of Rock Creek to the Baltimore Pike. Corps artillery could not drop trail directly along the line of battle because "the density of the growth of

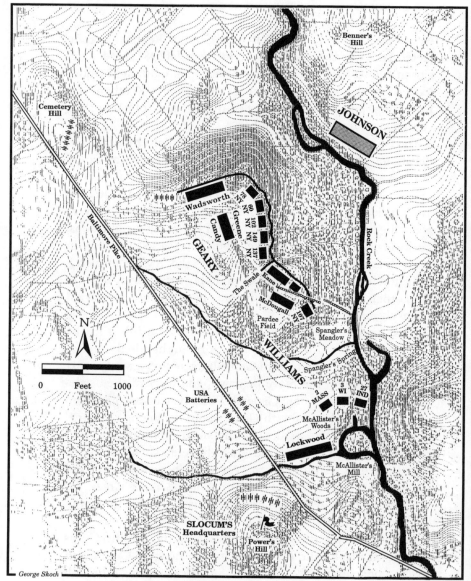

Situation on the Union Right, Late Morning, July 2, 1863

George Skoch

timber, [and] the irregularity and extremely broken character of the ground" prevented it from doing so with any advantage. Some guns were placed on Powers Hill west of the Baltimore Pike to offer long-range support. Although Meade defined the general position for the corps, credit for selecting this well-conceived emplacement belongs to Geary and Williams.[61]

Meade initially considered taking the offensive on his right. At 9:30 A.M., he ordered Slocum to examine the ground in front of Culp's Hill to determine if circumstances warranted an attack. Brigadier General Gouverneur K. Warren, the army's chief engineer, received a similar directive from Meade. Should prospects seem propitious, Meade intended to launch a powerful assult led by the Twelfth and Fifth corps, supplemented by the Sixth Corps once it arrived. Slocum replied that he already had conducted a reconnaissance (apparently when he visited Williams early in the morning) and recommended against an assault. He worried about Confederate formations on his right despite believing that the enemy's position possessed no particular advantages. Warren concurred with this judicious assessment.[62]

Although never acted upon, the concept of an offensive from the right prompted changes in the Twelfth Corps command structure during the remainder of the battle and created controversy that festered for months. Meade had suggested a combined attack of several corps, which meant that Slocum's seniority entitled him to direct the assault.[63] Williams once again assumed control of the Twelfth Corps and ordered Ruger to lead the First Division. Colonel Silas Colgrove of the 27th Indiana, a forty-seven-year-old lawyer and state legislator, inherited command of the Third Brigade; responsibility for the 27th passed to Lieutenant Colonel John R. Felser, a Hoosier merchant and last of the human dominoes in this chain.[64]

The Fifth and Sixth corps would deploy on the opposite end of Meade's line in the afternoon, emasculating Slocum's phantom wing. This irrelevant command arrangement continued

to live in Slocum's mind, however, and he illogically considered himself a wing commander for the rest of the battle.
Slocum thus proved as unwilling to shed authority on July 2
as he had been to accept it the day before.

This makeshift situation also posed problems for Williams.
Lockwood ranked Ruger and by rights should have served as
acting division commander. But Williams balked at assigning
responsibility for half the corps to an inexperienced stranger
unfamiliar with the other brigades of the First Division. Displaying a good attorney's imagination and mental flexibility,
Williams told Lockwood to "regard his command as an un-
attached brigade pending present operations" and to report
directly to the acting corps commander.[65]

While the high command pondered an offensive and shuffled
authority to accommodate Slocum's ephemeral wing, the men
of Greene's brigade labored on a more tangible task. Shortly
after the Second Division began occupying its new positions
on Culp's Hill, General Geary met with Greene and perhaps
his other brigade leaders to discuss the advisability of con-
structing earthworks along their line. Geary expressed doubts
about the utility of building works. Perhaps because the division's entrenchments at Chancellorsville had proved of little
use, many of the troops also viewed such field engineering as
a waste of time and energy. Apart from the question of utility,
Geary fretted about the loss of morale consequent on fighting
behind barricades. Pop Greene respectfully disagreed, believing
that saving lives superseded all other considerations. Geary
acquiesced to Greene's appeal and granted permission to go
ahead with the digging.[66]

Greene began immediately to fortify his line. The men grumbled a little at this early morning exercise, but soon everyone
pitched in with adequate enthusiasm. Many of the soldiers
hailed from western New York and possessed skills as woods-
men. Well supplied with axes, picks, and shovels, they soon
sent the sounds of falling timber and the stacking of rocks

and trees echoing along the slopes of Culp's Hill. By 9:00 A.M., a substantial line of logs and stones, shored up on the outer face with cordwood and earth, appeared along the entire Third Brigade front. The New Yorkers then placed a heavy abatis in advance of the line, so concealing it in the woods that it could not be seen at a distance of more than fifty yards.[67]

The troops continued to improve their defenses throughout the morning, including the construction of a traverse trench running at a ninety-degree angle east to west along the brigade's right flank. Greene ordered this innovation as a matter of local protection. The troublesome ravine ran below and parallel to his traverse and created a natural weak point where his right connected with Cobham's left. By the time Greene's New Yorkers laid down their tools at noon, defenses nearly five feet thick and substantial enough to stop a shell frowned from the upper and middle reaches of Culp's Hill.[68]

Much of the rest of the Twelfth Corps engaged in similar activity. The Pennsylvanians of Cobham's brigade arrived while Greene's New Yorkers pursued their labors. General Kane claimed that he left his ambulance long enough to indicate where the Second Brigade should build its earthworks. Taking their cue from Greene's troops, the three Keystone State regiments completed their own line in about three hours.[69] McDougall's brigade appeared next. Motivated by the desire to create a more formidable defense than at Chancellorsville, the troops of the 123d New York, 20th Connecticut, and 46th Pennsylvania extended Cobham's line to near the base of the hill. By midafternoon they completed this work. The brigade's other three regiments took cover behind the existing stone wall.[70] Williams, Ruger, and Colgrove all ordered the Third Brigade of the First Division to build works of logs, rails, and stones on both sides of the swale, although the fortifications in McAllister's Woods were substantially less elaborate than those on Culp's Hill.[71]

The Twelfth Corps thus entrenched from the top of Culp's Hill to Rock Creek and the Baltimore Pike. Just as with initial deployment of the corps, Slocum bore little responsibility for construction of these defenses. Greene overcame whatever initial objections Geary may have harbored, and the rest of the corps followed the aged New Yorker's example without debate.

Once ensconced behind their works, the men of the Twelfth Corps felt a sense of security. The Spangler's Meadow–McAllister's Woods area had been popular with local residents as a picnic grounds, and, as one poetic soldier recalled, "the oaks [formed] a grateful tent above our heads, as they had . . . over generations of pleasure groups; the pellucid waters of the spring [were] refreshingly cool." Some troops lounged quietly behind the breastworks, while others visited on the picket line or observed Confederates near Gettysburg from Wadsworth's vantage point on the crest of Culp's Hill.[72]

Unknown to these casual spectators, the four brigades of Edward "Alleghany" Johnson's Confederate division were preparing to end their pacific interlude. Instructed after midnight to occupy Culp's Hill by General Ewell, Johnson had begun to execute his orders when he learned that Williams's division inhabited the area and that the Fifth Corps was approaching from the east. Johnson correctly decided to consult with Ewell before moving forward. By the time Ewell heard about Johnson's concerns, General Lee already had postponed the advance. Ewell's offensive now would be triggered by an attack against the Union left led by Lieutenant General James Longstreet. Once Longstreet's guns opened fire, Ewell would conduct a demonstration against Culp's Hill that he could convert into a real attack if a favorable opportunity appeared.[73]

Johnson's division numbered more than six thousand troops on July 2. Its units included the famous Stonewall Brigade of Brigadier General James A. Walker, another brigade of Virginians under Brigadier General John M. Jones, the five Louisiana regiments of Francis T. Nicholls's brigade led at Gettysburg by

Major General Edward Johnson
(*Photographic History* 10:107)

Colonel Jesse M. Williams of the 2d Louisiana, and a mixed unit of North Carolinians, Marylanders, and Virginians commanded by Brigadier General George H. Steuart. Many of these regiments had fought in "Stonewall" Jackson's original division, and the troops enjoyed an esprit as exalted as their combat record.[74]

Major Joseph W. Latimer, a youngster of not quite twenty years known as "the boy major," commanded the artillery battalion attached to Johnson's division. Early in the morning, Latimer reluctantly had occupied Benner's Hill, across Rock Creek and one-half mile to the northeast of Culp's Hill, as the only practical position for his guns. The open height offered little shelter for his horses and caissons and provided inadequate room for proper deployment of all his pieces. Latimer crowded fourteen guns onto Benner's Hill and placed two twenty-pounder Parrotts across the Hanover Road to the north.[75]

The afternoon passed quietly, interrupted only by occasional skirmish fire along Rock Creek. Then at 4:00 P.M., Ewell ordered Johnson to commence his artillery bombardment against Culp's and Cemetery hills. Timed to coincide with the expected start of Longstreet's offensive on the opposite end of the battlefield, Latimer's barrage exploded with a metallic roar, sending shot and shell hurtling toward the Twelfth Corps infantry now huddled behind their entrenchments.[76]

Union artillery immediately engaged Latimer's battalion in a fierce duel. Colonel Charles S. Wainwright, in charge of the guns east of the Baltimore Pike, turned his batteries on Cemetery Hill against Southern cannon on Benner's Hill. One piece of Knap's Pennsylvania Battery had moved to the crest of Culp's Hill shortly before the bombardment began. Soon thereafter, two more 10-pounder Parrotts appeared under the command of Lieutenant John Geary, the general's son. Two 12-pounders from Battery K, 5th U.S. Artillery, joined these three rifles, and some of the Twelfth Corps ordnance on Power's Hill also focused on Latimer's exposed batteries.[77]

Confederate projectiles found their marks on Culp's Hill, forcing volunteers from the 60th and 78th New York to stand in for Geary's fallen gunners. But Latimer's cannoneers faced converging fire in an exposed area and suffered more severely than did the Federals. When a Rebel ammunition wagon exploded spectacularly thirty minutes into the fight, fire from

Benner's Hill slackened perceptibly. The artillery continued to exchange shots, albeit at a slower pace, until Latimer sustained a mortal wound late in the action. By 6:30 P.M., Latimer's successor withdrew his batteries to the rear, and once again quiet, along with the fading sun, descended on Slocum's front.[78]

It had been anything but quiet on the Union left since 4:00 P.M. Longstreet's attack finally commenced at that hour and succeeded in driving Daniel E. Sickles's Third Corps from its advanced positions west of Cemetery Ridge and Little Round Top. Meade responded by ordering reinforcements from other sectors of the battlefield, including the Twelfth Corps, to respond to the crisis on his left.[79]

The precise sequence of events by which the Twelfth Corps shifted to the southwest on the evening of July 2 remains one of the minor mysteries of the Gettysburg campaign. Countless writers have addressed the subject (most of them only fleetingly), drawing on a corpus of contradictory primary sources that seemingly support a variety of potential scenarios.

It is known that at 5:30 P.M., a time at which the duel between Latimer and Union cannoneers was winding down and the chaos of an uncertain outcome raged in the Wheatfield and the Peach Orchard, Meade's signal officers informed Slocum that they had seen "a heavy column of [Confederate] infantry" moving toward the Twelfth Corps. Shortly thereafter, Meade sent orders to Slocum, the text of which regrettably has been lost. Secondary testimony provides the best evidence about the contents of these orders, and the two most important witnesses are Generals Williams and Slocum. In an 1875 letter defending himself against criticisms lodged in a recently published history of the battle, Slocum unequivocally stated that "Gen. Meade sent me an order to remove the entire 12th Corps from its position on the right, to one on the left." Because, as described below, Slocum retained a part of his corps on the right and engaged in a fierce battle that evening with attacking

Confederates on Culp's Hill, many writers have applauded his "resolute insistence" that paid dividends for the Union army.[80]

Williams's version of events, however, casts doubt on the degree of Slocum's resolution, if not the happy outcome of his indecision. Nine months after the battle and again a year later, Williams recalled that at 5:30 or 6:00 P.M. Slocum sent him an order "to detach all I could spare, at least one Div. to support our left." Williams responded by ordering Ruger's First Division, situated closest to the southern end of the battlefield, to move out. Accompanying Ruger's troops, Williams met Slocum near "wing" headquarters at Power's Hill, explaining that he feared for the security of the Union right and had ordered Geary to extend the Second Division to cover Ruger's vacant works. Williams also ventured the opinion that it would be unwise to detach any more troops from the Twelfth Corps front. According to Williams, Slocum replied that Meade's orders were "urgent" and instructed him to send "all the troops [I] could spare" to the south, a clear indication of both Meade's acute sense of emergency and a degree of discretion Slocum neglected to mention in 1875. Slocum concurred with Williams's appraisal of the situation on the Union right, and Pap marched off to the left believing that Geary would remain on Culp's Hill. In fact, only after fighting ended on the second day would Williams discover that any of Geary's troops had decamped.[81]

Slocum's postwar account continues at variance with Williams's more contemporary story. The New Yorker stated that on receiving Meade's categorical directive to move the entire corps, he instantly set each brigade in motion. At the same time, he dispatched his adjutant general, Colonel Hiram C. Rodgers, to Meade's headquarters with a request that he be allowed to retain "at least a division" on the Culp's Hill front. According to Slocum, Rodgers returned shortly with Meade's permission to keep one brigade rather than a division on the right. Slocum selected Greene's brigade, last in line and yet to begin its march to the left, to remain on Culp's Hill with instructions to stretch as far as possible to protect the abandoned trenches.[82]

At this point it is useful to consult General Geary's recollection of events. His official report stated: "By a staff officer of Major-General Slocum, at 7 P.M. I received orders to move the division by the right flank, and follow the First Division, leaving one brigade to occupy the line of works of the entire corps. The First Division had gone nearly half an hour previously."[83] Geary's testimony contains two salient points. First, he mentioned no preliminary order from Slocum to move his entire division, later modified to omit Greene's brigade (neither did he say anything about orders from Williams to extend his front to McAllister's Woods). Second, Geary confirmed that thirty minutes transpired between Ruger's departure and his receipt of orders to shift two brigades to the south, time enough for Rodgers to have ridden from Power's Hill to Meade's headquarters at the Widow Leister's house, receive clarification from Meade, and report back to Slocum.

The final source on this subject is the most confusing and perhaps the least credible. Captain Charles P. Horton, General Greene's assistant adjutant general, remembered that at 6:00 P.M. the brigade received orders to move out and was in the act of doing so when engaged by Confederate skirmishers along Rock Creek. According to Horton, Greene halted his men, reinforced his skirmishers, and sent word of the situation to Geary. Geary allegedly ignored Greene's dilemma and simply reiterated his order for the Third Brigade to vacate Culp's Hill. As the courier bearing Geary's ill-advised instructions returned to Greene's position, he met Colonel Rodgers, who invoked Slocum's authority to countermand Geary's directive, told Greene to remain where he was, and promised to return the rest of Geary's division to Greene's support.[84]

What is to be made of this welter of conflicting accounts? If Meade's original orders to Slocum survived, decisions by the principal general officers of the Twelfth Corps could be readily reconstructed. In the absence of that evidence, however, certain speculative conclusions may be drawn. First, Meade unquestionably viewed the situation on his left with alarm and gave what in hindsight seems to be undue precedence to that flank over the security of the rest of his line. Although aware of potential danger on Slocum's front, the army commander indisputably wanted the Twelfth Corps to help defend the southern portion of the field. It is probable that Meade's orders conveyed a strong desire that Slocum detach as much of his corps as possible and preferably all of it.

Slocum must have read these orders with deep misgivings. He knew that unseen Confederate forces opposed him across Rock Creek, and he had the benefit of Williams's recommendation that at least one entire division be retained along his line. Facing uncertain conditions on the previous day, Slocum had reacted timidly and irresponsibly to discretionary orders; he faced the same quandary on the late afternoon of July 2. He sent Rodgers to Meade ostensibly to secure permission for Geary's division to remain in its fortifications on Culp's Hill, but he also wished to quantify Meade's orders—in other words, to eliminate any discretion contained in the original directive.

Slocum avers that he instantly placed his whole corps in motion, a contention that Horton indirectly confirms.[85] But both Geary and Williams state that the First Division departed before the Second Division received any instructions to move. Considering the self-justifying nature of Slocum's account and Horton's chronologically confused recitation of events, the weight of evidence indicates that Slocum, wisely enough, hedged his bet.

If Meade's order to Slocum encouraged but did not explicitly require shifting the entire Twelfth Corps to the left, Slocum could have retained all of Geary's division on the right without exceeding the scope of his authority. Such a decision probably would have avoided the near disaster Greene's brigade experienced later that evening. Slocum's refusal after the war to acknowledge the probable latitude contained in Meade's orders perhaps reflected sensitivity about what many considered a mistake at Culp's Hill. Meade bears principal responsibility for the fact that only Greene's brigade, surely an inadequate force, remained to defend the position. But Slocum had the chance to avert the error.

Meade, Slocum, and Geary played out this drama while the First Division hastened toward the Union left. Under the watchful eye of General Williams, who was unwilling to entrust command of the movement to any of his subordinates, Lockwood's brigade led the march followed by Colgrove and McDougall. The soldiers progressed at a brisk pace, at times practically running, motivated by the sound of rapid musketry that reminded L.R. Coy of the 123d New York of "a bunch of China crackers connected and fired at once." The troops turned south on the Baltimore Pike until they reached the Granite Schoolhouse Lane, a dirt road that skirted the southern base of Power's Hill. Following this track, the men eventually emerged onto the Taneytown Road. "Hurrying to the right up this road," wrote Williams, "I soon began to pass masses of disorganized portions of the 3d Corps."[86] Williams's sound instincts and the roar of battle explain the division's appearance near the scene of combat. Neither Meade nor Slocum had provided Williams with precise instructions about his destination, and the staff officer detailed by Slocum had no idea where to direct the reinforcements.[87]

Confederate artillery shells fell among the approaching troops, who at one point became alarmed at what seemed to be a battery of guns tearing down the road in panic. A German ordnance sergeant astride an empty caisson and in search of ammunition assured the Red Stars as he galloped by that "dis ish nod a retread!" The Twelfth Corps men were glad to hear it. They received additional comfort from an old woman who, as the shriek of the Rebel yell became audible on the distant winds, stood by the roadside and told the passing bluecoats, "Never mind, boys, they're nothing but men."[88]

Williams searched amidst throngs of stragglers and the slightly wounded along the east slope of Cemetery Ridge for someone in authority to advise him about the situation ahead. Although these fugitives offered enthusiastic encouragement, no one had knowledge about current tactical conditions. Williams's best geographical information came from Colonel Maulsby of the First Maryland Home Brigade, who had lived in nearby Westminster, Maryland, and knew the countryside around Gettysburg fairly well. With Maulsby's neophytes in the forefront, Williams pointed toward the first opening at the summit of the ridge.[89]

As Lockwood's brigade pressed forward near the crest, Lieutenant Colonel Freeman McGilvery rushed toward Williams expressing great delight at the appearance of the Twelfth Corps. McGilvery commanded the First Volunteer Brigade of the Artillery Reserve at Gettysburg and knew Williams from their service together earlier in the war. The cannoneer explained, "with the rapidity that such occasions require[d]," that his beleaguered artillery lacked infantry supports and that the Confederates already had captured some of his pieces. Williams ordered Lockwood to charge the woods in his front, specifying that Maulsby's Marylanders fix bayonets and move at the double quick.[90]

Colonel Maulsby promptly obeyed this directive—so promptly, in fact, that his men advanced without properly deploying from marching column into battle line. With Lockwood at the head of the formation and the 150th New York in close support, the 1st Maryland dashed west toward the Trostle Farm in the gathering twilight. Both Lockwood and Colonel Ketcham reported facing "the most terrific firing of shells and musketry" during the onslaught, an exaggerated impression that may have reflected their lack of combat experience. The Confederates already had fallen back by the time Lockwood's troops moved off

Cemetery Ridge, and as Maulsby said, "our friends on the other side did not stand long enough to give [our] bayonets a chance to show what metal they were made of." Considering the reckless tactics employed by the gallant, impetuous Marylanders, they were fortunate that no Confederate brigade challenged their attack.[91]

Maulsby's momentum carried his regiment into the fields east of the Peach Orchard. The 150th New York swept through the Trostle farmyard after the Marylanders, taking possession of three guns from Captain John Bigelow's Massachusetts battery captured earlier by the 21st Mississippi. Companies B and G of the Dutchess County men removed their prizes by hand while the rest of the regiment dutifully attended to the myriad wounded who littered the ground in the nearby orchard, fields, and woods.[92]

Meanwhile, Williams had ordered Ruger's division to take position on Cemetery Ridge south of where Lockwood began his attack. Ruger formed his brigades in two lines and pushed westward a short distance into Weikert's Woods, encountering no Confederate resistance. By now the sun's remaining influence had all but vanished. Williams instructed Ruger to halt and rode forward to retrieve Lockwood from his isolation near the Peach Orchard.[93] Thus ended the First Division's brief bravura on the Federal left that evening.

The Twelfth Corps had not played a crucial role in repulsing the Confederates. By the time Lockwood and the Red Stars arrived, the Southern tide had crested and begun to recede. Still, the First Division accomplished all that was asked of it, and Pap Williams discharged his responsibilities competently. Although some accounts suggest that General Meade personally led Lockwood's brigade forward, the commanding general in fact took no direct hand in guiding the First Division.[94]

However small Williams's part in rebuffing Lee's offensive on July 2, Geary contributed even less. What happened to the

First and Second brigades of Geary's division that evening is
foggy enough, but why it happened defies explanation.

Ordered to leave Greene's brigade on Culp's Hill and march
with Candy and Cobham to Williams's assistance on the army's left, Geary placed his troops in motion and eventually
reached the Baltimore Pike. Turning south with Candy's brigade in the lead, the White Stars marched past corps headquarters at Power's Hill and beyond the country road used by
Williams to reach Cemetery Ridge. They continued southward, crossed Rock Creek, and halted on a hill south of the
stream. As far as the Battle of Gettysburg was concerned,
Geary's two brigades had stepped off the map.[95] Slocum referred to Geary's march as "an unfortunate and unaccountable
mistake." A Wisconsin soldier termed Geary's performance "a
singular blunder," and the historian of the 2d Massachusetts
concluded that "it did not show much of a soldier's instinct
to take a road leading to the rear and follow it for about two
miles before halting."[96]

Geary's own testimony sheds little light on the puzzling
episode. Clearly he suffered from the same lack of information
that plagued Williams. "I received no specific instructions as
to the object of the move, the direction to be taken, or the
point to be reached, beyond the order to move by the right
flank and to follow the First Division," he wrote in his report.
Because Williams had a half-hour head start, Geary lost track
of his colleague's whereabouts and followed some stragglers
he assumed were trailing the Red Stars. Once across Rock
Creek, Geary claimed to have received an order at 7:30 P.M.
to hold the position "down to the creek at all hazards," at
which point he formed a line with his right on the Pike near
the Rock Creek bridge and his left on the creek itself.[97] This
order has no relevance unless it actually applied to Geary's
former position on Culp's Hill. If so, this could have been the
directive Williams said he issued when Slocum first told him
to move to the left.

Geary's initial confusion is understandable, if not justifiable. His inability to find the rest of the corps on Cemetery Ridge and willingness to keep his men uselessly idle cannot be excused. Why did Geary fail to send couriers to Slocum's headquarters or westward until they found the Union left? How could an experienced and brave man not deduce that his position south of Rock Creek contributed nothing toward mitigating the emergency that had summoned him from Culp's Hill? How could Slocum lose track of half his corps for hours and not send an adequate number of orderlies to locate it?[98] Had Geary's troops been needed on the Union left that evening, and Geary had no inkling that they were not, history would have remembered the general unkindly indeed. As matters developed, his folly cost the Federals nothing in a strategic or tactical sense. But his absence from Culp's Hill was not inconsequential. Five of the six Twelfth Corps brigades had decamped from the Union right, leaving only Greene's New York regiments to defend their positions. In a short time, Pop Greene would face one of the critical challenges of his long life.

Greene's imminent adversary, "Old Clubfoot" Johnson, had hidden his four Confederate brigades on low ground north of the Hanover Road that morning. There he awaited Ewell's signal to assail his designated target one mile away. Except for employing a few skirmishers east of Rock Creek, Johnson kept his infantry concealed and quiet throughout the day. He did direct Jones's Virginians to support Latimer near Benner's Hill during the afternoon artillery duel. When the Southern gunners retired from their unequal contest, Ewell sent Johnson the long-anticipated directive to attack. Ewell's other two divisions waited farther west, poised to move forward once Johnson successfully engaged the Yankees in his front.[99]

Happily for Ewell, he chose to attack at the very moment in which 83 percent of the Twelfth Corps was vacating its prepared positions. This spectacular timing appears to have been

Brigadier General George Sears Greene
(*Photographic History* 10:305)

entirely serendipitous. Although some Union pickets did withdraw from their posts near Rock Creek, no evidence indicates
that Ewell reacted to any specific information about Slocum's
dispositions. Instead, he merely adhered to Lee's timetable for
engagement of the Second Corps.[100] In any case, Lee intended
Ewell's offensive either to prevent Union reinforcements from

reaching Longstreet's sector or to exploit the absence of those forces in his own front. The exploitation was about to begin.

Johnson's advance encountered three immediate obstacles. First, the appearance of Union cavalry to the east prompted Old Clubfoot to detach the Stonewall Brigade to guard the division's left and rear. This deprived the Confederates of one-fourth of their strength.[101] Second, as the brigades of Jones, Williams, and Steuart, in that order, reached Rock Creek, they discovered waist-deep water that would take time to negotiate.[102] The crossing became even more difficult when Union skirmishers scattered about one hundred yards west of the creek and peppered the graycoats with a persistent and surprisingly effective fire.

Lieutenant Colonel John O. Redington of the 60th New York commanded the advanced Federal line. When he saw Johnson's troops forming for their strike across Rock Creek, he sounded a bugle summoning the 78th New York, known as the Cameron Highlanders and led by Lieutenant Colonel Herbert von Hammerstein, to come to his assistance. Redington maintained a brisk fire that compelled the Confederates to lie down in the grass on the creek's far bank. The Federals exchanged musketry for thirty minutes, slowly withdrawing up the slope of Culp's Hill as Jones and Williams crossed the stream and pursued in the gathering gloom. Fifty yards from the main Union line, the plucky marksmen dashed for the works and joined their comrades behind the entrenchments.[103]

While the skirmishers delayed Johnson's approach, Greene ordered his remaining regiments to fan out and extend their front to cover as much of the forsaken line as possible. The 60th stretched to the top of the hill on the left to occupy ground vacated by the 78th. The 102d expanded to its right the length of a regiment, a maneuver repeated by the 149th and 137th, which now held the portion of the line previously controlled by Cobham's men. The trenches McDougall's soldiers had built near the base of Culp's Hill remained empty. Greene's

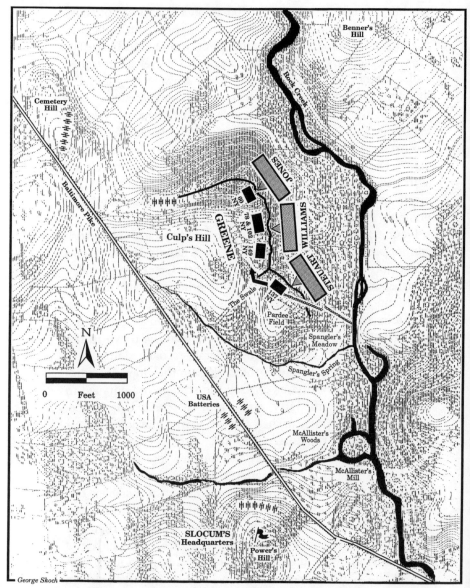

Confederate Assaults on the Union Right, Evening of July 2, 1863

men stood in one rank a foot or more apart and had no local reserve.[104] Realizing that his brigade would need help to resist a major Confederate assault, Greene notified Wadsworth and Howard, who promptly dispatched a total of seven regiments numbering 755 men.[105] Until these reinforcements arrived, only the New Yorkers would confront Johnson's three brigades.

The Confederates formed with Jones on their right opposing the 60th New York on the hill's steepest grade, Williams next in line opposite the 78th, 102d, and 149th, and Steuart trailing on the left aimed at the 137th New York farthest from the crest. Johnson mustered seventeen regiments three lines deep and outnumbered Greene more than three to one.[106]

Those odds were not as overwhelming as they might appear. Twilight obscured the Federal line until the Confederates reached pistol range. There Greene's concealed bluecoats staggered the brigades of Jones and Williams with a deadly volley. The terrain also favored the defenders. Jones's men had to scale the precipitous northern end of Culp's Hill in the face of rapid fire. Johnson's first attack failed, and the Virginians and Louisianians dropped back among the rocks to regroup.[107]

The initial Union reinforcements now began to arrive from Cemetery Hill, including the 61st Ohio, which took position alongside the determined New Yorkers. These troops appeared not a moment too soon because the Confederate line, "yelping and howling in its peculiar manner," emerged again from the smoke and darkness to renew the assault. "Out into the murky night like chain lightning [leapt] the zigzag line of fire" from the Union rifles. "A thousand tongues of flame thrust themselves into the darkness toward the foe, and winged death hisse[d] through the rebel ranks." This time the two Confederate brigades actually reached the works, but they could not hold them. In short order, Federals drove them back into the night.[108] More fresh regiments began to appear. Some relieved the New Yorkers, who withdrew temporarily to replenish ammunition and clean fouled muskets. Other units headed straight for the Federal right, where Colonel David Ireland's 137th New York had been conducting a private war with "Maryland" Steuart's command.[109]

A Scottish tailor from New York City, Ireland had posted his men in the most vulnerable portion of Greene's attenuated line. Not only was his right flank completely in the air, but the ground in his front also ascended more gently toward the Federal works, making the Confederate approach relatively easy. Ireland was in the process of sliding his regiment southward when Confederates exploded from the woods to his front and right. The attackers progressed by the guiding light of muzzle flashes from Ireland's line. Discovering that the works on Ireland's right lay unprotected, Steuart sent his men surging toward the pregnable area. Ireland ordered his right-most company to pivot west and block the incipient flank attack. These few troops obeyed, but after a short while fell back to establish another position at right angles to their breastworks.[110]

At this point the unfortunate 71st Pennsylvania (known as the "California Regiment") made its brief and undistinguished entrance onto the stage. General Hancock had heard the racket on Culp's Hill and deduced that the Union troops there needed assistance. He instructed a division commander to rush two regiments to the threatened sector, and the 106th and 71st Pennyslvania regiments moved rapidly to the right. The 106th misunderstood its mission, halting on Cemetery Hill. The 71st arrived at Culp's Hill, reporting to Ireland as the Confederate attack erupted in its presence.[111]

Considerable confusion exists today, as it did in 1863, about the actions of the California Regiment at Culp's Hill on July 2. Greene referred to it as an Eleventh Corps unit in an article written nearly a generation after the battle. Geary assigned it to the First Corps in his account of the fight. Ireland and Lieutenant Colonel Horton described its arrival in substantially different ways. In the absence of a definitive narrative, it appears that a staff officer led the Pennsylvanians to Ireland's end of the Union position just as Ireland had ordered his right flank to face south. The 71st briefly extended this line but soon departed—not in response to Confederate pressure but under orders from its commanding officer, Colonel Richard P. Smith. This withdrawal heightened the crisis faced by the 137th, but there is no evidence that the unseemly maneuver besmirched Colonel Smith's reputation.[112]

Ireland next played his last remaining card. Falling back again, this time with his entire regiment, he took position behind the traverse constructed earlier on Greene's orders. This deployment strengthened the 137th in relation to any threat from the south. Steuart's troops witnessed this realignment, which one of them termed a Yankee "skeedadle," and took possession of all the works built by Cobham and McDougall. Three companies of the 149th New York formed on Ireland's right, a maneuver momentarily misinterpreted as a retreat by the rest of the regiment until their colonel, Henry A. Barnum, stabilized the line. The New Yorkers defended their new front, which was also exposed in the tangled, rocky woods to its right, until the 14th Brooklyn arrived to assist them.[113]

Conventional Confederate wisdom asserted that Federals had occupied the works captured by Steuart's brigade. Union accounts disagreed, ascribing their foe's confusion to fierce flanking fire delivered by Ireland and his supports and to a mistaken interpretation of the 71st Pennsylvania's precipitate retreat as a forced withdrawal. Whatever the case, no regiment in Greene's brigade suffered more casualties or acquitted itself more honorably than did the 137th.[114]

The other New York regiments distinguished themselves as well. Greene's command turned away two more attacks on its right before Johnson relinquished the offensive between 10:00 and 11:00 P.M. In the process, the 149th's regimental flag sustained eighty-one shots through its silk and seven through its staff. The 60th captured Jones's brigade flag and one of the Virginia regimentals along with some five dozen prisoners

snatched from across the works in their front. "The appearance
of the men in the trenches," observed one New Yorker, "with
their clothes ragged and dirty, their faces black from smoke,
sweat and burnt powder, [and] their lips cracked and bleeding
from salt-petre in the cartridges bitten by them . . . resembled
more the inhabitants of the bottomless pit than quiet peaceful
citizens of the United States of America." An admiring
Henry W. Slocum attributed "the failure of the enemy to gain
possession of our works . . . entirely to the skill of General
Greene and the heroic valor of his troops."[115]

Slocum's praise rang true, but did Greene's stouthearted victory hold significance beyond the mere maintenance of his
position? Many writers have thought so, claiming that
Greene's triumph marked the turning point in the entire Battle
of Gettysburg. "The battle was at no other time so nearly lost
as it was in the emergency when old George Greene and his
men did the impossible and saved the day that won the war,"
enthused one observer. "Had Greene and his gallant little band
been defeated in this action," echoed a Pennsylvania veteran,
"the battle of Gettysburg might not have been the glorious
victory it was for our arms."[116]

Such analysts based their claims on the proximity of Johnson's division to the all-important Baltimore Pike on the evening of July 2. Once Geary and Williams abandoned their
positions on the Union right, no Federal troops barred the way
to that vital road. A four hundred-yard march would have
brought the Confederates to the pike and a nearby supply and
ammunition train. Meade's headquarters lay a short distance
beyond. Southern control of the pike would threaten the rear
of the Northern army on Cemetery Ridge and sever one of
two potential Federal routes of retreat. In short, goes the argument, "Ewell then held for a time in his hands the most
golden opportunity that ever fell to a subordinate commander
during a battle that was to decide the destinies of a Nation."
But instead of exploiting this decisive advantage, Johnson hun-

kered down behind his captured earthworks, and, fearing a trap, refused to venture forward and seize the day.[117]

In fact, Johnson enjoyed a very brief window of opportunity to reach the Baltimore Pike unopposed. If Ewell had started the offensive earlier to take advantage of waning sunlight, his troops would have encountered the entire Twelfth Corps, the departure of which coincidentally mirrored the Confederate advance. By the time Johnson suspended further efforts to capture Culp's Hill, Williams and Geary were already en route to their old lines. Furthermore, Union troops on Cemetery Hill and a brigade of reinforcements from the Sixth Corps under Brigadier General Thomas H. Neill could have opposed the Confederates. The only fresh unit available to Johnson was Walker's brigade, still posted to block Federal cavalry along the Hanover Road. As Edwin B. Coddington wrote, "The lost opportunity of the Confederates, which had been fleeting at best, to envelop the right of the Union army existed less in actuality than in the minds of broken-hearted veterans seeking the reason why." Ewell missed no chance to wreck the Army of the Potomac on July 2.[118]

Slocum ensured this by ordering the Twelfth Corps to return to its former position "immediately after the repulse of the enemy on the left." Williams had no idea that any of Geary's division had moved from Culp's Hill, but he quickly directed Ruger to shift the First Division back to its entrenchments. On the way, the acting corps commander spotted "a large collection of General and other officers," including Meade, in an open field near the Taneytown Road. Williams paused at this "pleasant gathering" to exchange congratulations on the day's results, while Ruger continued forward toward the Union right.[119]

The Third Brigade led the march under a full moon. Between the Taneytown Road and the Baltimore Pike, a staff officer from Slocum's headquarters informed Ruger that not only had most of the Second Division temporarily vacated Culp's Hill but also the remaining Federals had recently concluded a desperate struggle. Although this messenger erroneously reported that Geary's men had reoccupied their old lines, Ruger prudently ordered skirmishers from both Colgrove's and McDougall's brigades to ascertain the situation. Colgrove told Lieutenant Colonel Charles R. Mudge of the 2d Massachusetts to have scouts determine if Confederates occupied McAllister's Woods or ground across the swale at the base of Culp's Hill. When the works nearest Rock Creek proved to be empty, the 13th New Jersey, 27th Indiana, and 3d Wisconsin filled in from right to left securing the ground south of the swale.[120]

Company F of the 2d Massachusetts then cautiously probed across the open meadow and into the edge of the woods just beyond Spangler's Spring. The New Englanders heard voices in the darkness, and closer investigation revealed that Virginians from Steuart's brigade were filling their canteens at the spring. The Unionists captured nearly two dozen thirsty Confederates before returning to McAllister's Woods, where the entire regiment deployed facing north at right angles to their old lines. The 107th New York later formed on the left and rear of the 2d Massachusetts facing more easterly than to the north.[121]

Other Federals also groped their way toward old positions. Colonel McDougall dispatched Company I of the 123d New York and a portion of Company E of the 5th Connecticut to reconnoiter the First Brigade's former line. Finding Southerners along their entire portion of Culp's Hill, they avoided capture when a New York lieutenant shouted a warning. Apparently troops from the 20th Connecticut and 46th Pennsylvania also ventured forward in the shadows and encountered parched graycoats at Spangler's Spring. Everyone happily gathered water until an unwary Federal casually announced that "the rebels had caught 'hail columbia' over on the left." The Confederates took exception to this remark, a short mêlée ensued, and both sides took a few prisoners.[122]

McDougall withdrew his vanguard and deployed the brigade to extend Colgrove's left toward the Baltimore Pike. The 123d New York occupied a somewhat advanced position with the 3d Maryland, 145th New York, 20th Connecticut, 5th Connecticut, and 46th Pennsylvania forming ranks from right to left. Ruger's line now faced east toward the swale and Rock Creek, and north to cover the gap between the base of Culp's Hill and the Baltimore Pike one-quarter mile away.[123]

Lockwood's two regiments were the last of Ruger's troops to return to the right. They withdrew from their advanced positions at the west of the Trostle Farm, unsettled by the cries of the wounded they heard along the way. Arriving at the Baltimore Pike about midnight, they secured McDougall's left and provided support for newly posted Union artillery.[124]

In the meantime, Slocum's couriers finally located Geary and told him to return to Culp's Hill. Geary issued marching orders to the Second Division about 9:00 P.M.[125] Cobham's brigade countermarched on the Baltimore Pike with the 29th Pennsylvania in the lead and pivoted into the woods toward its old breastworks. Two hundred yards from the destination, a volley from the forest in Cobham's front claimed fourteen casualties. Cobham, assisted by General Kane, extracted his brigade and marched it farther north to a position behind Greene's survivors. The Pennsylvanians relieved the 137th New York, forming a longer line running west and oriented south toward McDougall's position one thousand feet away. Any Confederate troops now attempting to reach the Baltimore Pike would face a potentially blistering crossfire. Candy's brigade arrived last, probably about 1:00 A.M., and deployed in two lines. One rank supported the right of Greene's brigade and the other debouched behind and to the right of Cobham. Their presence allowed the 149th New York and Greene's other weary regiments to leave the trenches, refit, and steal some sleep on the hill's rocky slopes.[126]

The realignment of the Twelfth Corps between 10:00 P.M.
and 1:00 A.M. occurred while both Slocum and Williams attended a council of war convened at Meade's headquarters
shortly after 9:00 P.M. One of Meade's staff officers had found
Williams near the Baltimore Pike and summoned him to the
conference in his capacity as acting corps commander.[127] Slocum participated as Meade's senior lieutenant. When Meade
polled his subordinates regarding the army's next move, Slocum offered his oft-quoted advice to "stay and fight it out."
That is precisely the policy the generals adopted before the
meeting adjourned shortly before midnight.[128]

Williams finally rejoined his division, only to receive "the
astounding intelligence" that Confederates manned a large section of his works. Apparently Slocum had not been informed
about Greene's battle either and learned of the situation from
Williams. Williams placed two additional batteries on the rise
of ground west of the Baltimore Pike and opposite the lower
reaches of Culp's Hill. These guns joined ordnance already
in position on Power's and McAllister's hills to provide the infantry with substantial artillery support. Slocum instructed
Williams to "Drive [the Confederates] out at daylight," and
Williams spent the next several hours preparing to do so.[129]

Thus ends the story of the Twelfth Corps on the first two
days at Gettysburg, except for an unpleasant postscript. Meade
penned his report of the campaign in the fall of 1863; Slocum
and Williams, then serving in the western theater, had the opportunity to read it in late November.[130] The narrative slighted
the contribution of the Twelfth Corps in several respects, particularly in relation to Williams and the First Division, and
contained a number of factual errors. Williams confessed to being "pretty mad" about this public injustice, observing that
"Gen. Slocum is a mile or so ahead of me in indignation." Both
Slocum and Williams had thought highly of Meade in July;
however, Slocum's attitude toward army authority had soured
by November. Unhappy with his transfer from the Army of the

Confederate Skirmishers at the Foot of Culp's Hill
(*Battles and Leaders* 3:312)

Potomac to the West, Slocum had suffered the further affront of assignment under Major General Joseph Hooker, an officer he considered scarcely worthy of respect. Meade's inaccurate report provided the last straw for the New Yorker's prickly sensibilities.[131]

Slocum drafted a legalistic protest dripping with contempt and sent it to Meade requesting that an official correction be filed with the War Department. He told a private correspondent that he considered demanding a court of inquiry to secure proper credit for Williams and his division.[132] Meade eventually responded to Slocum's protest, apologizing for his failure to mention Williams and expressing regret for any disservice his report may have rendered. Although Williams accepted Meade's explanation, Slocum still harbored resentment, expressed later in condemnations of Meade's conduct at Gettysburg.[133]

A review of Twelfth Corps leadership on July 1–2 yields a mixed verdict. Slocum's own record has prospered from a lack of scrutiny. His vacillation and oversights on both days might have brought serious consequences. But because Ewell would not (or could not) exploit his advantages either day, Slocum generally has escaped censure from historical analysts. Among second- and third-level commanders, Williams and Greene stand out. Both performed splendidly under difficult circumstances requiring independent thinking. Thomas Ruger, George Cobham, Silas Colgrove, and Archibald McDougall reacted competently to increased responsibility. Charles Candy committed no serious error, and Henry Lockwood and his enthusiastic rookies made up in bravery and spirit what they lacked in polish and skill. John White Geary's inexplicable disappearance on the evening of July 2 dominates any evaluation of his generalship during the first two days at Gettysburg.

Regardless of the checkered record of its leadership and through no fault of its soldiers, the Twelfth Corps did not play a decisive role during these forty-eight hours. Its delayed appearance on July 1, though unwarranted and regrettable, did not materially affect the outcome of the fighting. Williams's contributions on the Union left on July 2 came after the die had been cast. Greene's tenacious defense of Culp's Hill possessed the most significance, but even there potential Confederate gains probably would have been transitory at best.

The Twelfth Corps left the Army of the Potomac in September 1863 for a new career in the West. It left behind a proud legacy earned on a half-dozen major battlefields. Gettysburg's first two days contributed but a modest portion to that distinguished record.

"No Troops on the Field Had Done Better"
John C. Caldwell's Division in the Wheatfield, July 2, 1863

D. SCOTT HARTWIG

I n the 128 years since the Battle of Gettysburg, veterans, students, and historians have filled volumes exploring the question of why the battle was lost or won. Such writers usually have focused on command at the army and corps level. There is nothing wrong with this emphasis, for the decisions and actions of senior officers shaped the battle and influenced thousands of lives. But these officers did not lead troops into battle. They managed resources, allocating men and material to obtain objectives. Command at this level can be likened to a sword. The hilt represents the army commander, the blade is the corps. The point of the sword represents those who directed soldiers in combat—the division, brigade, and regimental leaders. Although we know a great deal about what happened at the hilt and blade of the sword of command, we know relatively little about activity at the point. It is thus instructive to shift focus from the hilt and blade to the point. An examination of the experience of divisional command on July 2 illuminates the challenge of directing men in battle during the American Civil War.

The experience of Brigadier General John C. Caldwell and his First Division of the Second Corps, Army of the Potomac, illustrates the role of divisional leaders at Gettysburg. Caldwell's division serves as an excellent model for two reasons. First, Caldwell conducted the only division-sized Federal assault in what was almost exclusively a defensive battle for the Army of the Potomac. Second, because defenders enjoyed significant advantages due to weaponry and tactics, it stands to reason that directing an attack was a division commander's most difficult mission. Caldwell faced the particularly challenging situation of managing an attack in an extremely fluid battle in which he literally knew nothing about the ground or enemy strength. Although perhaps not typical, Caldwell's experience reveals the problems with which division commanders contended in directing and coordinating an assault.

The First Division ranked among the outstanding units in the Army of the Potomac. It had been organized in the fall of 1861 by Major General Edwin V. Sumner, who, despite limitations as a battlefield commander, understood how to train soldiers. When Sumner was promoted to corps command, the division passed to the equally tough Brigadier General Israel B. Richardson, who led it through the Seven Days battles and was mortally wounded during assaults against the Sunken Lane at Antietam. Brigadier General Winfield Scott Hancock succeeded Richardson, and the division fought magnificently under his direction in the grim attacks against Marye's Heights at Fredericksburg and during the Chancellorsville campaign. Sumner, Richardson, and Hancock left an indelible mark on the division, teaching the men sharp discipline and drill and imbuing them with an aggressive spirit. Hancock claimed at Gettysburg, without boast, that the division "had never flinched" on the field of battle.[1]

The First Division earned its enviable record at great cost. The only four-brigade division in the Union army at Gettysburg (none of the rest had more than three), it nonetheless counted a mere 3,200 effectives. Its largest brigade numbered 975 officers and men. The Second Brigade, famous as the Irish Brigade, mustered only 532 effectives. Four of its regiments were under one hundred men. Yet despite its skeleton strength, the division remained a formidable fighting unit because of excellent training and competent, respected leadership at every level. The First Division was a veteran organization in the best sense of the word. The term *veteran* often implies that all men so designated were "good" soldiers, yet many veteran units were quite marginal due to poor leadership, slack discipline, or heavy casualties. In contrast, a number of green outfits, notably Brigadier General George J. Stannard's brigade at Gettysburg, performed with distinction. Proficiency at battlefield drill, discipline, and leadership separated good and bad units in combat. In all of these categories the First Division had kept its fighting edge despite heavy losses. This was due, no doubt, to high standards for officers and men set by Sumner, Richardson, and Hancock.[2]

Hancock was promoted to command of the Second Corps following Chancellorsville, and Brigadier General John C. Caldwell replaced him by virtue of his seniority in the division. The thirty-year-old Caldwell hailed from Maine, where before the war he had been principal of Washington Academy at East Machias, a village in the northeastern corner of the state. He volunteered for service after the firing on Fort Sumter, and by April 28, 1862, had risen to the rank of brigadier general. When Oliver O. Howard was wounded at Seven Pines, his brigade was assigned to Caldwell, who led it competently in every battle that followed except Second Manassas. "Caldwell is an agreeable man and well liked," wrote one man who served with him before Gettysburg. "There is none of the assumed dignity and importance so common among officers. . . . He is much more familiar with his officers than General Meagher and is much better liked by them than M. by his." Despite his volunteer's background, Caldwell evidently enjoyed the confidence of Hancock, who otherwise would have supported someone else to command the First Division.[3]

Caldwell's experience in brigade leadership likely taught him that success on the battlefield depended on three basic factors—the ability to communicate, to move, and to engage

Brigadier General John Curtis Caldwell
(Courtesy of the National Archives)

the enemy. These factors also applied at the division level, but commanders faced larger responsibilities and far greater difficulty of application. In the era of muzzle-loading weapons and control of movements and firepower by voice or visual signals, a unit the size of the First Division posed complex challenges. Officers established control by maneuvering troops in dense formations so that commands by voice and signal could be heard or seen. Endless hours on the drill fields ingrained complex maneuvers that enabled a unit to move from column to line or line to column quickly and without disorder. The ultimate objectives of such training were to achieve maximum firepower on the firing line swiftly and to maintain cohesiveness in combat. In the noisy chaos of a Civil War battlefield, the best drilled and disciplined units minimized disorder and continued to deliver effective fire despite the hellish environment. Every man and officer grew accustomed to his place in a formation. A unit was a machine on the battlefield—soldiers were merely parts within it. With the exception of skirmishers, individuals received virtually no encouragement to demonstrate initiative and resourcefulness. The soldier's duty was to keep his place in the ranks and look to his officers for direction.

At the divisional level, Caldwell's task was to direct the movements of his brigades so that every rifle or musket in their ranks came to bear on the enemy. With four brigades, Caldwell's division was a formidable unit that could sustain itself in battle longer and perform more varied maneuvers than the typical two-brigade Federal division. But maneuvering four brigades in the deafening noise and smoky atmosphere of a battlefield severely tested the limits of mid–nineteenth century military communications. Although the Civil War has been called the first modern war, the voice, signal (hand or flag), or written options for communicating available to Caldwell had changed little since the time of Alexander the Great. A competent staff was critical to Caldwell's ability to command and control his brigades. Through staff officers he could follow the flow of the battle and maintain communications, by verbal and written messages, with his brigadiers. Seven officers made up Caldwell's personal staff, five of whom (two majors and three first lieutenants), together with a cavalry corporal who served as an orderly, accompanied him into battle. One other means of communication was Caldwell's headquarters flag, a large banner that marked the division's administrative point of control on the battlefield.[4]

The primitive nature of communications severely limited Caldwell's ability to manage a battle. Once under fire, the division's brigades largely passed from his control to that of their respective commanders. Caldwell was fortunate that four good officers headed his brigades. Brigadier General Samuel K. Zook and Colonel John R. Brooke had led brigades in battle; Colonel Edward Cross and Colonel Patrick Kelly, although new to brigade command, boasted extensive combat experience and had earned their positions through merit. All had learned their trade under the tutelage of Richardson and Hancock. Like their former division commanders they were tough, aggressive, and confident, qualities that trickled down to their field and line officers as well as to the men on the firing line.

Unfortunately, the small arms of the division did not match the quality of its personnel. Six of the division's eighteen regiments were completely or partly armed with .69 caliber smoothbore muskets and two others carried .54 caliber Austrian muskets. At least six regiments carried two different caliber muskets. The variety of weapons made replenishing ammunition on the battlefield a time-consuming and complicated procedure, and at this late date in the war reflected badly on the Federal ordnance department. The large number of smoothbores also reduced Caldwell's tactical choices. Regiments armed with smoothbores could not break up Confederate formations with medium- or long-range fire; their only option was to close quickly to a range at which their weapons could be effective, a potentially costly business if the enemy were well posted and armed with rifles.[5]

The First Division bivouacked near the rear of Little Round Top following an exhausting march on July 1. Roused from their slumber on the morning of the second, the men underwent a "careful and rigid inspection" of arms in anticipation of action that day. The division then moved from its bivouac, taking up several different positions before marching to the southern end of Cemetery Ridge. Arriving at 7:00 A.M., Caldwell's troops massed in columns of regiments by brigades on the left of Brigadier General John Gibbon's Second Division of the Second Corps and the right of Major General Daniel E. Sickles's Third Corps. This dense formation permitted close control and rapid mobility. Hancock undoubtedly ordered this alignment, for Gibbon's division and Brigadier General Alexander Hays's Third Division of the Second Corps deployed in the same formation. Facing a nebulous situation along his front (there was no guarantee that Lee would attack the Federals), Hancock wanted his divisions to move quickly if necessary.[6]

Caldwell placed the brigades of Cross, Kelly, and Brooke from left to right on the front line and held Zook in reserve behind Kelly. Captain James Rorty's Battery B, 1st New York Artillery (four 10-pounder Parrotts) unlimbered between Cross's and Kelly's brigades to provide artillery support. First Lieutenant Josiah M. Favill, a young member of Zook's staff, recalled that the division's position provided not a particle of cover: "We were posted on broad, high, open ground, gently sloping in front towards a small brook called Plum Run, some three or four hundred yards in front." Because their officers expected movement or action momentarily, the Federals constructed no earthworks or other protection. Orders allowed the soldiers to stack arms and rest but not to remove their accouterments. "Our men sat or lay down in their ranks, while the officers gathered in little groups, and discussed the probable outlook for the day," wrote Favill. Officers informed the soldiers that they were to be held in reserve, an announcement that prompted a battle-wise Irishman in Kelly's brigade to quip, "In resarve; yis, resarved for the heavy fighting."[7]

The Irishman's prediction seemed to ring hollow as the morning passed without incident. "Our horses quietly browsed in the rich grass," wrote Lieutenant Colonel St. Clair Mulholland of the 116th Pennsylvania, "and the men lay in groups, peacefully enjoying a rest after the rapid march of the day before." At 10:00 A.M. picket firing erupted beyond the Emmitsburg Road, continuing with varying intensity until after noon. "But 3 o'clock came and still no signs of the general engagement," noted Mulholland. There was, however, a disturbing development on Caldwell's left. Shortly before three o'clock, Sickles's Third Corps marched from its positions south of Caldwell to a point far in advance of the army's general line of battle. First Lieutenant W. S. Shallenberger of the 140th Pennsylvania observed "a division of the 3rd Corps . . . moving forward in line of battle by brigades. Beautifully the movement was executed—flags flying and bayonets glistening in the sunlight as they march[ed] against the foe." Caldwell watched the spectacle with Hancock, Kelly, and other officers who had gathered in front of the Irish Brigade. They could only guess at the meaning of the advance, but Hancock remarked with a smile, "Wait a moment, you will soon see them tumbling back."[8]

Whether Sickles should have moved forward is a question beyond the scope of this essay, but his new position forced Meade to modify his plans in order to support the exposed Third Corps. Sickles occupied a front too broad for his corps to defend properly; indeed, unsupported artillery held stretches of his line. This meant that units sent to reinforce Sickles would be broken up and rushed about to plug holes or respond to emergencies rather than entering the battle as organizations capable of delivering blows with their entire strength. Moreover, no single person coordinated the defense of the Union left—an arrangement that produced a critical void as troops from various corps hastened to support Sickles. It would be a battle on the Union side with no one at the hilt of the sword, a fact that would cost Caldwell and his men dearly.[9]

About 3:00 P.M., James Longstreet's Confederate artillery shattered the comparative tranquility of the battlefield with its pre-assault bombardment. "At half-past three the cannonade was furious," wrote Lieutenant Charles Hale of Colonel Cross's staff. The crash of musketry in the direction of Little Round Top carried to Caldwell's position by four o'clock. "It was a great relief," recalled Hale, "for the suspense was ended and we now knew that our lines out there in the front were fighting on the defensive."[10]

Longstreet's blow fell first at Devil's Den and Houck's Ridge, and within minutes Little Round Top also came under fierce attack. As more Southern brigades joined the battle, the action spread northward to John Rose's Wheatfield. Brigadier General George T. Anderson's brigade of eighteen hundred Georgians passed south of Rose's buildings, entered Rose Woods, and shouldered their way forward down a slope toward the open field of wheat. Opposing them were parts of two brigades from Sickles's corps—three regiments of Colonel Regis de Trobriand's Third Brigade of Major General David Bell Birney's First Division reinforced by elements of Colonel William R. Brewster's Second Brigade of Brigadier General Andrew A. Humphreys's Second Division. Two brigades of Brigadier General James Barnes's First Division of the Fifth Corps further bolstered these defenders just before Anderson's assault struck. Barnes's brigades crowded upon a stony hill, sparsely covered with trees, situated near the southwestern side of the Wheatfield. Their fire and that of the Third Corps units drove Anderson back after a fierce contest of musketry.[11]

Even before Anderson's repulse, Barnes observed trouble on his right flank. The New Englander had been uneasy about his position from the first, instructing his brigade commanders to look for lines of retreat almost as soon as they arrived on

Stony Hill. A large stretch of apparently unprotected ground to his right worried Barnes. Indeed, there was no infantry between him and the Peach Orchard. Sickles held the front from the orchard to Rose Woods with a line of artillery batteries unlimbered along the Wheatfield Road.[12]

The trouble looming on Barnes's flank came from Brigadier General Joseph B. Kershaw's brigade of South Carolinians, more than two thousand strong, which heralded the entry into the battle of Major General Lafayette McLaws's division. As Kershaw passed the Emmitsburg Road, he split his brigade, sending his left wing, under Colonel John D. Kennedy of the 2d South Carolina, in a northerly direction to attack the Peach Orchard and batteries along the Wheatfield Road. With his remaining two regiments, the 3d and 7th South Carolina, directly under his control, Kershaw swept through and around the Rose farm buildings and made straight for the Stony Hill. The Confederates paused briefly after passing the Rose farm buildings because the 3d had lapped over part of the 7th. Kershaw ordered the 7th to move by the right flank to uncover the 3d; this order somehow reached Kershaw's left wing, then threatening to overrun the guns along the Wheatfield Road. Without hesitation, the regiments under Colonel Kennedy broke off their attack and moved by the right flank, exposing their own left to guns along the Wheatfield Road. Quick to seize the opportunity, Federal cannoneers blasted the South Carolinians with canister and shrapnel, inflicting dreadful losses and sowing utter disorder in the ranks. Many of Kennedy's survivors made for the cover of a finger of Rose Woods that jutted out toward the Wheatfield Road. This brought them directly toward Barnes's flank, and he promptly ordered a retreat several hundred yards north to Trostle Woods, which ran along the northern border of the Wheatfield Road.[13]

Barnes's departure left de Trobriand's hard-pressed regiments alone to confront Anderson's renewed advance on their front and Kershaw's presence on their flank. Unable to stop the

Confederates, de Trobriand pulled his men back. Part of his brigade halted on a knoll in the center of the Wheatfield to support Captain George B. Winslow's Napoleons of Battery D, 1st New York Light Artillery. Canister from Winslow's guns sent Anderson's Georgians scrambling back for the cover of Rose Woods, but Kershaw's men soon brought fire to bear on the battery's right and a portion of Anderson's brigade worked through the eastern side of Rose Woods to menace its left. Winslow had no alternative but to withdraw. Confederates controlled the Wheatfield and Rose Woods, the center of Birney's front had been cracked wide open, and Federals at the Peach Orchard and Humphreys's line along the Emmitsburg Road occupied perilous positions.[14]

In the midst of this crisis, Sickles requested reinforcements from Meade. Meade sent a courier speeding to Hancock with instructions that he send a division to report to Major General George Sykes—clear evidence that Meade lacked confidence in Sickles. The courier found Hancock still in the company of Caldwell in front of Kelly's brigade. According to Lieutenant Colonel Mulholland, who was present at the meeting, Hancock quietly remarked, "Caldwell, you get your division ready." The First Division would report to Sykes "for service in the direction of Little Round Top." The order to "fall in" and "take arms" brought the four brigades to their feet, and in minutes the division was ready to move.[15]

"The direction we were to take was to the front and left," recalled Lieutenant Charles A. Fuller of the 61st New York. "There was no time to countermarch so as to bring the men right in front, so we simply left faced and started." The right of a regiment usually led the column of march, but to have accomplished this with the entire division, as Fuller noted, would have entailed a tedious countermarch of every regiment in the division. Caldwell dispensed with the familiar to save precious minutes. The division moved to the left in mass by column of regiments—a formation seldom employed within range of enemy small arms or artillery fire. It was the same formation all the brigades had assumed when they arrived on Cemetery Ridge, except each regiment in each brigade had simply faced to the left, formed into columns of fours, and commenced movement. This formation somewhat resembled the Greek phalanx, a huge moving mass, or "chunck," of men, many ranks deep. The disadvantages of the formation when exposed to artillery fire were too grim to contemplate. A single round of solid shot, case, or shell could fell dozens of men. Caldwell knew the risks but also appreciated the necessity for speed. Under the circumstances it was a risk worth taking. A movement in mass brought his division to the point of crisis quickly and in strength that could be applied against the enemy immediately. It also made the division easier to manage by drastically cutting the length of the column and hence the time it would take for Caldwell to communicate with his brigade commanders.[16]

Cross's brigade took the lead, followed in turn by Kelly, Brooke, and Zook. The men moved rapidly, frequently at the double-quick, in the direction of Little Round Top. Caldwell placed his headquarters at the front of the column, a position that allowed him to exert maximum control over his division. From there he could receive instructions from Sykes, whom he sent Lieutenant Daniel K. Cross of his staff to locate, and transmit them down the length of his column to each brigade commander without any disruption in the flow of information. He also could move the head of the column, and hence the entire division, in any direction with a single order.[17]

The wisdom of Caldwell's movement in mass became more apparent as the division neared the battle zone. Lieutenant Favill remembered that as the division marched forward "the tumult became deafening, the mountain side echoed back the musketry, so that no word of command could be heard, and little could be seen but long lines of flame, and smoke and struggling masses of men." Noise, carnage, confusion, and

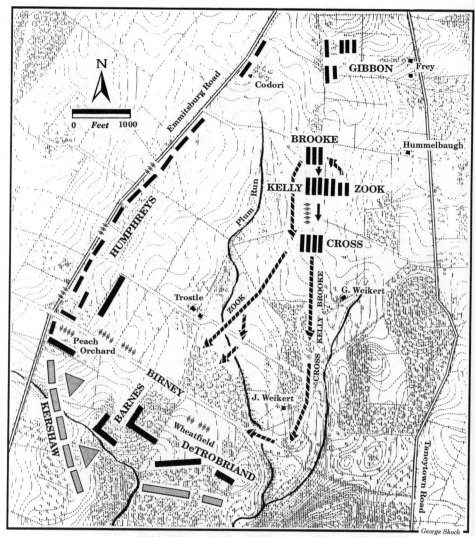

N

0   *Feet*   1000

Emmitsburg Road

Codori

GIBBON   Frey

Hummelbaugh

BROOKE

KELLY   **ZOOK**

CROSS

HUMPHREYS

Plum Run

Trostle

ZOOK

G. Weikert

CROSS KELLY BROOKE

Peach
Orchard

BIRNEY

KERSHAW

BARNES

J. Weikert

Wheatfield

DeTROBRIAND

Taneytown Road

George Skoch

Caldwell's Division Shifts to the Left

smoke—all were factors that historians who sit in judgment of soldiers like Caldwell often neglect to take into account. Yet he and his subordinates had to make instant decisions within this hostile environment. If they erred, and circumstances and means of communication ensured that they would, the consequences might be grim. Caldwell's situation was all the more difficult because, even with Sykes's orders, he knew virtually nothing about the ground, enemy positions and strength, or Federal dispositions in the area toward which he moved.[18]

The division passed by the George Weikert farm, through Weikert's Woods, over two stone walls, and into an open and slightly marshy pasture near the northernmost end of the Plum Run Valley (also known as the "Valley of Death"). The column crossed the pasture toward Trostle Woods, which screened the Wheatfield. Lieutenant Cross had failed to locate Sykes, and Caldwell had dispatched Lieutenant William P. Wilson to search for the Fifth Corps commander. Wilson enjoyed better luck (although he never said where he found Sykes) and returned with a member of Sykes's staff. They met Caldwell at the head of the column as it entered Trostle Woods. Caldwell learned that he should take his division to Rose's Wheatfield rather than toward Little Round Top. The instructions from Sykes called for the First Division "to advance to the south side of the Wheat-field, drive the enemy back, and if possible establish the original line on the crest." Sykes's staff officer rode a young horse, and every Confederate shell that screamed into the vicinity set the animal "to plunging furiously." Lieutenant Charles Hale, who accompanied Colonel Cross and attempted to hear the orders carried by Sykes's staff officer, recalled that the horse kicked so furiously "that we had to give him all the room there was." Hale could pick up only the officer's last statement, delivered as his horse gave a plunge: "The enemy is breaking directly on your right—Strike him quick." Now at least vaguely aware of the enemy's position,

Caldwell could formulate a plan for committing his own men. But his battle report suggests that he still knew little of the ground and general disposition of friendly troops.[19]

Caldwell confronted a knotty tactical problem in attempting to strike swiftly against Confederates on the right. With the left of each regiment at the head of each column, deployment in the formation they were trained to assume in combat would entail moving the regiments by the left flank, then facing them to the right into the line of battle. The units would then have to march by the right flank to get back into the vicinity of the Wheatfield. Caldwell deemed all of this an unnecessary loss of time and instructed Colonel Cross to move his men onto the Wheatfield Road by the right flank, which brought them into line along the northern edge of the Wheatfield and southern edge of Trostle Woods. When each of Cross's regiments had deployed in a brigade front, they left-faced. This left the file closers in front of the line of battle and placed the rear rank in front and front rank in rear. "Of course there was instant confusion," observed Lieutenant Hale, "for it brought the line of battle facing by the rear rank, with the file closers pushing and crowding through." The 148th Pennsylvania "found itself in the anomalous condition of being not only faced by the rear rank, but inverted by wings—companies A and B in the center, and center companies far out of place at the extreme." The right guide of the regiment was in the center and the colors were in the rear rank on the right. "To any but well drilled and disciplined troops" this odd formation "would have been disastrous," wrote Colonel Daniel Bingham of the 64th New York. A member of the 148th recalled that "this eccentricity of formation, I am happy to say, did not, in the slightest manner, affect the conduct of our regiment. Previous drill and discipline had provided for just such condition." Caldwell had gambled that his men possessed the training and discipline to fight effectively despite being employed in an awkward and unfamiliar forma-

Colonel Edward E. Cross
(*Photographic History* 8:102)

tion. The situation demanded additional Federals on the firing line, and Caldwell's improvisation placed them there quickly.[20]

Cross's advance through Trostle Woods onto the Wheatfield Road and then into the Wheatfield was, as Lieutenant Hale testified, "all done without a halt, and without the loss of a minute in maneuvering." "The entire brigade moved with the mobility of a single battalion: four regiments, closed intervals, four sets of field officers—an aggregated strength of about one thousand," stated Hale admiringly. "Just in the nick of time it was hurled against the enemy and struck a tremendous blow. That was the very way the brigades of the First Division had been trained to fight." Cross advanced his brigade to the brow of a slight ridge cutting across nearly the center of the Wheat-field. Most of the soldiers stood in the open, except for those of the 5th New Hampshire and two-thirds of the 148th Pennsyl-vania, who enjoyed cover along the eastern side of Rose Woods. Lieutenant Charles A. Fuller, a file closer in the 61st New York, recalled that as the brigade reached the crest of this ridge he saw in front "one or two men come toward us on a run, and throw themselves down behind this partial stone wall (which bordered the southern end of the Wheatfield). But a brief time passed when a solid line of men in gray appeared and placed themselves as had the first comers." It was Anderson's Geor-gians. "Here the battle opened with great energy," a member of the 148th Pennsylvania recollected. Cross's regiments opened a fire described by Caldwell as "terrific" on the gray-clad line in front. They drew a heavy fire in return and also felt pressure on their right flank from members of the 7th South Carolina, who had refused their right flank and were concealed by the arm of Rose Woods bordering the western edge of the Wheatfield. "The Rebs had their slight protection, but we were in the open," noted Lieutenant Fuller, "without a thing better than wheat straw to catch a minnie bullet that weighed an ounce. Of course our men began to tumble." Smoke quickly blanketed the field, and many men in the brigade lay down to gain some protection and to look for targets under the grimy canopy.[21]

While Cross's men slugged it out with Anderson, Kershaw, and perhaps elements of Semmes's brigade, Caldwell brought up his Second Brigade. Kelly's regiments also faced by the rear rank in their formation; due to the rapidity with which the

Cross's Brigade Enters the Wheatfield

George Skoch

brigade went into action, it pushed into the Wheatfield on Cross's right. It was probably while bringing Kelly into action that Caldwell learned he had lost control over Zook's brigade. Despite precautions to maintain control over his command, the limits of battlefield communications left Caldwell power-less to prevent others from seizing a major element of his force.[22]

Zook's brigade had occupied the rear of the First Division as it marched south to enter the battle. It was intercepted en route by Major Henry E. Tremain of Sickles's staff. Because Birney clamored for reinforcements in the area of the Wheat-field, Sickles had dispatched Tremain to find Hancock and hurry Caldwell's division forward if it had not already started. Tremain spotted fresh troops marching to the front and rode straight to them. Informed that they belonged to the First Division, Tremain considered trying to locate Caldwell but decided that it would take too long. The captain knew minutes were precious because of the crisis near the Wheatfield. On learning from a regimental commander that Zook led the bri-gade, Tremain spurred to the head of the column and asked the general if he would detach his brigade and go into action immediately. Tremain later recorded what transpired next:

> He replied, politely but with soldierly mien, that his orders were to follow the column. Repeating the request I asked him to assume the responsibility of compliance, promising to protect him and to return him as soon as possible with a formal order from the proper officer.
> It was a critical interview. There was no time to parley. . . . It was obvious, too, that Zook, as well as myself, fully appre-ciated that neither the request nor instant compliance with it could be deemed within the strict limits of military regularity. "Sir," said General Zook, with a calm, firm look, inspiring me with its significance, "if you will give me the order of General Sickles I will obey it." My response then was: "General Sickles' order, general, is that you file your brigade to the right and move into action here." . . . Few men would have acted as Zook did.

Brigadier General Samuel Kosciuszko Zook
(*Photographic History* 10:135)

Yet had he acted otherwise it might have changed the fate of
the day. Who knows? It was such acts of sagacity and nobleness
that won Gettysburg.

One might be tempted to add that such acts can just as well
lose battles. It was fortunate for the Federals that Sickles and
Sykes, though not working together in coordinating the battle,
at least recognized the Wheatfield as the point needing immediate reinforcement. This brought Zook into battle with
his own division quite by chance, and, equally by chance, on
the right of the divisional line Caldwell was then forming.
What Caldwell might have done with Zook had Tremain not
intervened is purely speculative. The strongest brigade of the
First Division with 975 effectives, Zook's command probably
would have been held in reserve. But the actions of Tremain
and Zook could not be undone, and Caldwell lived with the
arrangement.[23]

In less than ten minutes Caldwell had placed three brigades
totaling 2,350 men on the firing line. He had assistance from
Captain Tremain, but given the noise, smoke, and poor communications, it was still an impressive performance. Control
at the battle front now passed to the hands of Cross, Zook,
and Kelly. As divisional commander, Caldwell would keep his
finger on the pulse of action to determine when and where to
commit Brooke's brigade, which constituted his reserve, while
also looking beyond the immediate battle his men were fighting. Were his flanks adequately protected? Was support available to sustain his division's momentum? How would he secure
what had been gained already? What was the nature of the
ground? What were the dispositions of friendly troops in the
area? These were questions for which Caldwell sought answers
while the battle raged in front.[24]

The action had developed in promising fashion until fierce
resistance by the brigades of Kershaw, Anderson, and Semmes
slowed Federal progress to a near halt. Zook's regiments had

Colonel Patrick Kelly
(MOLLUS-MASS/U.S. Army Military History Institute,
Carlisle Barracks, Pa.)

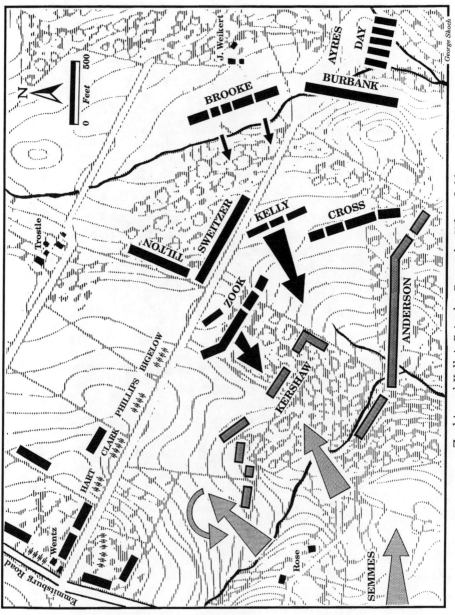

Zook's and Kelly's Brigades Enter the Wheatfield

passed over and through the brigades of Barnes's division in Trostle Woods, crossed the Wheatfield Road and its fences, and entered the "rocky woodland" of Rose Woods on the western edge of the Wheatfield. Perhaps forty yards to Zook's left rear was Kelly's brigade, moving forward to go into action on Cross's right. Lieutenant Colonel Mulholland, whose 116th Pennsylvania occupied the right of Kelly's line, noted that as Zook's troops "approached the line of timber covering the hill they received a withering fire from the concealed enemy, which staggered them for a moment." Josiah M. Favill of Zook's staff recalled that "we soon came to a standstill and a close encounter, when the firing became terriffic and the slaughter frightful. We were enveloped in smoke and fire, not only in front, but on our left, and even at times on the right." Among the first to fall was Zook, who sustained a mortal wound. Command passed to Lieutenant Colonel C. G. Freudenburg of the 52d New York. He ordered the brigade to press forward before falling wounded himself. "Our men fired promiscuously, steadily pressing forward," wrote Lieutenant Favill, "but the fighting was so mixed, rebel and Union lines so close together, and in some places intermingled, that a clear idea of what was going on was not readily obtainable."[25]

Because Kershaw's men focused on Cross's right and on Zook, Kelly's Irish Brigade was able to close to within fifty feet of the Confederates. As the Federals approached Kershaw's line, wrote Mulholland, "suddenly someone in the ranks cried out 'there they are.'" Kelly's Irishmen had been fortunate. Every regiment but the 28th Massachusetts carried smoothbores, but at fifty feet even their inferior weapons could inflict significant damage. Mulholland believed that "the effect of our fire was deadly in the extreme, for under such circumstances a blind man could not have missed his mark." Yet the Irishmen made no headway against Kershaw's 7th and 3d South Carolina. Stubborn Confederate resistance helped check the Northern advance, but disorder on the Union side abetted the South

Carolinians. The brigades of Zook and Kelly converged as they pushed into the woods; their left and right, respectively, over-lapped and became hopelessly intermingled in "a deplorable state of confusion." The "dense woods" and "large bowlders of rocks" that strewed the woods also retarded efforts to maintain forward momentum, as did the proximity of Anderson's Georgians, posted along the southern edge of the Wheatfield where they could bring fire on Kelly's flank.[26]

Cross's brigade might have relieved the pressure on Anderson; however, by the time Zook had been shot, so too had Cross. Before the New Hampshire colonel could launch an assault, he was mortally wounded at a point near the left of his brigade. Command in these difficult circumstances devolved on the senior officer, Colonel Boyd McKeen, a good soldier who proved unable to establish control over the brigade and mount an offensive. McKeen also learned that cartridges were running low, which he reported to division headquarters.[27]

Caldwell responded promptly to McKeen's report by ordering Brooke to relieve the First Brigade. Just ten minutes had elapsed since the division had entered the battle, which attests to the rapidity of Cross's fire. Brooke quickly moved his brigade into action, passing into the Wheatfield and replacing the right of Cross's brigade. Only the 61st New York, 81st Pennsylvania, and right seven companies of the 148th Pennsylvania withdrew. The left three companies of the 148th and the 5th New Hampshire remained in the woods trading fire with Anderson's men and elements of the 1st Texas and 15th Georgia. Brooke's regiments halted on the ridge, by then liberally sprinkled with the dead and wounded of the First Brigade, and returned the fire of Anderson's Georgians. While his men blazed away at their front, Brooke made his way over to Kelly's brigade, which was stalled somewhat to his right rear. At Brooke's encouragement, Kelly started his men forward and Brooke ordered his own soldiers to charge. "That was the right thing at the right time and we were off with a yell," wrote Stephen A. Osborne of the

Colonel John Rutter Brooke
(*Photographic History* 10:303)

145th Pennsylvania on Brooke's right. But from the point of view of Colonel Daniel Bingham of the 64th New York, on Brooke's left center, the order was not so easily executed. "The men were firing as fast as they could load," asserted Bingham, "the din was almost deafening, it was very difficult to have orders understood, and it required considerable effort to start the line forward into another charge. The officers and non-commissioned officers displayed the greatest gallantry." So too did the color guards; indeed, it may have been the movement of the 64th New York's color guard that enabled Brooke to get his brigade moving. According to Colonel Bingham, the two color bearers of his regiment "rushed several rods ahead" of the regimental line "so that they were dimly perceivable through the cloud of smoke." This act started the 64th New York and 2d Delaware forward "with a cheer"—which may have inspired the rest of the brigade to advance.[28]

Brooke's surging line received a volley from Anderson's Georgians as it neared Rose Woods and the southern border of the Wheatfield. "It staggered us," wrote Stephen Osborne, "but only for a moment, then on we went right over the Johnnies, leaving almost as many prisoners as there were of us." After nearly an hour of intense fighting, Anderson's men were physically exhausted and too disorganized to stop Brooke's fresh regiments. "Pressing forward, firing as we went," reported Brooke, his regiments steadily advanced into Rose Woods. Elements of Anderson's regiments made a stand across Rose's Run among a "hornet's nest of rocks and underbrush" along the ridge that rises south of the run. The Georgians delivered a "deadly" fire into Brooke's advancing line from their position of cover. But the Federals were not to be stopped, as they "swept onward loading and firing" and rolled over the point of resistance, netting more than one hundred prisoners.[29]

At this rocky ledge Brooke's assault confronted part of Semmes's brigade drawn up in line "within pistol range." Sheltering themselves among rocks and behind the lip of the ridge, the Federals drove the Southerners to cover but proved unable to press their attack farther. Brooke paused to assess his situation. His assault into Rose Woods had precipitated a forward movement by the entire division. When Anderson's men withdrew on the southern end of the field, Kelly's Irish could advance against Kershaw's right. A gap extending for nearly one hundred yards between Kershaw's 7th South Carolina and the 50th Georgia of Semmes (which had come into the ravine at the base of the Stony Hill in response to a request from Kershaw) presented an opportunity. Kelly's men discovered the gap and worked around the flank of the Carolinians while their comarades and Zook's brigade, who were jumbled together "in one confused mass," pressed Kershaw's front. The 7th fought until the right and left wings were nearly doubled on each other. "This was some of the most severe fighting our division had ever done," wrote Lieutenant Colonel Mulholland. At last the 7th gave way, leaving the 3d South Carolina, reinforced by about fifty men of the 50th Georgia, to fight on desperately until overwhelmed and forced to retire with Kershaw to the Rose Farm. Kelly's and Zook's men swarmed over the position defended by Kershaw's men, taking "a great many prisoners" from the 3d and 7th and finding "many dead" Confederates "nearly all hit in the head or upper part of the body."[30]

While Brooke, Kelly, and Zook ground their way forward, the extreme left of the division, Cross's 5th New Hampshire and seven companies of the 148th Pennsylvania, also pressed ahead. They gained a position in Rose Woods overlooking the ravine on Brooke's left rear and sparred with elements of Henry L. Benning's and Jerome B. Robertson's brigades. Brooke, meanwhile, found his situation not yet desperate but growing perilous. In its fight for possession of the Stony Hill, Kelly's brigade had diverged to the right and lost connection with Brooke's right, leaving it in the air. Despite the efforts of the 5th and 148th, Brooke's left also was exposed. He sent a runner (or rider) back to apprise Caldwell of the situation and request support for his brigade's threatened flanks.[31]

Caldwell reacted promptly to Brooke's call for help. He sent Lieutenant Wilson of his staff over to some troops visible in Trostle Woods along the northern boundary of the Wheatfield Road. It was Colonel Jacob B. Sweitzer's brigade of Barnes's division. Wilson made no headway with Sweitzer, so Caldwell rode over in person. Sweitzer recalled that Caldwell rode up "in haste and said his brigade [*sic*] was driving the enemy like H——l over yonder in the woods, pointing... beyond the Wheatfield, and asked if I would give him the support of my

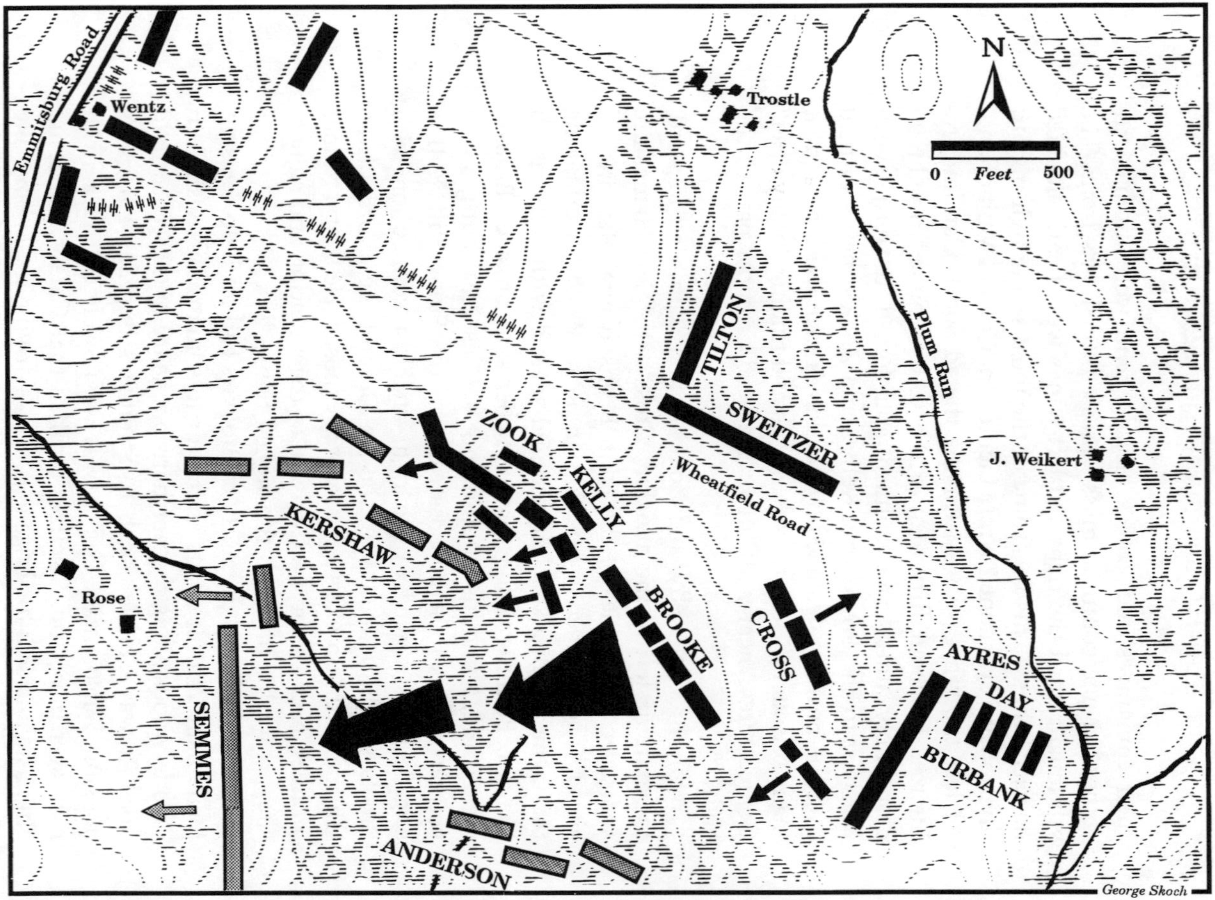

Brooke's Brigade Enters the Wheatfield

George Skoch

N

0 Feet 500

Trostle

Plum Run

J. Weikert

SWEITZER

TILTON

Wheatfield Road

CROSS

AYRES

DAY

BURBANK

BROOKE

KELLY

ZOOK

KERSHAW

ANDERSON

Wentz

SEMMES

Emmitsburg Road

Rose

brigade." Sweitzer did not know Caldwell (he could see that he was a general) but referred the stranger to Barnes with the assurance that he would obey his commander's orders "with pleasure." Caldwell repeated his request to Barnes, who agreed to release Sweitzer, then proceeded to waste precious minutes by shouting a few "patriotic remarks" to Sweitzer's men before he ordered them forward. Sweitzer marched forward armed only with the knowledge that friendly troops were in the woods at the southern end of the Wheatfield and he was to support them. Caldwell sent no staff officer to direct Sweitzer—probably because they all were employed elsewhere. Even if a staff officer had been available, it might not have helped Sweitzer reach the point of most desperate need. Given the combination of intense confusion and primitive communications, Caldwell's simple request that Sweitzer's brigade support the troops fighting in the woods probably conveyed all that was necessary and possible at this stage of the battle.[32]

Caldwell looked to his left flank once Sweitzer's line had moved forward. While Caldwell's division had advanced through the Wheatfield and Rose Woods, Brigadier General Romeyn B. Ayres and two brigades of U.S. regulars from the Second Division of the Fifth Corps descended the northern shoulder of Little Round Top, crossed the Plum Run Valley, and climbed Houck's Ridge. Ayres's mission was to clear the ridge of Confederates, whose sniping fire was "annoying" Federals on Little Round Top. Unfortunately for Ayres, he fell victim to the absence of a controlling hand in this area of the battlefield. His division faced due west, whereas to his front Caldwell's general orientation was southwest—placing the two formations nearly at right angles to each other. Ayres also worried about deadly fire against his exposed left from Confederates concealed in high ground above Devil's Den. He responded to this emergency by refusing the left of his left regiment, the 17th U.S., and ordering the rest of the division to lie down. Pinned on the left and blocked by Caldwell's and

Sweitzer's troops in their front and left front, Ayres's regulars endured the unnerving and maddening experience of taking fire without the ability to contribute materially to the fight.[33]

Caldwell sought to free the regulars. From Sweitzer's position he galloped over to Ayres, whom he found behind a stone wall that ran south from the Wheatfield Road. The two generals arranged to have Ayres's Second Brigade wheel to its left to come into line with the First Division's general orientation. This would secure Caldwell's left flank. "Thus far everything had progressed favorably," wrote Caldwell. "I had gained a position which, if properly supported on the flanks, I thought impregnable from the front."[34]

Caldwell had performed with commendable ability to this point. His soldiers entered the battle with speed and power, checked the penetration in Birney's front, threw three Southern brigades back in disorder, and gained ground beyond the original line. He had sought to protect gains by communicating to Barnes and Ayres his need for support while seeking coordination at least between the regulars and his own division. Barnes and Ayres, in contrast, made no effort to communicate with Caldwell. Nor did the commander of the First Division receive much help from Fifth Corps headquarters, though he acted under Sykes's orders. Caldwell alone attempted to exert some semblance of control over the struggle for the Wheatfield. But this effort at the divisional level—at the point of the sword—suffered from lack of direction at the corps level because neither Sykes nor Sickles applied a firm hand to the contest. In consequence, a confusing battle went from heady success to disaster in a matter of minutes.

About the time Caldwell's drive reached its high-water mark, Brigadier General William Barksdale's brigade of Mississippians slammed into the hinge of Sickles's line at the Peach Orchard and broke it wide open. While Barksdale swung north to roll up the Federals along the Emmitsburg Road, Brigadier General W. T. Wofford's brigade of Georgians, which had followed in support of Barksdale, passed through the orchard and continued straight east, guiding on the Wheatfield Road. They picked up Kershaw's shattered left wing along their advance and bore down on Caldwell's exposed right. Caldwell knew nothing of this approaching Confederate storm. By the time he appreciated the danger, the situation had developed beyond his capacity to influence events—or to save his command.

While conversing with Ayres at the stone wall that sheltered regulars of the Second Brigade, Caldwell saw parties of troops falling back across the Wheatfield. Lieutenant William H. Powell of Ayres's staff observed this phenomenon with concern and warned Ayres, "General, you had better look out, the line in front is giving way." Powell recalled that Caldwell turned and remarked "in rather a sharp manner, 'That's not so sir; those are my troops being relieved.'" The two generals went on with their conversation, but Powell interrupted them again a few minutes later, advising Ayres "to look out for your command. I don't care what any one says, those troops in front are running away." Caldwell and Ayres paused to scan the front. Without a further word, Caldwell spurred his horse north along the stone wall to the Wheatfield Road, then west in the direction of his right flank. He could not have traveled far before discovering "that all the troops on my right had broken and were fleeing to the rear in great confusion." Caldwell and his orderly, Corporal Uriah N. Parmelee—apparently the only member of his staff still accompanying the division commander—sought in vain to check the fleeing fugitives. Soon they were borne along with the flotsam of retreat and defeat.[35]

Zook's and Kelly's brigades dissolved under pressure applied against their flank by regiments under Wofford and Kershaw. The Confederates harassed retreating Federals with "terrific" and "most destructive" musketry, according to Lieutenant J. J. Permeus of the 140th Pennsylvania, who added that "neither valor nor discipline could withstand such a fire and such odds." Federals rushed to the rear to escape the trap closing on them. Permeus recalled that "as we fell back through the Wheatfield we suffered dreadfully, losing more, I think, than on the advance." Colonel Patrick Kelly reported that his command "narrowly escaped being captured." As Confederates crushed the right of the First Division, Lieutenant Wilson of Caldwell's staff, either on his own or at his chief's direction, rode rapidly to warn Brooke of impending disaster that threatened to isolate and destroy his brigade. Brooke promptly ordered a retreat. "We went back, if not as fast and noisy as we went, still the most of us made fair time," wrote Stephen A. Osborne. Confederate troops were in the Wheatfield by the time Brooke's men emerged from Rose Woods. "I found the enemy had nearly closed in my rear," Brooke reported, "and had the movement not been executed at the time it was, I feel convinced that all would have been lost by death, wounds, or capture."[36]

The collapse of the First Division unleashed the fury of the Southern assault first on Sweitzer's brigade and then on Ayres's regulars. The regulars attempted to steady the crumbling Wheatfield line by changing the Second Brigade's front to the south-southwest. This brought the right of the brigade out into the Wheatfield and exposed it to a flank fire from Wofford's soldiers. The regulars hastily pulled out of danger, removing the last island of organized resistance against the triumphant Confederate tide in the Wheatfield.[37]

Caldwell reported that his men fell back "generally in good order, but necessarily with some confusion." Lieutenant Colonel C. H. Morgan of Hancock's staff exhibited less charity when he wrote that he encountered the First Division, "or the remnants of it flying to the rear, without no shadow of an organization." Morgan's efforts to stop the fleeing troops duplicated Caldwell's earlier failure: "All attempt to rally them [elements of Third Corps] or any of Caldwell's division within reach of the enemy's bullets was useless."[38]

The First Division finally regrouped along the Taneytown Road, but it was well into the night before officers restored order and organization. Losses had been severe—177 killed, 880 wounded, and 208 missing, or nearly 40 percent of the division. Brigade commanders Cross and Zook would die of their wounds, and Brooke lay painfully disabled. Only Kelly emerged from the battle unscathed. George Sykes complained to Hancock that the division had "done badly"; however, the record spoke otherwise. The First Division fought with courage and spirit. Only the depth of its penetration into the Wheatfield and Rose Woods exposed it to disaster when the Peach Orchard fell.[39]

Nor could it be said that Caldwell handled his division poorly. Indeed, he contributed a nearly flawless performance. When the call came for help on Sickles's hard-pressed front, Caldwell put his soldiers in motion within minutes. Risking casualties by moving his men in mass, he delivered them to the point of crisis rapidly and in strength. Caldwell labored under severe constraints: Sykes provided only sketchy instructions, the ground was unfamiliar, and information about Confederate strength and dispositions consisted of vague gestures by a staff officer. Exhibiting a flexible mind and translating decisions into action, Caldwell placed three brigades into the battle in ten minutes, a notable feat given the available communications. He saved precious minutes by deploying his brigades into battle faced by the rear rank, a formation that might have led to disaster with mediocre troops. Caldwell gambled that his well-drilled troops would not be adversely affected, and their stout performance vindicated his judgment. As already noted, no other Federal general in the Wheatfield battle area attempted to achieve control by coordinating with adjacent division commanders. When disaster struck, limitations of communication rendered Caldwell powerless to extricate his men from the field in better order. Even modern communications might not have made a great difference. If Caldwell's

experience taught anything, it was that the Federals desperately needed someone above divisional command to monitor
the battle and exercise a controlling influence. Such a presence
likely would have spared not only Caldwell's First Division but
also the divisions of Barnes and Ayres their bitter defeats.

Caldwell endured criticism by Sykes and some of his own
subordinates for not putting his men "into action very
handsomely"—a comment related to the facing-by-the-rear-
rank deployment. "Much incensed" by Sykes's accusation,
Hancock ordered an investigation into the conduct of the First
Division. "Subsequent investigation showed that no troops on
the field had done better," wrote Lieutenant Colonel Morgan.
Although the investigation exonerated Caldwell, Hancock may
have harbored a seed of doubt about his lieutenant. In the
reorganization of the army in March 1864, Caldwell lost his
command. Alexander Webb, a brigadier in the Second Corps
painfully sparing in his praise for anyone, wrote on March 26,
1864, "Caldwell leaves in [?]. He feels very badly. I am very
fond of him and am sorry to see him owsted."[40]

Caldwell had executed the basic principles of command in
combat admirably. He had communicated as effectively as possible, moved his men skillfully, and engaged them with positive results. But another element of command applied
particularly to those who led, not ordered, men into battle—
an element that could be neither taught nor learned but had
to be accepted. How Caldwell mastered it is unknown. Chap-
lain J. W. Stuckenberg of the First Division offered a graphic
example in his wartime diary:

> In [the] 1st Division there were two operating stands, where the
> Surgeons were constantly consulting about operations and were
> performing amputations. Heaps of amputated feet & hands,
> arms & legs were seen lying under the tables and by their sides.
> Go around among the wounded and you witness the most sad-
> dening and sickening sights. Some are writhing with pain, and
> deeply moaning and groaning and calling for relief which cannot

be afforded them. The finest forms are horribly disfigured & mutilated. Wounds are found in all parts of the body. . . . Some of the wounds are dressed, some not. From some the blood still oozes in others maggots are perhaps found. Perhaps they are poorly waited on, there not being nurses enough. No physician may have examined their wounds and dressed them. Their physical wants may not have been attended to. They long for home & their friends, but they cannot get to the one, the other cannot come to them. Through neglect, perhaps, they die. They are buried in their clothes, without shroud, without coffin, perhaps without religious services and a board to mark their resting place.[41]

Like any division, brigade, or regimental commander, Caldwell had to watch his men die in large numbers. Perhaps the most difficult challenge of command was to acknowledge this grim fact and persevere.

Notes

"If the Enemy Is There, We Must Attack Him": R. E. Lee and the Second Day at Gettysburg

1. Joan K. Walton and Terry A. Walton, eds., *Letters of LeRoy S. Edwards Written During the War Between the States* (N.p., [1985]), [57]; Arthur James Lyon Fremantle, *Three Months in the Southern States: April–June, 1863* (1863; reprint, Lincoln: Univ. of Nebraska Press, 1991), 231–32.

2. Randolph H. McKim, *A Soldier's Recollections: Leaves from the Diary of a Young Confederate* (1910; reprint, Washington, D.C.: Zenger Publishing, 1983), 182; Stephen Dodson Ramseur to Ellen Richmond, Aug. 3, 1863, folder 7, Stephen Dodson Ramseur Papers, Southern Historical Collection, Wilson Library, University of North Carolina, Chapel Hill, North Carolina (repository hereafter cited as SHC).

3. Robert Garlick Hill Kean, *Inside the Confederate Government: The Diary of Robert Garlick Hill Kean*, ed. Edward Younger (New York: Oxford Univ. Press, 1957), 84; Wade Hampton to Joseph E. Johnston, July 30, 1863, quoted in Herman Hattaway and Archer Jones, *How the North Won: A Military History of the Civil War* (Urbana: Univ. of Illinois Press, 1983), 414.

4. James Longstreet to Augustus Baldwin Longstreet, July 24, 1863, reproduced in part in J. William Jones et al., eds., *Southern Historical Society Papers*, 52 vols. and 3-vol. index (1876–1959; reprint, Wilmington, N.C.: Broadfoot Publishing, 1990–92), 5:54–55 (hereafter cited as *SHSP*). This letter also appeared in the *New Orleans Republican* on Jan. 25, 1876, in the *New York Times* four days later, and in Longstreet's article "The Campaign of Gettysburg" in the *Philadelphia Weekly Times*, Nov. 3, 1877 (the *Weekly Times* article also appeared under the title "Lee in Pennsylvania" in Editors of the *Philadelphia Weekly Times*, *The Annals of the War Written by Leading Participants North and South* [Philadelphia, 1879], 414–46 [the last work cited hereafter as *Annals of the War*]).

5. William Swinton, *Campaigns of the Army of the Potomac: A Critical History of Operations in Virginia, Maryland and Pennsylvania, from the Commencement to the Close of the War, 1861–1865* (1866; rev. ed., New York: Charles Scribner's Sons, 1882), 340–41. Swinton credited "a full and free conversation" with Longstreet as his source for "revelations of the purposes and sentiments of Lee." In Editors of the *Philadelphia Weekly Times*, "Lee in Pennsylvania,"

433, Longstreet used almost precisely the same language as Swinton when he observed: "There is no doubt that General Lee, during the crisis of that campaign, lost the matchless equipoise that usually characterized him, and that whatever mistakes were made were not so much matters of deliberate judgment as the impulses of a great mind disturbed by unparalleled conditions."

6. Edward A. Pollard, *The Lost Cause: A New Southern History of the War of the Confederates* (New York: E. B. Treat and Company, 1866), 406–7. Pollard's assessment of Lee is a bit harsher in his *Lee and His Lieutenants, Comprising the Early Life, Public Services, and Campaigns of General Robert E. Lee and His Companions in Arms, with a Record of Their Campaigns and Heroic Deeds* (New York: E. B. Treat and Company, 1867).

7. James D. McCabe, Jr., *Life and Campaigns of General Robert E. Lee* (St. Louis: National Publishing, 1866), 393–95.

8. Jubal A. Early, *The Campaigns of Gen. Robert E. Lee. An Address by Lieut. General Jubal A. Early, before Washington and Lee University, January 19th, 1872* (Baltimore: John Murphy and Company, 1872), 30–32. Fitzhugh Lee, J. William Jones, and William Nelson Pendleton were among Longstreet's chief critics. For the early arguments in the Gettysburg controversy, see vols. 4–6 of the *SHSP.* Useful modern treatments include Thomas L. Connelly, *The Marble Man: Robert E. Lee and His Image in American Society* (New York: Alfred A. Knopf, 1977); William Garrett Piston, *Lee's Tarnished Lieutenant: James Longstreet and His Place in Southern History* (Athens: Univ. of Georgia Press, 1987); and Glenn Tucker, *Lee and Longstreet at Gettysburg* (Indianapolis: Bobbs-Merrill, 1968.)

9. Frank E. Everett, Jr., "Delayed Report of an Important Eyewitness to Gettysburg—Benjamin G. Humphreys," *The Journal of Mississippi History* 46 (Nov. 1984): 318.

10. U.S. War Department, *The War of the Rebellion: A Compilation of the Official Records of the Union and Confederate Armies,* 127 vols., index, and atlas (Washington, D.C.: GPO, 1880–1901), ser. I, vol. 27, pt. 2:318 (hereafter cited as *OR;* all references are to volumes in Series I).

11. Ibid., 318–19.

12. Robert E. Lee, Jr., *Recollections and Letters of General Robert E. Lee* (1904; reprint, Wilmington, N.C.: Broadfoot Publishing, 1988), 102. Lee wrote to Major William M. McDonald of Berryville, Virginia.

13. Transcript of conversation between R. E. Lee and William Allan, Apr. 15, 1868, pp. 13–15, William Allan Papers, SHC. Lee apparently misconstrued Longstreet's comment about an agreement not to fight an offensive battle, interpreting it as a claim that Lee had agreed to fight no battle at all.

14. Transcript of conversation between R. E. Lee and William Allan, Feb. 18, 1870, pp. 20–21, Williams Allan Papers, SHC.

15. John D. Imboden, "The Confederate Retreat from Gettysburg," in *Battles and Leaders of the Civil War,* ed. Robert Underwood Johnson and Clarence Clough Buel, 4 vols. (New York: Century, 1887), 3:421 (this set hereafter cited

as *B&L*), Henry Heth, "Letter from Major-General Henry Heth, of A. P. Hill's Corps, A.N.V.," in *SHSP* 4:154–55.

16. Fremantle, *Three Months*, 269. For other eyewitness versions of Lee's accepting full responsibility for the defeat while greeting survivors of the Pickett-Pettigrew assault, see Charles T. Loehr, *War History of the Old First Virginia Infantry Regiment, Army of Northern Virginia* (1884; reprint, Dayton, Ohio: Press of Morningside Bookshop, 1978), 38 (Loehr recalls Lee saying to Pickett, "General, your men have done all that men could do, the fault is entirely my own."), and Robert A. Bright, "Pickett's Charge. The Story of It as Told by a Member of His Staff," in *SHSP* 31:234 (Bright has Lee say, "Come, General Pickett, this has been my fight and upon my shoulders rests the blame.").

17. R. E. Lee to Jefferson Davis, Aug. 8, 1863, in *OR*, vol. 51, pt. 2:752. Lee also alluded to public disapproval in his talk with John Seddon: "Major Seddon, from what you have observed, are the people as much depressed at the battle of Gettysburg as the newspapers appear to indicate?" Seddon answered in the affirmative, whereupon Lee stated forcefully that popular sentiment misconstrued events on the battlefield—Fredicksburg and Chancellorsville were hollow victories yet lifted morale, whereas Gettysburg accomplished more militarily but lowered morale. Heth, "Letter from Major-General Henry Heth," 153–54.

18. Heth, "Letter from Major-General Henry Heth," 159–60; Thomas Jewett Goree to James Longstreet, May 17, 1875, in Thomas Jewett Goree, *The Thomas Jewett Goree Letters*, vol. 1, *The Civil War Correspondence*, ed. Langston James Goree V (Bryan, Texas: Family History Foundation, 1981), 285–86. Longstreet asked Goree for his recollections of Gettysburg in a letter of May 12, 1875. A portion of Goree's reply of May 17 (with several errors of transcription) appears on p. 400 of Longstreet's *From Manassas to Appomattox: A Memoir of the Civil War in America* (Philadelphia: J. B. Lippincott, 1896).

19. James Power Smith, "General Lee at Gettysburg," in *Papers of the Military Historical Society of Massachusetts*, 14 vols. and index (1895–1918; reprint, Wilmington, N.C.: Broadfoot Publishing, 1989–90), 5:393. The charge that Lee considered Longstreet slow was common in Lost Cause literature. For example, Fitzhugh Lee's "A Review of the First Two Days' Operations at Gettysburg and a Reply to General Longstreet by Fitzhugh Lee," in *SHSP* 5:193, quotes an unnamed officer who stated that Lee called Longstreet "the hardest man to move I had in my army" and Douglas Southall Freeman, *R. E. Lee: A Biography*, 4 vols. (New York: Charles Scribner's Sons, 1934–36), 3:80, cites W. Gordon McCabe, who in old age remarked to Freeman that Lee had told his son Custis that Longstreet was slow. No direct evidence from Lee's hand supports this contention; however, William Preston Johnston made a memorandum of a conversation with Lee on May 7, 1868, in which he claimed that Lee, in the context of a discussion of the second day of the Battle of the Wilderness, observed that "Longstreet was often slow." William G. Bean, ed., "Memoranda of Conversations Between General Robert E. Lee and William

Preston Johnston, May 7, 1868, and March 18, 1870," *Virginia Magazine of History and Biography* 73 (Oct. 1965):478. Because it is impossible to confirm when Johnston reconstructed his conversations with Lee, his undated memorandum should be used with care.

20. Longstreet, *From Manassas to Appomattox*, 384. The best analysis of Longstreet's part in the Gettysburg controversy is Piston, *Lee's Tarnished Lieutenant*, esp. chaps. 7–9. Piston concludes (p. 150) that "Longstreet's efforts to defend his military reputation had been futile."

21. Edward Porter Alexander, *Fighting for the Confederacy: The Personal Recollections of General Edward Porter Alexander*, ed. Gary W. Gallagher (Chapel Hill, N.C.: Univ. of North Carolina Press, 1989), 277–78. See also idem, *Military Memoirs of a Confederate: A Critical Narrative* (New York: Charles Scribner's Sons, 1907), 387–89.

22. Freeman, *R. E. Lee* 3:81–82.

23. Ibid., 82–84, 159–60. Douglas Southall Freeman offered a significantly different analysis in *Lee's Lieutenants: A Study in Command*, 3 vols. (New York: Charles Scribner's Sons, 1942–44), 3:173–74, finding that Longstreet's "attitude was wrong but his instinct was correct. He should have obeyed orders, but the orders should not have been given."

24. Clifford Dowdey, *Death of a Nation: The Story of Lee and His Men at Gettysburg* (New York: Alfred A. Knopf, 1958), 155, 239–40. The reviewer was Richard B. Harwell, whose blurb appears on the dustjacket of Dowdey's *Lee* (Boston: Little, Brown, 1965).

25. Frank E. Vandiver, "Lee During the War," in *1984 Confederate History Symposium*, ed. D. B. Patterson (Hillsboro, Tex.: Hill Junior College, 1984), 17. Vandiver listed a series of physical factors: "Lee at Gettysburg was infirm, had been thrown from his horse a couple of weeks before and had sprained his hands; he may have been suffering from infectious myocarditis, did have diarrhea and stayed mainly in his tent." There is slim evidence to support such a catalog of ailments.

26. J. F. C. Fuller, *Grant and Lee: A Study in Personality and Generalship* (1933; reprint, Bloomington: Indiana Univ. Press), 197. Fuller disliked Lee's tactical plan because it "depended on the earliest possible attack and the most careful timing to effect co-operation; further, *Lee's* troops were by no means concentrated, and to make things worse he issued no written orders."

27. H. J. Eckenrode and Bryan Conrad, *James Longstreet: Lee's War Horse* (1936; reprint, Chapel Hill: Univ. of North Carolina Press, 1986), 213.

28. Edwin B. Coddington, *The Gettysburg Campaign: A Study in Command* (New York: Charles Scribner's Sons, 1968), 362.

29. Harry W. Pfanz, *Gettysburg: The Second Day* (Chapel Hill: Univ. of North Carolina Press, 1987), 26–27; Alan T. Nolan, *Lee Considered: General Robert E. Lee and Civil War History* (Chapel Hill: Univ. of North Carolina Press, 1991), 98.

30. Walter H. Taylor, *Four Years with General Lee* (1877; reprint, Bloomington: Indiana Univ. Press, 1962), 93.

31. For discussions of Lee on the first day at Gettysburg, see Alan T. Nolan, "R. E. Lee and July 1 at Gettysburg," and Gary W. Gallagher, "Confederate Corps Leadership on the First Day at Gettysburg: A. P. Hill and Richard S. Ewell in a Difficult Debut," in *The First Day at Gettysburg: Essays on Confederate and Union Leadership,* ed. Gary W. Gallagher (Kent, Ohio: Kent State Univ. Press, 1992).

32. The quotations are from the first of Longstreet's three accounts in Editors of the *Philadelphia Weekly Times,* "Lee in Pennsylvania," 421. See also James Longstreet, "Lee's Right Wing at Gettysburg," in *B&L* 3:339–40, and Longstreet, *Manassas to Appomattox,* 358–59. Douglas Southall Freeman, among others who sought to discredit Longstreet, made much of the fact that each of the three narratives employed somewhat different language in recounting this episode. Freeman, *R. E. Lee* 3:74–75. The most important point, however, is that all three versions concur in juxtaposing Longstreet's defensive and Lee's offensive inclinations.

33. Smith, "General Lee at Gettysburg," 391. This account was reprinted under the same title in *SHSP* 33:135–60.

34. James Power Smith, "With Stonewall Jackson in the Army of Northern Virginia," in *SHSP* 43:57–58. Smith presented a slightly different version of the discussion between Lee and Longstreet here, adding: "I was the only other person present at this interview between Lee and Longstreet on the afternoon of the first day of the Battle of Gettysburg." The version cited in the preceding note does not mention Lee's disappointment at Longstreet's reply.

35. G. Moxley Sorrel, *Recollections of a Confederate Staff Officer* (1905; reprint, Wilmington, N.C.: Broadfoot Publishing, 1987), 157; Raphael J. Moses, "Autobiography," pp. 60–61, No. 529, SHC; Fremantle, *Three Months,* 256.

36. The quotation is from Thomas J. Goree to My Dear Mother, July 12, 1862, in Goree, *Goree Letters,* 164. In *Lee and His Lieutenants,* 420, Edward A. Pollard described the relationship between Lee and Longstreet as "not only pleasant and cordial, but affectionate to an almost brotherly degree; an example of beautiful friendship in the war that was frequently remarked by the public."

37. Armistead L. Long to Jubal A. Early, Apr. 5, 1876, reproduced in "Causes of the Defeat of Gen. Lee's Army at the Battle of Gettysburg—Opinions of Leading Confederate Soldiers," in *SHSP* 4:66; transcript of conversation between R. E. Lee and William Allan, Apr. 15, 1868, pp. 13–14, William Allan Papers, SHC; Taylor, *Four Years with General Lee,* 96.

38. Jubal A. Early, "Leading Confederates on the Battle of Gettysburg. A Review by General Early," in *SHSP* 4:271–75. For descriptions of the ground in the official reports of Second Corps officers, see *OR,* vol. 27, pt. 2:445 (Ewell), 469–70 (Early), and 555 (Rodes).

39. Early, "A Review by General Early," 273–74.

40. George Campbell Brown Memoir, pp. 70–71, Brown-Ewell Papers, Tennessee State Library and Archives, Nashville, Tennessee. Brown admitted that he could not fix precisely the time of his meeting with Lee, suggesting that it might even have taken place on the night of July 2. His "strong impression"

was that it was on the night of the first, however, and it seems far more likely that Lee was considering a flanking movement then—with Longstreet's arguments fresh in his mind—rather than after the second day's fighting.

41. Early, "A Review by General Early," 272–73; *OR* vol. 27, pt. 2:446.

42. *OR*, vol. 27, pt. 2:318–19.

43. Jedediah Hotchkiss, *Make Me a Map of the Valley: The Civil War Journal of Stonewall Jackson's Topographer*, ed. Archie P. McDonald (Dallas, Tex.: Southern Methodist Univ. Press, 1973), 157; *OR*, vol. 27, pt. 2:317.

44. Moses, "Autobiography," 61; *OR* vol. 27: 2:318.

45. Alexander, *Fighting for the Confederacy*, 233; David Gregg McIntosh, "Review of the Gettysburg Campaign. By One Who Participated Therein," in *SHSP* 37:140.

46. Jubal A. Early, *Lieutenant General Jubal Anderson Early, C.S.A.: Autobiographical Sketch and Narrative of the War Between the States* (1912; reprint, Wilmington, N.C.: Broadfoot Publishing, 1989), 257–58; George Templeton Strong, *Diary of the Civil War, 1860–1865*, ed. Allan Nevins (New York: Macmillan, 1962), 327.

47. For a sampling of this correspondence, see *OR*, vol. 27, pt. 3:494–508.

48. Alexander, *Fighting for the Confederacy*, 234.

49. Ibid.

50. Gideon Welles, *Diary of Gideon Welles, Secretary of the Navy Under Lincoln and Johnson*, ed. Howard K. Beale, 3 vols. (New York: W. W. Norton, 1960), 1:328, 330.

51. *OR*, vol. 27, pt. 1:61.

52. Heth, "Letter from Major-General Henry Heth," 160; Fremantle, *Three Months*, 256.

53. Justus Scheibert, *Seven Months in the Rebel States During the North American War, 1863*, ed. William Stanley Hoole (Tuscaloosa, Ala.: Confederate Publishing, 1958), 118.

54. Lee, *Recollections and Letters*, 109; *OR*, vol. 27, pt. 2:309.

55. Alexander, *Fighting for the Confederacy*, 91–92.

The Peach Orchard Revisited:
Daniel E. Sickles and the Third Corps on July 2, 1863

1. The most extensive treatment of Sickles's actions at Gettysburg on July 2, 1863, and the debate they provoked is Richard A. Sauers, *A Caspian Sea of Ink: The Meade-Sickles Controversy* (Baltimore, Md.: Butternut and Blue, 1989). Although openly pro-Meade and anti-Sickles, Sauers's work nevertheless is highly useful for its tracing of the controversy over time and its organization of the voluminous materials on the subject.

2. The fullest biographies of Sickles are Edgcumb Pinchon, *Dan Sickles: Hero of Gettysburg and "Yankee King of Spain"* (Garden City, N.Y.: Doubleday, Doran and Company, 1945), and W. A. Swanberg, *Sickles the Incredible* (New

York: Charles Scribner's Sons, 1956). Pinchon is more dramatic, Swanberg more thoroughly researched and dependable. The preceding paragraphs are drawn from Swanberg, *Sickles the Incredible,* 77–87.

3. Swanberg, *Sickles the Incredible,* 88–105.

4. Ibid., 1–76; Pinchon, *Dan Sickles,* 67–137. A prominent member of Sickles's defense team was Edwin M. Stanton, soon to be Lincoln's secretary of war.

5. Swanberg, *Sickles the Incredible,* 106–46. Although troublesome to both men, the arguments between Sickles and Hooker involved relatively petty issues. See Walter H. Hebert, *Fighting Joe Hooker* (Indianapolis: Bobbs-Merrill, 1944), 66–67. One of these altercations led Hooker to write: "In my official intercourse with veteran politicians suddenly raised to high military rank, I have found it necessary to observe their correspondence with especial circumspection." *OR* 5:637. The vote to confirm Sickles's commission was 19 to 18.

6. Swanberg, *Sickles the Incredible,* 146–66. For the performance of Hooker's division, of which Sickles's brigade was a part, in the Peninsula campaign, see Hebert, *Fighting Joe Hooker,* 92–112.

7. Sickles's assignment to command the Third Corps was announced as temporary on February 5, 1863, then made permanent on April 15, 1863. *OR,* vol. 25, pt. 2:51, 211–12. Meade's letters expressing his opinion of Sickles can be found in George Meade, *The Life and Letters of George Gordon Meade,* 2 vols. (New York: Charles Scribner's Sons, 1913), 1:351, 354.

8. Swanberg, *Sickles the Incredible,* 177–90. The classic account of Chancellorsville is John Bigelow, Jr.'s, *The Campaign of Chancellorsville: A Strategic and Tactical Study* (New Haven: Yale Univ. Press, 1910); for portions especially relevant to Sickles's situation, see 279–81, 324–27, 344–46. Sickles's after-action report is in *OR,* vol. 25, pt. 1:384–95. His casualties are listed in ibid., 180. Meade's comment is in Meade, *Life and Letters* 1:373.

9. On the Hooker-Meade disagreement, see Swanberg, *Sickles the Incredible,* 195–96; Hebert, *Fighting Joe Hooker,* 218; Meade, *Life and Letters,* 377–78, 381–82. For Hooker's relief and replacement by Meade, see Hebert, *Fighting Joe Hooker,* 231–46; Freeman Cleaves, *Meade of Gettysburg* (Norman, Okla.: Univ. of Oklahoma Press, 1960), 115–25; and Coddington, *The Gettysburg Campaign,* 130–33.

10. Coddington, *The Gettysburg Campaign,* 210, 218–19; Edward J. Nichols, *Toward Gettysburg: A Biography of General John F. Reynolds* (State College: Pennsylvania State Univ. Press, 1958), 180–82; David M. Jordan, *Winfield Scott Hancock: A Soldier's Life* (Bloomington: Indiana Univ. Press, 1988), 81. Hancock's assignment to command the Second Corps had come only on June 24, 1863. *OR,* vol. 27, pt. 3:299.

11. Coddington, *The Gettysburg Campaign,* 224–28; Sauers, *Caspian Sea of Ink,* 11–12; *OR,* vol. 27, pt. 3:395–96, 399. The rebuke to Sickles can be found in *OR,* vol. 27, pt. 3:399. Coddington argues that Meade was correct in his censure of Sickles but that Hancock did not merit such treatment, even though he also

failed to attain his target and thereby delayed another corps. Coddington, *The Gettysburg Campaign*, 669 n. 99. Although there are some differences in the two cases, it is difficult not to see a double standard at work in the mind of the new army commander.

12. *OR*, vol. 27, pt. 3:420. Again, the tone taken with Sickles is quite different from that taken with other corps commanders, most of whom fell short of Meade's goal for June 29.

13. *OR*, vol. 27, pt. 3:419, 424–25, 458–59, 463–66, 468; Henry Edwin Tremain, *Two Days of War: A Gettysburg Narrative and Other Excursions* (New York: Bonnell, Silver and Bowers, 1905), 1–20; Swanberg, *Sickles the Incredible*, 202–3; Coddington, *The Gettysburg Campaign*, 231–32; Sauers, *Caspian Sea of Ink*, 19–21. The brigades left behind were Col. P. Regis de Trobriand's Third Brigade of the First Division and Col. George C. Burling's Third Brigade of the Second Division.

14. *OR*, vol. 27, pt. 1:482, 531; Sauers, *Caspian Sea of Ink*, 22–24; Swanberg, *Sickles the Incredible*, 204–6.

15. George Gordon Meade, *With Meade at Gettysburg* (Philadelphia: John C. Winston, 1930), 96–100; Sauers, *Caspian Sea of Ink*, 25–27; Coddington, *The Gettysburg Campaign*, 330, 337–41; Pfanz, *Gettysburg: The Second Day*, 58–59. For a division commander's comments on the drafting of the contingency plan, see John Gibbon, *Personal Recollections of the Civil War* (New York: G. P. Putnam's Sons, 1928), 139–40.

16. Meade, *With Meade at Gettysburg*, 100–102; Sauers, *Caspian Sea of Ink*, 27–28; Coddington, *The Gettysburg Campaign*, 343–44; Pfanz, *Gettysburg: The Second Day*, 82–83; *OR*, vol. 27, pt. 1:482, 531.

17. *OR*, vol. 27, pt. 3:486–87; Joint Committee on the Conduct of the War, *Report of the Joint Committee on the Conduct of the War, at the Second Session Thirty-eighth Congress* (Washington, D.C.: GPO, 1865), 1:331–32, 449 (hereafter cited as *CCW*); Meade, *With Meade at Gettysburg*, 105–6; Meade, *Life and Letters* 2:354; Coddington, *The Gettysburg Campaign*, 344; Sauers, *Caspian Sea of Ink*, 29; Pfanz, *Gettysburg: The Second Day*, 60, 93.

18. *CCW* 1:449–50; Henry J. Hunt, "The Second Day at Gettysburg," in *B&L* 3:301–3. Hunt's analysis of Meade's and Sickles's positions is as follows: "The direct short line through the woods, and including the Round Tops, could be occupied, intrenched, and made impregnable to a front attack. But, like that of Culp's Hill, it would be a purely defensive one, from which, owing to the nature of the ground and the enemy's commanding position on the ridges at the angle, an advance in force would be impracticable. The salient line proposed by General Sickles, although much longer, afforded excellent positions for our artillery; its occupation would cramp the movements of the enemy, bring us nearer his lines, and afford us facilities for taking the offensive. It was in my judgment tactically the better line of the two, provided it were strongly occupied, for it was the only one on the field from which we could have passed from the defensive to the offensive with a prospect of decisive results. But General Meade had not, until the arrival of the Sixth Corps, a

sufficient number of troops at his disposal to risk such an extension of his lines; it would have required both the Third and Fifth corps, and left him without any reserve. Had he known that Lee's attack would be postponed until 4 P.M., he might have occupied this line in the morning; but he did not know this, expected an attack at any moment, and, in view of the vast interests involved, adopted a defensive policy, and ordered the occupation of the *safe* line." For a most judicious modern analysis of both the ground and the Sickles-Hunt colloquy, see Pfanz, *Gettysburg: The Second Day*, 93–97.

19. *OR*, vol. 27, pt. 1:482–83, 515, 531–32; *CCW* 1:297–98, 390–91. Humphreys placed the time of his advance at about 4:00 P.M., but this seems much too late. For Sickles's motivation in making the advance, see also Swanberg, *Sickles the Incredible*, 209–11, Coddington, *The Gettysburg Campaign*, 346, Pfanz, *Gettysburg: The Second Day*, 102–3, and Sauers, *Caspian Sea of Ink*, 30, 35–36. The Confederate unit discovered by Berdan was Cadmus M. Wilcox's brigade of R. H. Anderson's division of the Confederate Third Corps, not part of Longstreet's First Corps.

20. *CCW* 1:298–99; Tremain, *Two Days of War*, 56–65; Meade, *With Meade at Gettysburg*, 107–9, 114–15; Coddington, *The Gettysburg Campaign*, 345–46; Sauers, *Caspian Sea of Ink*, 36–38; Swanberg, *Sickles the Incredible*, 212–19; Pfanz, *Gettysburg: The Second Day*, 139–44. The exact details of these Sickles-Meade encounters are hopelessly snarled among the accounts of various participants and partisans. Nevertheless, the results are the same.

21. *CCW* 1:304; Swanberg, *Sickles the Incredible*, 220–35; *OR*, vol. 27, pt. 1:16.

22. *CCW* 1:295–394 (Sickles), 305–12 (Doubleday), 329–58 (Meade), 417–35 (Butterfield), 435–39 (Meade); *OR*, vol. 27, pt. 1:122–39; ibid. 33:3; Swanberg, *Sickles the Incredible*, 247–58; Sauers, *Caspian Sea of Ink*, 41–58. The identity of Historicus is unknown, although he must have been close to Sickles, if not the general himself. W. A. Swanberg believed Sickles to be Historicus, as did Coddington, in *The Gettysburg Campaign*, 721–22 n. 98. For another candidate, John B. Bachelder, see Cleaves, *Meade of Gettysburg*, 229–30.

23. The most exhaustive treatment to date of Sickles's arguments is Sauers, *Caspian Sea of Ink*, and the sources cited therein. Chapters 4 and 5 delineate the postwar development of the controversy and the changing arguments of participants, partisans, and historians. Chapters 6–9 explore Sickles's four main arguments. Sauer's discussion has a strong (and admitted) pro-Meade bias, which on occasion tends to reduce the strength of his case.

24. Although biased against Meade because he believed the army commander had treated him badly at Gettysburg, Major General Abner Doubleday stated the truth before the Joint Committee on the Conduct of the War when he testified: "General Meade is in the habit of violating the organic law of the army to place his personal friends in power." *CCW* 1:311. Few could quarrel with the choice of Reynolds, but Hancock had been only a division commander as late as Chancellorsville and did not outrank those corps commanders placed under his charge by Meade. Of course, Hooker had rewarded his own friends such as Sickles when he had held army command. This natural human practice

nevertheless tended to polarize the Army of the Potomac into warring factions, to the detriment of successful prosecution of the public business.

25. Sickles's testimony and arguments on the weakness of his original position are digested and summarized in Sauers, *Caspian Sea of Ink*, 121–26. This position apparently stretched from Patterson Woods in the north to just beyond the location of the First New Jersey Brigade monument in the south. A walking tour of this area and that immediately in front of it is highly instructive. The ground is indeed low, is partially masked in front, and is clearly lower than the Peach Orchard ridge to the west. Standing in the area just north of the G. Weikert House, it is easy to see why Sickles was so attracted to the Peach Orchard position. The best defensive solution to the terrain puzzle presented to Sickles is elusive even today. An excellent description of the terrain in which Sickles had to operate can be found in Hunt, "The Second Day at Gettysburg," 295–96. As for Meade's inattention to his left, even his biographer finds this lapse to be an error. Cleaves, *Meade of Gettysburg*, 146.

26. Henry J. Hunt's "The Second Day at Gettysburg," 302–3 provides the clearest statement of the issues and a judicious analysis of both protagonists.

27. For the respective frontages of the Second and Third corps, see Sauers, *Caspian Sea of Ink*, 128. Strengths of the two corps are carefully estimated in John W. Busey and David G. Martin, *Regimental Strengths and Losses at Gettysburg* (Hightstown, N.J.: Longstreet House, 1986), 16. In his vigorous attack on Sickles's action, Coddington argued that the Third Corps was actually stronger than the Second Corps. Coddington, *The Gettysburg Campaign*, 725 n. 132. As for Warren, both he and Meade went to the left only in response to Sickles's advance. Had Sickles remained in the position favored by Meade, it is likely that the army commander's focus would have remained on his right. *CCW* 1:377.

"If Longstreet . . . Says So, It Is Most Likely Not True": James Longstreet and the Second Day at Gettysburg

1. *Petersburg Index-Appeal* of undetermined date cited in a clipping in Reel 59, Frame 91, Jedediah Hotchkiss Papers, Library of Congress, Washington, D.C. (repository hereafter cited as LC).

2. Thomas Jewett Goree to his mother, Dec. 14, 1861, in Goree, *Goree Letters*, 111.

3. W. W. Blackford, *War Years with Jeb Stuart* (New York: Charles Scribner's Sons, 1945), 47; diary of Matilda Hamilton of "Prospect Hill," near Fredericksburg, Dec. 28, 1862, typescript in author's possession.

4. A. P. Stewart in "Soldier's Note Book," *Atlanta Journal*, Nov. 13, 1890; *Official Register of the . . . U.S. Military Academy . . . June, 1842* (New York: J. P. Wright, Book, Job and Law Printer, 1842), 8.

5. [Francis Grose], *Advice to the Officers of the British Army* (London: Printed by W. Richardson, 1783), 8; Sir Edward Thornton and James A. Garfield as quoted in William S. McFeely, *Grant: A Biography* (New York: W. W. Norton, 1981), 383, 434.

6. Gallagher's observation quoted above, p. 22; Freeman, *R. E. Lee* 3:331.

7. James Longstreet to Joseph E. Johnston, Oct. 5, 1862, Longstreet Papers, Perkins Library, Duke University, Durham, North Carolina (repository hereafter cited as PLD).

8. Moses, "Autobiography," 54; Sorrel, *Recollections*, 54; James Longstreet to Joseph E. Johnston, Oct. 5, 1862, Longstreet Papers, PLD.

9. Freeman, *Lee's Lieutenants* 2:620 n. 60 (where the year is misdated by typographical error); Cadmus M. Wilcox to E. P. Alexander, March 10, Feb. 6, 1869, Alexander Papers, SHC.

10. Lafayette McLaws to Charles Arnall, Feb. 2, 1897, Roll 34, Hotchkiss Papers, LC.

11. Ibid.; Freeman, *Lee's Lieutenants* 1:259–60.

12. Longstreet, *Manassas to Appomattox*, 196; James Longstreet to T. T. Munford, Nov. 8, 13, 1891, Box 26, Munford-Ellis Family Papers, PLD.

13. James Longstreet to Fitz John Porter, Apr. 1878, Porter Papers, LC; Longstreet, *Manassas to Appomattox*, 187.

14. James Longstreet to Lafayette McLaws, June 3, 1863, McLaws Papers, SHC.

15. James Longstreet, "Lee's Invasion of Pennsylvania," in *B&L* 3:246; James Longstreet, "The Mistakes of Gettysburg," in *Annals of the War*, 620.

16. *OR*, vol. 27, pt. 2:358; John Bell Hood to James Longstreet, June 28, 1875, in *SHSP* 4:148.

17. Undated transcript of Samuel R. Johnston's letter to Lafayette McLaws, in the latter's hand, McLaws Papers, PLD.

18. Ibid.; Alexander, *Fighting for the Confederacy*, 236.

19. Longstreet, "Lee in Pennsylvania," 423; George Campbell Brown Memoir, p. 83; Henry Herbert Harris Diary, July 14, 1863, typescript at Fredericksburg and Spotsylvania National Military Park from original owned by a descendant living in Fredericksburg.

20. Alexander, *Fighting for the Confederacy*, 278; A. L. Long, *Memoirs of Robert E. Lee* (Richmond, Va.: B. F. Johnson & Co., 1886), 281–82.

21. Alexander, *Fighting for the Confederacy*, 237.

22. John Bell Hood to James Longstreet, June 28, 1875, in *SHSP* 4:149.

23. Sorrel, *Recollections*, 169; Longstreet, *Manassas to Appomattox*, 368.

24. Longstreet, *Manassas to Appomattox*, 368.

25. Sorrel, *Recollections*, 157–58.

26. Lafayette McLaws to My Dear Wife, July 7, 1863, McLaws Papers, SHC.

27. For considerable detail on this episode, see Lafayette McLaws to I. R. Pennypacker, July 31, 1888, A. K. Smiley Public Library, Redlands, California. After the war, when it suited him again, Longstreet reclaimed these orders to withdraw as his own.

28. Longstreet, "Lee in Pennsylvania," 414.

29. Undated newspaper clipping, Roll 59, Frame 83, Hotchkiss Papers, LC. Several similar clippings are in adjacent frames of the same source.

30. Lafayette McLaws to Lizzie Ewell, Feb. 29, 1864, Ewell Papers, LC; Lafayette McLaws to Charles Arnall, Feb. 2, 1897, Roll 34, Hotchkiss Papers, LC.

31. The only published summary of the charges is in Robert K. Krick, "The McLaws-Knoxville Court Martial," a short article without notes in *A Collection of Essays Commemorating the 125th Anniversary of the Siege of Knoxville* (Knoxville, Tenn.: Knoxville Civil War Round Table, 1988), 11–14. The important manuscripts are in the McLaws Papers, PLD and SHC.

32. Clifford Dowdey, *The Seven Days: The Emergence of Lee* (Boston: Little, Brown, 1964), 84.

33. Evander M. Law to Lafayette McLaws, Apr. 29, 1864, McLaws Papers, SHC.

34. R. E. Lee to James Longstreet, Jan. 19, 1865, MS 1F1613a2, Virginia Historical Society, Richmond, Virginia.

35. Thomas Miller Ryland Diary, March 19, 1865, typescript in the author's possession from original owned by a descendant in Warsaw; Charles B. Fleet memoir in Elizabeth M. Hodges, *C. B. Fleet: The Man and the Company* [Lynchburg, Va.? 1985?], 42.

36. Transcript of conversation between R. E. Lee and William Allan, Apr. 15, 1868, p. 15, William Allan Papers, SHC.

37. Hunter H. McGuire to Jedediah Hotchkiss, March 30, 1893, Jan. [day illegible], 1897, Roll 34, Hotchkiss Papers, LC.

38. Richard Taylor, *Destruction and Reconstruction* (New York: D. Appleton and Company, 1879), 231.

"A Step All-Important and Essential to Victory": Henry W. Slocum and the Twelfth Corps on July 1-2, 1863

1. Historical image and historical reality can be entirely different. Howard, Sickles, and Schimmelfennig all have their Gettysburg defenders.

2. Charles E. Slocum, *The Life and Services of Major-General Henry Warner Slocum* (Toledo: Slocum Publishing, 1913), 112. Howard made these remarks at a memorial service for Slocum in Plymouth Church, Brooklyn, on April 24.

3. *OR*, vol. 25, pt. 1:185. The corps lost 2,822 men at Chancellorsville.

4. On Slocum's life and military career, see Ezra J. Warner, *Generals in Blue: Lives of the Union Commanders* (Baton Rouge: Louisiana State Univ. Press, 1964), 451–53; *Dictionary of American Biography* 17:216–17 (hereafter cited as *DAB*); and Coddington, *The Gettysburg Campaign*, 45.

5. Slocum, *Life and Services*, 292–93.

6. For information on Williams, see Warner, *Generals in Blue*, 559–60, and *DAB* 20:247–48. Warner speculates that Williams failed to retain corps com-

mand after Antietam because the authorities preferred to reserve such positions for regular army officers. Williams's letters appear in Alpheus S. Williams, *From the Cannon's Mouth: The Civil War Letters of General Alpheus S. Williams*, ed. Milo M. Quaife (Detroit: Wayne State Univ. Press, 1959).

7. *OR*, vol. 25, pt. 2:583; Warner, *Generals in Blue*, 272. Knipe commanded Pennsylvania militia during the Gettysburg campaign; McDougall returned to his regimental command shortly after the battle.

8. Warner, *Generals in Blue*, 415–16. The other Western regiments were the 27th Indiana and 5th, 7th, 29th, and 66th Ohio.

9. J. L. Cornet, "The Twenty-Eighth in Ten States and Twenty-Five Battles," *National Tribune*, Dec. 25, 1886; Warner, *Generals in Blue*, 169–70.

10. Stewart Sifakis, *Who Was Who in the Civil War* (New York: Facts on File, 1988), 104; Roger D. Hunt and Jack R. Brown, *Brevet Brigadier Generals in Blue* (Gaithersburg, Md.: Olde Soldier Books, 1990), 98. Candy's brigade included the 5th, 7th, 29th, and 66th Ohio and the 28th and 147th Pennsylvania.

11. Warner, *Generals in Blue*, 256–57; Hunt and Brown, *Brevet Brigadier Generals in Blue*, 119.

12. William M. Balch, "Did General George S. Greene Win the Civil War at the Battle of Gettysburg?" *National Tribune*, Aug. 20, 1931; Warner, *Generals in Blue*, 186–87; Wayne E. Motts, "To Gain A Second Star: The Forgotten George S. Greene," *Gettysburg: Historical Articles of Lasting Interest* 3 (July 1990):65–67. The only general officer at Gettysburg who had seen more sunrises than Greene was Brig. Gen. William "Extra Billy" Smith, a brigade commander in the Army of Northern Virginia.

13. John W. Busey and David G. Martin, *Regimental Strengths at Gettysburg* (Baltimore: Gateway Press, 1982), 88. Williams reported 3,770 men present in his division on June 30, and Geary stated that he took 3,922 soldiers into the battle. See Coddington, *The Gettysburg Campaign*, 713 n. 186 and *OR*, vol. 27, pt. 1:833.

14. *OR*, vol. 27, pt. 1:758; William F. Fox, "Slocum and His Men. A History of the Twelfth and Twentieth Army Corps," in *In Memoriam Henry Warner Slocum 1826–1894* (Albany, N.Y.: J. B. Lyon, 1904), 174; Williams, *From the Cannon's Mouth*, 224.

15. Oration of Capt. Joseph Matchett in John P. Nicholson, ed., *Pennsylvania at Gettysburg*, 2 vols. (Harrisburg, Pa.: E. K. Meyers, State Printer, 1893), 1:283–84; *OR*, vol. 27, pt. 1:758; ibid., pt. 3:420–21.

16. George K. Collins, *Memoirs of the 149th Regt. N.Y. Vol. Inft.* (Syracuse, N.Y.: Published by the Author, 1891), 133 (first quotation); Matchett in *Pennsylvania at Gettysburg* 1:284 (second quotation); *OR*, vol. 27, pt. 1:796; George A. Thayer, "Gettysburg, As We Men on the Right Saw It," reprinted in Ken Bandy and Florence Freeland, comps., *The Gettysburg Papers*, 2 vols. (Dayton, Ohio: Press of Morningside House, 1978), 2:803; Charles F. Morse, *History of the Second Massachusetts Regiment of Infantry; Gettysburg: A Paper Read at the Officers Reunion in Boston, May 10, 1878* (Boston: George H. Ellis Printer, 1882), 6; William Henry Harrison Tallman, "Memoir," typescript in the vertical files at

Gettysburg National Military Park (repository hereafter cited as GNMP). The precise time of departure and order of march from Littlestown to Two Taverns is difficult to establish. Williams says his troops left their camps "at daylight . . . my division leading." Various Second Division sources report they left Littlestown about 8:00 A.M., but Geary claims to have departed with his troops at 5:00 A.M. See *OR*, vol. 27, pt. 1:825; Williams, *From the Cannon's Mouth*, 224; Richard Eddy, *History of the Sixtieth New York State Volunteers* (Philadelphia: Published by the Author, 1864), 259.

17. Tallman, "Memoir."

18. *OR*, vol. 27, pt. 3:416; Jesse H. Jones, "Saved the Day. Greene's Brigade Behaves Nobly at Gettysburg," *National Tribune*, March 7, 1895 (quotation); Coddington, *The Gettysburg Campaign*, 311.

19. Morse, "History of the Second Massachusetts," 6; Eddy, *History of the Sixtieth New York*, 259; Thayer, "Gettysburg," 803; *OR*, vol. 27, pt. 1:825; Lt. Col. Charles P. Horton to John B. Bachelder, Jan. 23, 1867, typescript in Bachelder Papers, GNMP; Coddington, *The Gettysburg Campaign*, 707 n. 138.

20. Collins, *Memoirs of the 149th Regt.*, 134; Morse, *History of the Second Massachusetts*, 6; Julian Wisner Hinkley, *A Narrative of Service with the Third Wisconsin Infantry* (Madison: Wisconsin History Commission, 1912), 82.

21. Charles P. Horton to John B. Bachelder, Jan. 23, 1867, Bachelder Papers, GNMP; Eddy, *History of the Sixtieth New York*, 259; John Hamilton SeCheverell, *Journal History of the Twenty-Ninth Ohio Veteran Volunteers, 1861–1865* (Cleveland, 1883), 69.

22. Thayer, "Gettysburg," 803; *Maine at Gettysburg: Report of the Maine Commissioners Prepared by the Executive Committee* (Portland, Maine: Lakeside Press, 1898), 520; Henry W. Slocum to Messrs T. H. Davis & Co., Sept. 8, 1875, Samuel P. Bates Papers, copy at GNMP. See also Coddington, *The Gettysburg Campaign*, 311.

23. Edmund R. Brown, *The Twenty-Seventh Indiana Volunteer Infantry in the War of the Rebellion* (Monticello, Ind., 1899), 367; *OR*, vol. 27, pt. 3:463. It is difficult to determine the precise time or even the sequence of arrival for Howard's couriers and the unidentified civilian. Slocum failed to acknowledge the receipt of messages from Howard in his accounts of events at Two Taverns.

24. *OR*, vol. 27, pt. 3:458–59.

25. Slocum received along with the circular a communication from Maj. Gen. Daniel Butterfield, Meade's chief of staff, providing further instructions about executing the withdrawal should Reynolds trigger the movement. Ibid., 462.

26. Coddington, *The Gettysburg Campaign* 311; William F. Fox, "Life of General Slocum," in *In Memoriam Henry Warner Slocum*, 77.

27. Slocum, *Life and Services*, 102 (quotations); Fox, "Life of General Slocum," 78–79. Howard would not have received a copy of the Pipe Creek Circular by the time he sent his messengers.

28. Samuel P. Bates, *The Battle of Gettysburg* (Philadelphia: T. H. Davis & Co., 1875), 93.

29. Henry W. Slocum to Messrs. T. H. Davis & Co., Sept. 8, 1875, copy in Samuel R. Bates Papers, GNMP (first quotation); Coddington, *The Gettysburg Campaign*, 708-9 n. 149 (second quotation); Oliver O. Howard, "Campaign and Battle of Gettysburg," *Atlantic Monthly Magazine* 38 (July 1876):60; Abner Doubleday to Samuel P. Bates, Apr. 24, 1874, Samuel P. Bates Papers, copy at GNMP; Meade, *Life and Letters* 2:249.

30. Coddington, *The Gettysburg Campaign*, 312, 708 n. 142: *OR*, vol. 27, pt. 1:825. William Fox reported that he spoke with the hotel keeper at Two Taverns, a Mr. Snyder, after the battle. Snyder told Fox that Slocum and his staff were at dinner in the hotel when an orderly bearing Howard's dispatch appeared. Slocum read the message and left the table quickly. "In ten minutes they were all gone." It is uncertain if Snyder meant all the officers left the hotel or the entire corps left Two Taverns. Fox implies the latter, although this would have been highly unlikely. Slocum's departure from the hotel would not be tantamount to an instant march by the corps. Fox, "Slocum and His Men," 175-76.

31. Tallman, "Memoir."

32. Collins, *Memoirs of the 149th Regt.*, 134; Samuel Toombs, *Reminiscences of the War* (Orange, N.J.: Printed at the Journal Office, 1878), 72, 74-75; Morse, "History of the Second Massachusetts," 6-7.

33. Slocum, *Life and Services*, 102; Alpheus S. Williams to John B. Bachelder, Nov. 10, 1865, typescript in Bachelder Papers, GNMP. It is puzzling that Slocum would not have heard about Reynolds's death from one of Howard's couriers at Two Taverns.

34. Alpheus S. Williams to John B. Bachelder, Nov. 10, 1865, typescript in Bachelder Papers, GNMP; L. R. Coy to his wife, July 2, 1863, typescript copy in 123d N.Y. file at GNMP; Matchett in *Pennsylvania at Gettysburg* 1:284.

35. Alpheus S. Williams to John B. Bachelder, Nov. 10, 1865, typscript in Bachelder Papers, GNMP; Williams, *From the Cannon's Mouth*, 224-25; *OR*, vol. 27, pt. 1:811. It is curious that Williams would be directed to go to the right when the point of danger in the late afternoon of July 1 clearly lay on Cemetery Hill. Perhaps Slocum acted on information he received from Howard's couriers while en route to Gettysburg and issued before the Federal line collapsed north and west of town. Harry W. Pfanz has identified the road used by Williams to be the one that left the Baltimore Pike at the Horner Farm and led past the Deardorff Farm to the Hanover Road about one mile east of Benner's Hill. See *Atlas to Accompany the Official Records of the Union and Confederate Armies* (Washington, D.C.: GPO, 1891-95), Plate XL. See also Coddington, *The Gettysburg Campaign*, 709 n. 151.

36. *OR*, vol. 27, pt. 1:825, 848. The Second Brigade probably alighted at Powers Hill.

37. *OR*, vol. 27, pt. 1:825, 839; William F. Fox, ed., *New York Monuments Commission for the Battlefields of Gettysburg and Chattanooga. Final Report on*

the Battlefield of Gettysburg, 3 vols. (Albany: J. B. Lyon, Printers, 1900, 1902), 2:634, 1:446–47, 2:628 (hereafter cited as *N.Y. at Gettysburg*); Maj. Moses Veale in *Pennsylvania at Gettysburg* 2:566.

38. Williams, *From the Cannon's Mouth*, 225; OR, vol. 27, pt. 1:773, 777, 811; Hinkley, *Third Wisconsin*, 83–84.

39. Coddington, *The Gettysburg Campaign*, 310, 302, 315. Coddington states that Howard "had a justifiable grievance against General Henry W. Slocum" for being "unnecessarily slow" on July 1. However, he adds that it was "questionable whether Slocum could have pushed on to Gettysburg in time to affect the outcome of the battle on July 1 even if he had not hesitated in his movements." The Twelfth Corps covered the four miles from its bivouacs north of Two Taverns to Rock Creek in less than two hours. Had Slocum ordered a departure when first notified of the battle at Gettysburg, it is reasonable to believe that Williams could have reached Cemetery and East Cemetery hills by 4:00 P.M. and supplemented Col. Orland Smith's Eleventh Corps brigade, which served as a lonely anchor around which the First and Eleventh corps rallied. Of course, had Slocum investigated the sounds of battle prior to the arrival of messengers at Two Taverns, the corps could have appeared at Gettysburg earlier.

40. OR, vol. 27, pt. 1:703; Oliver Otis Howard, *Autobiography of Oliver Otis Howard*, 2 vols. (New York: Baker & Taylor, 1908), 1:416. Although Howard's first message may be considered implicit, there is no question that the communication carried by Capt. Daniel Hall at 2:45 P.M. clearly called for Slocum's help. See Charles W. Howard, "The First Day at Gettysburg," in Military Order of the Loyal Legion of the United States, Illinois Commandery, *Papers* 4 (Chicago: Cozzens & Beaton, 1907), 253–54; OR, vol. 27, pt. 1:126.

41. Howard, "The First Day at Gettysburg," 258.

42. Col. C. H. Morgan's "Statement," typescript in Bachelder Papers, GNMP.

43. Edwin Eustace Bryant, *History of the Third Regiment of Wisconsin Veteran Volunteer Infantry* (Madison, Wisc.: Published by the Veteran Association of the Regiment, 1891), 183–84; Lewis A. Stegman, "Slocum at Gettysburg," *National Tribune*, June 17, 1915; Coddington, *The Gettysburg Campaign*, 313. For Slocum's explanation, see Howard's report in OR, vol. 27, pt. 1:704.

44. Morgan, "Statement"; OR, vol. 27, pt. 1:696, 704. Hancock stated that Slocum arrived between 5:00 and 6:00 P.M.; Howard placed the time at about 7:00 P.M. See OR, vol. 27, pt. 1:368–69, 704.

45. There is some question about Slocum's position subsequent to Meade's arrival. Clearly, he no longer commanded the army. Williams stated that in the late afternoon of July 1 he "had been notified that I was in command of the 12th Corps, Gen. Slocum temporarily taking command of the right wing, in place of Reynolds." At 9:20 P.M. Slocum sent a message to Meade as commander of the Twelfth Corps. At 3:40 A.M. on July 2, Slocum communicated to Williams instructing that officer to advance his "division." It appears that Slocum considered himself back in charge of the Twelfth Corps, and not a wing, during the predawn hours of July 2. Williams, *From the Cannon's Mouth*, 225; OR, vol. 27, pt. 3:468, 484.

46. Oration of Rev. J. Richards Boyle, in *Pennsylvania at Gettysburg* 2:592–93; *OR*, vol. 27, pt. 1:846–49; "Notes of a Conversation with General Kane," typescript in Bachelder Papers, GNMP.

47. Geary stated that "at 5 A.M. on the 2d, having been relieved by the Third Army Corps . . . the division was placed on the right of the main line of battle." Col. John H. Patrick of the 5th Ohio, also in command of the 147th Pennsylvania at this time, reported that he received orders at 5:00 A.M. from his brigade commander, Col. Candy, to "return to the brigade" from their advanced positions west of Little Round Top. This would suggest that Geary received orders to move prior to 5:00 A.M. Col. Henry A. Barnum of the 149th New York says that the division began its march at 4:00 A.M., but this seems too early. Sunrise on July 2 came at 4:15 A.M. *OR*, vol. 27, pt. 1:825, 839, 868; Pfanz, *Gettysburg: The Second Day*, 58.

48. Elevations and distances may be calculated from the U.S. Geological Survey topographical maps. Coddington, *The Gettysburg Campaign*, 330; *OR*, vol. 27, pt. 2:504. Except for a thicker understory today, the area looks much as it did in 1863.

49. Collins, *Memoirs of the 149th Regt.*, 136; Jones, "Saved the Day."

50. Motts, "To Gain a Second Star," 68. The 60th New York initially occupied Greene's left, but shortly after the original deployment a portion of the 78th New York moved to the 60th's left. The rest of the 78th New York served on the picket line near Rock Creek. *OR*, vol. 27, pt. 1:860, 862–63. Busey and Martin, *Regimental Strengths at Gettysburg*, 96, credit Greene's brigade with 1,350 men. The ravine below Greene's right is still readily discernable on the ground.

51. Moses Veale in *Pennsylvania at Gettysburg* 2:566–67; *OR*, vol. 27, pt. 1:854. Regimental monuments and markers on Culp's Hill, though not infallible, are of some use when placing regiments on the ground. Busey and Martin, *Regimental Strengths at Gettysburg*, 95, give Kane's strength as nine hundred; *OR*, vol. 27, pt. 1:833, credits the brigade with only seven hundred men in the engagement.

52. Henry E. Brown, *The 28th Regt. P.V.V.I., The 147th Regt. P.V.V.I., and Knap's Ind. Battery "E." at Gettysburg, July 1,2,3, 1863* (N.p., n.p.: 1892), 5; J. L. Cornet, "The Twenty-Eighth in Ten States," *National Tribune*, Dec. 25, 1886; *OR*, vol. 27, pt. 1:836.

53. Williams, *From the Cannon's Mouth*, 226; *OR*, vol. 27, pt. 1:773, 777–78; Alpheus S. Williams to John B. Bachelder, Nov. 10, 1865, typescript in Bachelder Papers, GNMP. The Fifth Corps division that supported Williams belonged to Brig. Gen. James Barnes.

54. *OR*, vol. 27, pt. 1:778, 783. McDougall stated that his brigade did not leave for its new position until 11:00 A.M. Morse, "The Twelfth Corps at Gettysburg," in Military Order of the Loyal Legion of the United States, Massachusetts Commandery, *Papers* 14 (1918; reprint, Wilmington, N.C.: Broadfoot Publishing, 1990), 23, describes the swale as follows: "This so-called swale was a low, flat meadow, about a hundred yards wide, between the two rocky,

wooded hills. Through this swale trickled a small stream, at that time nearly dry, which flowed into Rock Creek." The regimental positions behind the stone wall are given in *OR*, vol. 27, pt. 1:800. The regimental order on the front line is probably correct and conforms with the regimental monuments on the field.

55. Byrant, *History of the Third Regiment*, 185; *OR*, vol. 27, pt. 1:819; Edmund J. Raus, Jr., *A Generation on the March—The Union Army at Gettysburg* (Lynchburg, Va.: H. E. Howard, 1987), 76. For a synopsis of Carman's contributions to Antietam historiography, see Stephen W. Sears, *Landscape Turned Red: The Battle of Antietam* (New Haven: Ticknor & Fields, 1983), 373.

56. Thayer, "Gettysburg," 806; Morse, "The Twelfth Corps at Gettysburg," 23; Morse, "History of the Second Massachusetts," 7; *OR*, vol. 27, pt. 1:815, 823; Bryant, *History of the Third Regiment*, 185; Brown, *The Twenty-Seventh Indiana*, 370. Most of the battlefield tablets refer to the small rocky knoll south of the swale as "McAllister's Woods," although few of the memoirs or contemporary accounts assign it any specific name.

57. Sifakis, *Who Was Who*, 391–92.

58. *OR*, vol. 27, pt. 1:775; pt. 3:496–97; Pfanz, *Gettysburg: The Second Day*, 62–63; Raus, *A Generation on the March*, 29, 84; Busey and Martin, *Regimental Strengths at Gettysburg*, 92; *N.Y. at Gettysburg* 3:1030. Although the two Maryland regiments had been in service since mid-1861, only the 1st Maryland Potomac Home Brigade had seen any action and this of a limited nature. For a summary of the brigade's combat history prior to the Gettysburg Campaign, see John C. Burns, "Maryland and the Struggle for the Union Right at Gettysburg," 11–12, typescript dated 1973, GNMP.

59. Stephen G. Cook and Charles E. Benton, eds., *The "Dutchess County Regiment" in the Civil War* (Danbury, Conn.: Danbury Medical Printing Co., 1907), 22, 26; *N.Y. at Gettysburg* 3:1032; John H. Shane, "Getting into the Fight at Gettysburg," *National Tribune*, Nov. 27, 1924.

60. Cook and Benton, *The "Dutchess County Regiment,"* 27, 29–30; *N.Y. at Gettysburg* 3:1032–33, 1039; Henry J. Hunt, "The Second Day at Gettysburg," in *B&L* 3:294; Williams, *From the Cannon's Mouth*, 227; Alpheus S. Williams to John B. Bachelder, Apr. 7, 1864, typescript in Bachelder Papers, GNMP.

61. *OR*, vol. 27, pt. 1:870; Burns, "Maryland and the Union Right at Gettysburg," 13. For Meade's role in determining the Twelfth Corps deployment on the morning of July 2, see *OR*, vol. 27, pt. 1:759.

62. *OR*, vol. 27, pt. 3:486–87; Coddington, *The Gettysburg Campaign*, 337; Hunt, "The Second Day at Gettysburg," 297; Toombs, *Reminiscences*, 75; Fox, "A History of the Twelfth and Twentieth Army Corps," 177–78.

63. Analyzing the command structure of the Twelfth Corps on the morning of July 2 can be a thorny undertaking. Although it may be argued that Slocum retained his position as a "wing commander" assigned him by Meade's Pipe Creek Circular on July 1, the circumstances anticipated by the circular never occurred, so Slocum did not exercise wing authority on July 1. Meade's communications to Slocum on the morning of July 2 addressed him as Twelfth

Corps commander, not a wing leader, and Slocum responded in like fashion. See *OR*, vol. 27, pt. 3:486–87. General Ruger indirectly supported this understanding in ibid., pt. 1:778.

64. Brown, *The Twenty-Seventh Indiana*, 369; *OR*, vol. 27, pt. 1:778, 811–12, 815; Raus, *A Generation on the March*, 20.

65. Alpheus S. Williams to John B. Bachelder, Apr. 21, 1864, typescript in Bachelder papers, GNMP; Williams, *From the Cannon's Mouth*, 228.

66. Collins, *Memoirs of the 149th Regt.*, 137; Jones, "Saved the Day"; *In Memoriam George Sears Greene Brevet Major-General, United States Volunteers, 1801–1899* (Albany, N.Y.: J. B. Lyon, State Printers, 1909), 42. Geary mentioned nothing about hesitating to authorize construction of the works but stated instead that "breastworks were immediately thrown up along our entire line." *OR*, vol. 27, pt. 1:826.

67. Collins, *Memoirs of the 149th Regt.*, 137; Jones, "Saved the Day"; Balch, "General George S. Greene"; Charles P. Horton to John B. Bachelder, Jan. 23, 1867, typescript in Bachelder papers, GNMP. Harry Pfanz called my attention to the fact that elements of Brig. Gen. James S. Wadsworth's division of the First Corps built earthworks on Culp's Hill during the evening of July 1. This circumstance reduces the innovation, if not the correctness, of Greene's desire to fortify his line.

68. Charles P. Horton to John B. Bachelder, Jan. 23, 1867, typescript in Bachelder Papers, GNMP; Collins, *Memoirs of the 149th Regt.*, 137; McKim, *A Soldier's Recollections*, 197.

69. *OR*, vol. 27, pt. 1:847, 849, 854; "Notes of a Conversation with General Kane," GNMP.

70. *OR*, vol. 27, pt. 1:773, 783, 798, 803; Henry C. Morhous, *Reminiscences of the 123d Regiment, New York State Volunteers* (Greenwich, N.Y: People's Journal Book and Job Office, 1879), 47; John W. Storrs, *The Twentieth Connecticut* (Naugatuck, Conn.: Press of the Naugatuck Valley Sentinel, 1886), 82–83.

71. Williams, *From the Cannon's Mouth*, 226; *OR*, vol. 27, pt. 1:773, 778, 812; Morse, "The Twelfth Corps at Gettysburg," 24.

72. Thayer, "Gettysburg," 807 (quotation); Morse, "History of the Second Massachusetts," 8; Collins, *Memoirs of the 149th Regt.*, 138; Storrs, *The Twentieth Connecticut*, 83.

73. Coddington, *The Gettysburg Campaign*, 367; Hunt, "The Second Day at Gettysburg," 293–94.

74. Busey and Martin, *Regimental Strengths at Gettysburg*, 151; *OR*, vol. 27, pt. 2:286.

75. *OR*, vol. 27, pt. 2:543; Burns, "Maryland and the Union Right at Gettysburg," 14–15; Robert K. Krick, *Lee's Colonels* (Dayton, Ohio: Press of Morningside Bookshop, 1979), 212.

76. *OR*, vol. 27, pt. 2:543; Burns, "Maryland and the Union Right at Gettysburg," 15–16; Bryant, *History of the Third Regiment*, 186; *OR*, vol. 27, pt. 1:863.

77. Coddington, *The Gettysburg Campaign*, 428; *OR*, vol. 27, pt. 1:826, 870, 899.

78. *In Memoriam, George Sears Greene*, 40; *OR*, vol. 27, pt. 1:863, 773, 870; Bryant, *History of the Third Regiment*, 186–87; Coddington, *The Gettysburg Campaign*, 428; *OR*, vol. 27, pt. 2:544. Capt. Charles I. Raine replaced Latimer, who died on August 1.

79. See Pfanz, *Gettysburg: The Second Day*, for the definitive study of Long-street's assaults against Sickles.

80. *OR*, vol. 27, pt. 3:489; Henry W. Slocum to Messrs. T. H. Davis & Co., Sept. 8, 1875, copy in Samuel P. Bates Papers, GNMP (Slocum responded to Samuel P. Bates's *The Battle of Gettysburg*, 191); *N.Y. at Gettysburg* 3:1335; *In Memoriam, George Sears Greene*, 41, 85; Fox, "A History of the Twelfth and Twentieth Army Corps," 178. Coddington, *The Gettysburg Campaign*, 764 n. 115, was among the first historians to analyze Slocum's actions carefully as well as critically.

81. Alpheus S. Williams to John B. Bachelder, Apr. 21, 1864, Nov. 10, 1865, typescripts in Bachelder Papers, GNMP.

82. Henry W. Slocum to Messrs. T. H. Davis & Co., Sept. 8, 1875, copy at GNMP.

83. *OR*, vol. 27, pt. 1:826.

84. Charles P. Horton to John B. Bachelder, Jan. 23, 1867, typescript in the Bachelder Papers, GNMP. Horton placed the Confederate attack against Culp's Hill considerably earlier than most other witnesses, calling into question the accuracy of his account.

85. Ibid.; Henry W. Slocum to Messrs. T. H. Davis & Co., Sept. 8, 1875, copy at GNMP.

86. Alpheus S. Williams to John B. Bachelder, Apr. 21, 1864, Nov. 10, 1865, typescripts in Bachelder Papers, GNMP; Morse, "The Twelfth Corps at Get-tysburg," 26; *OR*, vol. 27, pt. 1:783; L. R. Coy to his wife, July 2, 1863, typescript copy in 123d New York file, GNMP; Williams, *From the Cannon's Mouth*, 228.

87. Williams, *From the Cannon's Mouth*, 228; Coddington, *The Gettysburg Campaign*, 418, 757 n. 51.

88. Morhous, *123rd Regiment, New York*, 48; *N.Y. at Gettysburg* 2:858; Morse, "History of the Second Massachusetts," 8–9. This woman was the same "crone" who encouraged the Third Brigade as it marched into position in the morning (see reference to Bryant in note 55). It is possible that this episode occurred after Ruger's division reached Cemetery Ridge.

89. Alpheus S. Williams to John B. Bachelder, Nov. 10, 1865, typescript in Bachelder Papers, GNMP; *OR*, vol. 27, pt. 1:804; Coddington, *The Gettysburg Campaign*, 757 n. 51; Burns, "Maryland and the Union Right at Gettysburg," 18.

90. Alpheus S. Williams to John B. Bachelder, Nov. 10, 1865, typescript in Bachelder Papers, GNMP; Williams, *From the Cannon's Mouth*, 228; *OR*, vol. 27, pt. 1:774; Morse, "The Twelfth Corps at Gettysburg," 27; *N.Y. at Gettysburg* 3:1042. McGilvery and Williams had served together at Cedar Mountain in 1862.

91. *OR*, vol. 27, pt. 1:804, 809; *N.Y. at Gettysburg* 3:1043; Williams, *From the Cannon's Mouth*, 228. In his official report, Williams implied that Lockwood did form a line of battle. *OR*, vol. 27, pt. 1:774. See Pfanz, *Gettysburg: The Second Day*, 408–9, for a summary of this action.

92. *OR*, vol. 27, pt. 1:766, 804–6; Cook and Benton, "The Dutchess County Regiment," 32. See Pfanz, *Gettysburg: The Second Day*, 341–46, for a description of the capture of Bigelow's guns.

93. *OR*, vol. 27, pt. 1:766, 774, 804; Morse, "The Twelfth Corps at Gettysburg," 27; Alpheus S. Williams to John B. Bachelder, Nov. 10, 1865, typescript in Bachelder Papers, GNMP; Jeffrey G. Charnley, "Neglected Honor: The Life of General A. S. Williams of Michigan (1810–1878)," (Ph.D. diss., Michigan State Univ., 1983), 188–89; Coddington, *The Gettysburg Campaign*, 419.

94. In *OR*, vol. 27, pt. 1:371, Maj. Gen. Winfield S. Hancock testified that "General Meade brought up in person a part of the Twelfth Corps, consisting of two regiments of Lockwood's brigade." However, neither Williams nor Lockwood mentioned Meade's presence before the advance and Meade himself claimed no such credit. In *The Gettysburg Campaign*, 758 n. 57, Coddington postulates that although Hancock knew both Meade and Williams well, in the smoke of battle Hancock or one of his staff officers probably confused Williams with the army commander due to their superficial physical similarities.

95. *OR*, vol. 27, pt. 1:826. Candy's brigade in reserve on Culp's Hill would have been closer to the Baltimore Pike than Cobham's brigade. The accounts of this march imply but do not specify that Candy took the lead.

96. *OR*, vol. 27, pt. 1:759; Bryant, *History of the Third Regiment*, 189; Morse, "The Twelfth Corps at Gettysburg," 26.

97. *OR*, vol. 27, pt. 1:826; Coddington, *The Gettysburg Campaign*, 764 n. 118. See Alpheus S. Williams to John B. Bachelder, Nov. 10, 1865, typescript in Bachelder Papers, GNMP, and *OR*, vol. 27, pt. 1:774 for possible origins of this order.

98. Coddington, *The Gettysburg Campaign*, 433–34. Capt. Horton testified that "staff officers and orderlies were sent in all directions to find the missing force." But the delay in doing so speaks either to the timeliness or efficiency of these searchers. Charles P. Horton to John B. Bachelder, Jan. 23, 1867, typescript in Bachelder Papers, GNMP.

99. *OR*, vol. 27, pt. 2:504; Coddington, *The Gettysburg Campaign*, 430. Coddington describes Johnson's position as being "in the triangular shaped area between the York and Hanover roads and about a mile from Culp's Hill. Jones's brigade moved forward about half a mile when it was detached to support the artillery." Coddington, *The Gettysburg Campaign*, 762 n. 105.

100. See *OR*, vol. 27, pt. 2:446–47, 504, and Coddington, *The Gettysburg Campaign*, 428–29, 762 n. 101. In *In Memoriam, George Sears Greene*, 44–45, Capt. Lewis R. Stegman argues that when the Union skirmish line was weakened to prepare for the move to Cemetery Ridge, Confederate officers must

have reported the departure to their superiors resulting in Johnson's attack on Culp's Hill. Stegman offers no evidence to support his opinion.

101. *OR*, vol. 27, pt. 2:504, 518–19; pt. 1:956. The Union cavalry belonged to Brig. Gen. David McMurtrie Gregg, commander of the Second Division.

102. *OR*, vol. 27, pt. 2:447; Burns, "Maryland and the Union Right at Gettysburg," 23. A dam across Rock Creek near McAllister's Mill had flooded some of the creek upstream into a virtual millpond. For a reference to the pond, see *OR*, vol. 27, pt. 1:856.

103. *OR*, vol. 27, pt. 1:862, 865, pt. 2:504; *In Memoriam, George Sears Greene*, 43; *N.Y. at Gettysburg* 2:627; Balch, "General George S. Greene." Von Hammerstein was a twenty-seven-year-old German native and veteran of the Austrian army. Raus, *A Generation on the March*, 71.

104. *In Memoriam, George Sears Greene*, 43–44; Jesse H. Jones, "The Breastworks at Culp's Hill," in *B&L* 3:316.

105. *OR*, vol. 27, pt. 1:731, 856; *In Memoriam, George Sears Greene*, 86–87, 47; Morse, "The Twelfth Corps at Gettysburg," 28; Coddington, *The Gettysburg Campaign*, 431, 763 n. 108. Greene neglected to mention the 157th New York of the Eleventh Corps as coming to his assistance, but Maj. Gen. Carl Schurz specifically did so in his report. The total number of reinforcements comes from Greene, but such precise tabulations should be used with some caution. The other regiments involved were the 6th Wisconsin, 14th Brooklyn (84th New York), 147th New York, 82d Illinois, 61st Ohio, and 45th New York. Heavy casualties on July 1 had reduced the strength of these regiments.

106. *OR*, vol. 27, pt. 2:513; *In Memoriam, George Sears Greene*, 45–46. Map 9 in Coddington, *The Gettysburg Campaign*, between 412 and 413 reverses Jones and Nicholls (Williams), a mistake repeated on other Gettysburg maps. Johnson's regiments included the 10th, 21st, 23d, 25th, 37th, 42d, 44th, 48th, and 50th Virginia, First Maryland Battalion, 1st and 3d North Carolina, and 1st, 2d, 10th, 14th, and 15th Louisiana regiments.

107. Charles P. Horton to John B. Bachelder, Jan. 23, 1867, typescript in Bachelder Papers, GNMP.

108. Ibid.; Collins, *Memoirs of the 149th Regt.*, 138; Jesse H. Jones, "A Story of the Fierce Fighting on the Right at Gettysburg," *National Tribune*, June 6, 1901.

109. Charles P. Horton to John B. Bachelder, Jan. 23, 1867, typescript in Bachelder Papers, GNMP.

110. S. Z. Ammen, "Maryland Troops in the Confederacy," unattributed newspaper articles, photocopies in the possession of Harry W. Pfanz; Fox, "A History of the Twelfth and Twentieth Army Corps," 179; *OR*, vol. 27, pt. 1:826, 856, 866; *N.Y. at Gettysburg* 1:451.

111. Coddington, *The Gettysburg Campaign*, 427, 761 n. 95. Brig. Gen. John Gibbon received Hancock's order and passed it along to Brig. Gen. Alexander S. Webb, who selected the 71st and 106th Pennsylvania regiments from his brigade.

112. George S. Greene, "The Breastworks at Culp's Hill," in B&L 3:317; OR, vol. 27, pt. 1:826, 866; Charles P. Horton to John B. Bachelder, Jan. 23, 1867, typescript in Bachelder Papers, GNMP. Horton claimed that Smith told him he had received orders to return the 71st Pennsylvania to its position with the Second Corps. Smith made no such claim in his report, and in fact stated he returned to camp "against orders." OR, vol. 27, pt. 1:432. In The Gettysburg Campaign, 431, Coddington observes that "the disappearance of the 71st Pennsylvania in no way affected the outcome of the struggle."

113. OR, vol. 27, pt. 1:866–88; Charles P. Horton to John B. Bachelder, Jan. 23, 1867, typescript in Bachelder Papers, GNMP; Winfield Peters, "A Maryland Warrior and Hero," in SHSP 29:247; Coddington, The Gettysburg Campaign, 431–32; Collins, Memoirs of the 149th Regt., 139; N.Y. at Gettysburg 2:689.

114. Typical Confederate claims that the Federal works were carried by storm are in McKim, A Soldier's Recollections, 198, and OR, vol. 27, pt. 2:504; for a Union rejoinder, see Charles P. Horton to John B. Bachelder, Jan. 23, 1867, typescript in Bachelder Papers, GNMP. The 137th lost 137 men at Gettysburg, as many as the 149th, 60th, and 78th combined. The brigade experienced some losses on July 3, but most of the casualties in the 137th came on July 2. OR, vol. 27, pt. 1:185.

115. OR, vol. 27, pt. 1:868, 763, 861, 764 (second quotation); Eddy, History of the Sixtieth New York, 261; Collins, Memoirs of the 149th Regt., 143 (first quotation). Few Union defenders performed more memorably than Color Sgt. William C. Lilly of the 149th, who repeatedly spliced his unit's fractured flagstaff and raised the tattered banner during the fighting. Lilly's gallant determination is memorialized in bronze relief on the regiment's monument on Culp's Hill.

116. Balch, "General George S. Greene"; John O. Foering in Pennsylvania at Gettysburg 1:189–90.

117. Eugene Powell, "Rebellion's High Tide Dashed Against the Immovable Rocks of Gettysburg. The Splendid Work on Culp's Hill by the 12th Corps," in National Tribune, July 5, 1900 (quotation); In Memoriam, George Sears Greene, 46; Alexander, Fighting for the Confederacy, 243; Slocum, Life and Services, 107. For other opinions about the consequences of Johnson's victory that night, see Morse, "The Twelfth Corps at Gettysburg," 28–29; Jones, "The Breastworks at Culp's Hill," in B&L 3:316; Greene, "The Breastworks at Culp's Hill," in B&L 3:317; McKim, A Soldier's Recollections, 198–99; Fox, "Life of Slocum," 81; and Motts, "To Gain a Second Star," 65.

118. Coddington, The Gettysburg Campaign, 432–33. Most assertions that Ewell missed an opportunity at Gettysburg concern July 1.

119. OR, vol. 27, pt. 1:759, 761, 778, 780; Alpheus S. Williams to John B. Bachelder, Apr. 21, 1864, typescript in Bachelder Papers, GNMP, Williams, From the Cannon's Mouth, 228.

120. OR, vol. 27, pt. 1:780, 813; Morse, "The Twelfth Corps at Gettysburg," 30; Morse, "History of the Second Massachusetts," 9–10; Toombs, Reminiscenses, 79.

121. Morse, "The Twelfth Corps at Gettysburg," 30–32; *OR*, vol. 27, pt. 1:816–17, 820; Alonzo H. Quint, *The Record of the Second Massachusetts Infantry, 1861–65* (Boston: James P. Walker, 1867), 179–80; George A. Thayer, "On the Right at Gettysburg. A Survivor's Story of the Gallant But Unavailing Charge by the 2nd Mass. Infantry," *National Tribune*, July 24, 1902.

122. *OR*, vol. 27, pt. 1:783, 790–91; *N.Y. at Gettysburg* 2:858; Morhous, *123rd Regiment, New York*, 48; Matchett in *Pennsylvania at Gettysburg* 1:285; Storrs, *The Twentieth Connecticut*, 88. Storrs describes a full-blown battle around Spangler's Spring, a claim unsubstantiated by other evidence.

123. L. R. Coy to his wife, Sarah, July 6, 1863, typescript, GNMP; *OR*, vol. 27, pt. 1:774–75. See *OR*, vol. 27, pt. 1:780, for a slightly different regimental order.

124. *OR*, vol. 27, pt. 1:806, 809–10; *N.Y. at Gettysburg* 3:1033, 1040.

125. *OR*, vol. 27, pt. 1:827. Geary probably placed the time of this order somewhat early.

126. Ibid., 827–28, 847, 849, 851, 854, 857, 836; *Pennsylvania at Gettysburg* 1:204, 2:593; "Notes of a Conversation with General Kane"; William Rickards to John B. Bachelder, Apr. 12, 1864, typescript in Bachelder Papers, GNMP; Coddington, *The Gettysburg Campaign*, 434–35, 765 n. 121; Greene, "Breastworks at Culp's Hill," 317; Collins, *Memoirs of the 149th Regt.*, 140.

127. Alpheus S. Williams to John B. Bachelder, Nov. 10, 1865, typescript in Bachelder Papers, GNMP. Meade would later forget that he had sent for Williams, or perhaps the staff officer invited Williams on his own accord.

128. Slocum, *Life and Services*, 109; Brown, *The Twenty-Seventh Indiana*, 376. See Coddington, *The Gettysburg Campaign*, 449–53, for a description of the council.

129. Williams, *From the Cannon's Mouth*, 229; *OR*, vol. 27, pt. 1:775, 870; Fox, "A History of the Twelfth and Twentieth Army Corps," 181; Coddington, *The Gettysburg Campaign*, 466–68.

130. Meade's report is in *OR*, vol. 27, pt. 1:114–19.

131. Williams, *From the Cannon's Mouth*, 272; Coddington, *The Gettysburg Campaign*, 772–73 n. 57. Slocum had written Col. Joseph Howland on July 17, 1863, that he thought highly of Meade and hoped that "he will continue to do as well as he has thus far." Miscellaneous Manuscripts of Col. Joseph Howland, New York Historical Society. Coddington believes that Maj. Gen. Daniel Butterfield, a Sickles partisan and inveterate critic of Meade's generalship at Gettysburg, probably influenced Slocum against Meade when Butterfield and Slocum served together in Tennessee during the winter of 1863–64.

132. *OR*, vol. 27, pt. 1:764–65; Henry W. Slocum to LeRoy H. Morgan, quoted in Williams, *From the Cannon's Mouth*, 284–87.

133. *OR*, vol. 27, pt. 1:769–70; Alpheus S. Williams to John B. Bachelder, Nov. 10, 1865, typescript in Bachelder Papers, GNMP; Coddington, *The Gettysburg Campaign*, 773 n. 57.

"No Troops on the Field Had Done Better":
John C. Caldwell's Division in the Wheatfield, July 2, 1863

The author is deeply indebted to Col. Terrance McClain (U.S. Army, Ret.) for his keen insight into the challenge of command in combat, and to Eric A. Campbell for making available all of his files on Caldwell's division at Gettysburg.

1. Undated statement by C. H. Morgan to John B. Bachelder, Bachelder Papers, New Hampshire Historical Society, Concord, New Hampshire (hereafter cited as Bachelder Papers, NHHS).

2. Busey and Martin, *Regimental Strengths at Gettysburg*, 242.

3. J. W. Stuckenberg Diary, Gettysburg College Library (repository hereafter cited as GCL).

4. Robert L. Brake, "List of Staff Officers, Army of the Potomac at the Battle of Gettysburg," GNMP. Included on Caldwell's staff were ambulance and ordnance officers, neither of whom accompanied him into battle.

5. Dean Thomas, *Ready, Aim, Fire: Small Arms Ammunition in the Battle of Gettysburg* (Gettysburg, Pa.: Thomas Publications, 1981), 60.

6. John P. Nicholson, ed., *Pennsylvania at Gettysburg: Ceremonies at the Dedication of the Monuments Erected by the Commonwealth of Pennsylvania*, 2 vols. (Harrisburg, Pa.: William S. Ray, State Printer, 1904), 1:727; *OR*, vol. 27, pt. 1:379.

7. Josiah M. Favill, *Diary of a Young Officer* (Chicago: R. R. Donnelly & Sons, 1909), 244–45; Nicholson, *Pennsylvania at Gettysburg* 1:683; Francis A. Walker, *History of the Second Army Corps in the Army of the Potomac* (New York: Charles Scribner's Sons, 1886), 543.

8. Nicholson, *Pennsylvania at Gettysburg* 1:622–23.

9. The need to coordinate the various units on the Union left eventually became apparent to Meade, who placed Hancock in command of both the Second and Third corps after Sickles was wounded. Hancock could do little with the Third Corps, however, because its organization was largely destroyed by that time.

10. Charles A. Hale, "With Colonel Cross in the Gettysburg Campaign," *Civil War Times Illustrated* 13 (August 1974):35.

11. For a more detailed description of this action, see chapter 11 in Pfanz, *Gettysburg: The Second Day.*

12. *OR*, vol. 27, pt. 1:601.

13. Ibid., pt. 2:368; Joseph B. Kershaw, "Kershaw's Brigade at Gettysburg," in *B&L*, 3:336.

14. New York Monuments Commission for the Battlefields of Gettysburg and Chickamauga, *Final Report on the Battlefield of Gettysburg*, 3 vols. (Albany, N.Y.: J. B. Lyon, 1900), 3:1206–7 (cover title, by which this item is hereafter cited, *New York at Gettysburg*); Major John P. Dunne to Pennsylvania State

Adjutant General, July 29, 1863, RG 19, Pennsylvania State Archives (copy GNMP); John Haley to John B. Bachelder, Bachelder Papers, NHHS.

15. Nicholson, *Pennsylvania at Gettysburg* 1:623; William P. Wilson undated statement to John B. Bachelder, Bachelder Papers, NHHS.

16. Charles A. Fuller, *Personal Recollections of the War of 1861–1865* (Sherburne, N.Y.: New Job Printing House, 1906), 92; *OR*, vol. 27, pt. 1:391.

17. William P. Wilson undated statement to John B. Bachelder, Bachelder Papers, NHHS.

18. Favill, *Diary of a Young Officer*, 346.

19. William P. Wilson undated statement to John B. Bachelder, Bachelder Papers, NHHS; Hale, "With Colonel Cross," 35; *OR*, vol. 27, pt. 1:379. Caldwell reported that he was positioned "on the right of the Fifth and the left of the Third Corps." His position was actually between Ayres's and Barnes's divisions of the Fifth Corps and in the center of the line Birney's division had occupied.

20. Hale, "With Colonel Cross," 35; *New York at Gettysburg* 1:460; "From the 64th New York," *Cattaraugus Freeman*, July 30, 1863 (hereafter cited by title of newspaper only); Nicholson, *Pennsylvania at Gettysburg* 1:728–29; Joseph W. Muffly, *The Story of Our Regiment: A History of the 148th Pennsylvania Volunteers* (Des Moines, Iowa: Kenyon Printing, 1911), 734.

21. Hale, "With Colonel Cross," 36; Fuller, *Personal Recollections*, 94–95; Muffly, *History of the 148th Pennsylvania*, 537; *OR*, vol. 27, pt. 1:379; Kershaw, "Kershaw's Brigade," 336.

22. *OR*, vol. 27, pt. 1:379.

23. Tremain, *Two Days of War*, 81–84.

24. J. W. Stuckenberg Diary, GCL.

25. Favill, *Diary of a Young Officer*, 246; Nicholson, *Pennsylvania at Gettysburg* 1:624, 694.

26. Nicholson, *Pennsylvania at Gettysburg* 1:624–25; *OR*, vol. 27, pt. 1:392, 398. See also Kershaw's account in "Kershaw's Brigade" and his report in *OR*, vol. 27, pt. 2:366–70.

27. Hale, "With Colonel Cross," 36; *OR*, vol. 27, pt. 1:381–82.

28. John R. Brooke to Francis A. Walker, Nov. 14, 1885, Bachelder Papers, NHHS; *OR*, vol. 27, pt. 1:382, 400; *Cattaraugus Freeman*, July 30, 1863; Stephen A. Osborne, "Recollections of the Civil War," *Shenango Valley News*, Apr. 2, 1915, copy at United States Military History Institute, Carlisle, Pennsylvania.

29. Osborne, "Recollections of the Civil War"; *Cattaraugus Freeman*, July 30, 1863; *OR*, vol. 27, pt. 1:400; Nicholson, *Pennsylvania at Gettysburg* 1:701; A. E. Clark, "A Yankee at Gettysburg," *National Tribune*, Oct. 10, 1918. The 145th Pennsylvania reported sending one hundred prisoners to the rear. Brooke stated simply that his brigade captured a "great number." It is likely that many of these prisoners escaped shortly after their capture when the Wheatfield was overrun by Wofford's and Kershaw's brigades. Col. W. W. White of the 7th Georgia, who wrote the report for Anderson's command, placed the number of missing in the brigade at 51. See reports in *OR*, vol. 27, pt. 1:413–16 (Capt.

John W. Reynolds and Capt. Moses W. Oliver of the 145th), 400 (Brooke), and in ibid., pt. 2:397 (White).

30. D. Sheldon Winthrop, *The Twenty-Seventh (Conn.)* (New Haven, Conn.: Morris & Benham, 1866), 386; Nicholson, *Pennsylvania at Gettysburg* 1:625; *OR*, vol. 27, pt. 1:386–92, 398; Kershaw, "Kershaw's Brigade," 336; Joseph B. Kershaw to John B. Bachelder, Apr. 3, 1878, Bachelder Papers, NHHS. Kershaw reported a total of thirty-two missing and captured. *OR*, vol. 27, pt. 2:370.

31. William P. Wilson undated statement to John B. Bachelder, William P. Wilson to John B. Bachelder, March 25, 1884, Bachelder Papers, NHHS; *OR*, vol. 27, pt. 1:401.

32. Jacob B. Sweitzer account of operations, Joshua L. Chamberlain Papers, LC (copy at GNMP); *OR*, vol. 27, pt. 1:379, 602, 611.

33. *OR*, vol. 27, pt. 1:634. The fierce criticism of Sickles's handling of the battle on July 2 may have diverted attention from the performance of George Sykes, whose direction of his corps was mediocre at best.

34. Ibid., 379, 634.

35. William H. Powell, *The Fifth Army Corps* (New York: G. P. Putnam's Sons, 1896), 534–38; *OR*, vol. 27, pt. 1:379–80.

36. J. J. Permeus to John B. Bachelder, Nov. 3, 1871, Bachelder Papers, NHHS; Osborne, "Recollections of the Civil War"; *OR*, vol. 27, pt. 1:401.

37. *OR*, vol. 27, pt. 1:634.

38. Ibid., 380; C. H. Morgan undated statement to John B. Bachelder, Bachelder Papers, NHHS.

39. Busey and Martin, *Regimental Strengths at Gettysburg*, 242; C. H. Morgan undated statement to John B. Bachelder, Bachelder Papers, NHHS.

40. C. H. Morgan undated statement to John B. Bachelder, Bachelder Papers, NHHS; Alexander Webb to his wife, March 26, 1864, cited in Coddington, *The Gettysburg Campaign*, 751 n. 41.

41. J. W. Stuckenberg Diary, GCL.

Bibliographic Essay

The principal sources on which the authors based their essays appear in the notes. For readers interested in a more general canvass of works pertinent to the second day at Gettysburg, a few suggestions will point the way toward the mass of available material. Richard A. Sauers, comp., *The Gettysburg Campaign, June 3–August 1, 1863: A Comprehensive, Selectively Annotated Bibliography* (Westport, Conn., 1982) surveys the literature as of a decade ago. The basic military documents are in U.S. War Department, *The War of the Rebellion: A Compilation of the Official Records of the Union and Confederate Armies* (127 vols., index, and atlas; Washington, D.C., 1880–1901). Series I, volume 27, parts 1–3 of the *Official Records* (or the ORs as they are often called) contain almost thirty-five hundred pages of orders, correspondence, and reports relating to Gettysburg. *The Gettysburg Papers*, comp., Ken Bandy and Florence Freeland (2 vols., Dayton, Ohio, 1978), reprint a number of postwar Union accounts; the *Southern Historical Society Papers*, ed. J. William Jones et al. (52 vols., 1877–1959; reprint [with 3-vol. index], Wilmington, N.C., 1990–92), include dozens of articles about Gettysburg by former Confederates who figured prominently in the controversy over Longstreet's performance. *Gettysburg Sources*, comp. James L. McLean, Jr., and Judy W. McLean (3 vols., Baltimore, Md., 1986–90), reprints a variety of material by Union and Confederate participants. The biannual scholarly publication *Gettysburg: Historical Articles of Lasting Interest* (Dayton, Ohio, 1989–) attests to the widespread interest in the campaign.

An exceptionally thorough and judicious study of the fighting along the southern end of the field on July 2 is Harry W. Pfanz's *Gettysburg: The Second Day* (Chapel Hill, N.C., 1987). Few monographs in the entire tactical literature on the Civil War rival Pfanz's work in either narrative grace or depth of research. Also useful are Oliver W. Norton's often-cited *The Attack and Defense of Little Round Top, Gettysburg, July 2, 1863* (1913; reprint, Dayton, Ohio, 1983) and Richard A. Sauers's *A

Caspian Sea of Ink: The Meade-Sickles Controversy (Baltimore, 1989), which examines with a favorable eye toward Meade the debate over the activities of the Third Corps at Gettysburg. No specialized work on fighting around Culp's Hill exists, though Edwin B. Coddington's massive *The Gettysburg Campaign: A Study in Command* (New York, 1968), covers those events in some detail. Less impressive but nonetheless worthwhile single-volume treatments of the battle are Clifford Dowdey's neo-Confederate *Death of a Nation: The Story of Lee and His Men at Gettysburg* (New York, 1958) and Glenn Tucker's gripping *High Tide at Gettysburg: The Campaign in Pennsylvania* (Indianapolis, 1958). *Gettysburg: The Confederate High Tide* (Alexandria, Va., 1985), by Champ Clark and the Editors of Time-Life Books, stands out among pictorial works. In a class by itself is Michael Shaara's novel *The Killer Angels* (New York, 1974), with its brilliant sketches of Lee, Longstreet, Joshua Chamberlain, and other commanders.

Three books of value for visitors to the battlefield are William A. Frassanito, *Gettysburg: A Journey in Time* (New York, 1975), which uses a selection of period and modern photographs to locate historic sites, Jay Luvaas and Harold W. Nelson, eds., *The U.S. Army War College Guide to the Battle of Gettysburg* (Carlisle, Pa., 1986), now somewhat out of date because the National Park Service recently changed its tour route at Gettysburg, and Edmund J. Raus, Jr., *A Generation on the March—The Union Army at Gettysburg* (Lynchburg, Va., 1987), which provides information on every Union unit and their monuments on the field.

Only a few titles from the abundant printed firsthand testimony can be mentioned here. James Longstreet's fiercely defensive memoir *From Manassas to Appomattox* (Philadelphia, 1896) denies his culpability for Confederate failure on the second day; George Meade's *Life and Letters of George Gordon Meade* (2 vols., New York, 1913) includes a long section on his father's role at Gettysburg; Alpheus S. Williams's richly rewarding *From the Cannon's Mouth: The Civil War Letters of General Alpheus S. Williams,* ed. Milo M. Quaife (Detroit, 1959), is essential on the Union Twelfth Corps; and *The War Between the Union and the Confederacy* (1905; reprint, Dayton, Ohio, 1974), by Colonel William C. Oates of the 15th Alabama, contains a colorful though somewhat unreliable narrative of the Confederate assault against Little Round Top. Unusual as a participant's account because of its striking combination of insight and lack of bias is Edward Porter Alexander's *Fighting for the Confederacy: The Personal Recollections of General Edward Porter Alexander* (Chapel Hill, N.C., 1989), ed.

Gary W. Gallagher, and volume 3 of *Battles and Leaders of the Civil War*, ed. Robert Underwood Johnson and Clarence Clough Buel (4 vols., New York, 1887), includes useful but sometimes self-serving articles by Longstreet, Sickles, Meade, George S. Greene, and Joseph B. Kershaw. A rich source for testimony from several North Carolina units is Walter Clark, ed., *Histories of the Several Regiments and Battalions from North Carolina in the Great War 1861–'65* (5 vols., 1901; reprint, Wilmington, N.C., 1991–92).

Biographical studies contain a wealth of information on the second day's battle. Douglas Southall Freeman's *R. E. Lee: A Biography* (4 vols., New York, 1934–35) vigorously attacks Longstreet and concludes that Gettysburg would have been a Confederate victory if "Stonewall" Jackson had been present; Freeman tempered his criticism of Longstreet and reached more balanced conclusions about Lee's leadership in *Lee's Lieutenants: A Study in Command* (3 vols., New York, 1942–44). Especially valuable for its careful discussion of postwar controversies is William Garrett Piston's *Lee's Tarnished Lieutenant: James Longstreet and His Place in Southern History* (Athens, Ga., 1987). Freeman Cleaves's *Meade of Gettysburg* (Norman, Okla., 1960) favors its protagonist on the question of Sickles's movement to the Peach Orchard; W. A. Swanberg's engagingly written *Sickles the Incredible* (New York, 1956) strives for balance with a difficult subject. A pair of unabashedly admiring books shed some light on Henry W. Slocum and his troops—Charles Elihu Slocum's *The Life and Services of General Slocum* (Toledo, Ohio, 1913) and New York Monuments Commission, *In Memorium: Henry Warner Slocum, 1826–1894* (Albany, N.Y., 1894).

Finally, three multivolume works merit the attention of anyone interested in the second day at Gettysburg. Shelby Foote's *The Civil War: A Narrative* (3 vols., New York, 1958–74), the second volume of which covers Gettysburg, sets a standard for sheer literary power that no other author has matched. A close second to Foote in terms of narrative skill is Bruce Catton's *Glory Road* (Garden City, N.Y., 1952), part of his "Army of the Potomac Trilogy"; less engagingly written but valuable for its analytical contribution is Kenneth P. Williams's *Lincoln Finds a General* (5 vols., New York, 1949–59), volume 2 of which deals with Gettysburg.

Index

Contributors

GARY W. GALLAGHER is Head of the Department of History at Pennsylvania State University. He has published widely on the Civil War, including three previous books of essays edited for Kent State University Press—*Antietam: Essays on the 1862 Maryland Campaign*, *Struggle for the Shenandoah: Essays on the 1864 Valley Campaign*, and *The First Day at Gettysburg: Essays on Confederate and Union Leadership*.

A. WILSON GREENE holds degrees in American History from Florida State University and Louisiana State University. Executive Director of the Association for the Preservation of Civil War Sites, he is the author of articles on various aspects of the Civil War as well as *J. Horace Lacy: The Most Dangerous Rebel of the County* and *Whatever You Resolve to Be: Essays on Stonewall Jackson*.

D. SCOTT HARTWIG, who studied under E. B. Long at the University of Wyoming, has published several articles on the battle of Gettysburg as well as *The Battle of Antietam and the Maryland Campaign of 1862: A Bibliography*. He is presently at work on a full-scale study of the 1862 Maryland campaign.

ROBERT K. KRICK grew up in California but has lived and worked on the Virginia battlefields for twenty years. He is the author of dozens of articles and nine books, the most recent being *Stonewall Jackson at Cedar Mountain*, a selection of the History Book Club.

WILLIAM GLENN ROBERTSON, who holds graduate degrees from the University of Virginia, is a member of the faculty at the United States Army Command and General Staff College at Fort Leavenworth. Among his many publications are *Back Door to Richmond: The Bermuda Hundred Campaign* and *The Petersburg Campaign: The Battle of Old Men and Young Boys, June 9, 1864*.

THE SECOND DAY AT GETTYSBURG
was composed in 10/13 Trump Medieval
on a Penta system with CG8600 and L300 output
by Reporter Typographics, Inc.;
printed by sheet-fed offset
on 60-pound Glatfelter Natural Smooth acid-free stock,
Smyth sewn and bound over 88-point binder's boards
in Holliston Roxite B binding cloth
with 80-pound Rainbow endpapers,
and wrapped with dustjackets printed in two colors
on 80-pound enamel stock with film lamination;
also notch bound with paper covers printed in two colors
on 12-point coated-one-side stock with film lamination
by Braun-Brumfield, Inc.;
designed by Will Underwood;
and published by
THE KENT STATE UNIVERSITY PRESS
KENT, OHIO 44242